CREATIVE ANARCHY

HOW TO BREAK THE RULES
OF GRAPHIC DESIGN
FOR CREATIVE SUCCESS

Denise Bosler

HOW BOOKS
Cincinnati, Ohio
www.howdesign.com

For more excellent books and resources for designers, visit www.howdesign.com.

18 17 16 15 14   5 4 3 2 1

ISBN-13: 978-1-4403-3332-3

Distributed in Canada by Fraser Direct
100 Armstrong Avenue
Georgetown, Ontario, Canada L7G 5S4
Tel: (905) 877-4411

Distributed in the U.K. and Europe by F&W Media International, LTD
Brunel House, Forde Close, Newton Abbot, TQ12 4PU, UK
Tel: (+44) 1626 323200, Fax: (+44) 1626 323319
Email: enquiries@fwmedia.com

Distributed in Australia by Capricorn Link
P.O. Box 704, Windsor, NSW 2756 Australia
Tel: (02) 4560-1600

Edited by Scott Francis
Designed by Claudean Wheeler
Production coordinated by Greg Nock

a content + ecommerce company

PART 1:

LEARN THE RULES

CREATIVE ANARCHY

INTRODUCTION

WHY DESIGN MATTERS

Design is about making life beautiful, functional, productive and profitable. It influences our decision-making process with the stealth of a *jōnin* ninja—most of the time we don't even realize it's there. From a highway sign to the note taped to the office refrigerator reminding everyone to take home leftover food, design is everywhere. It can empower and embolden (Helvetica) or trivialize and weaken (Comic Sans). Poor design creates chaos: Think of the Palm Beach County, Florida, ballot cards in the 2000 U.S. presidential election. Great design, like the simple red ribbon icon for AIDS awareness, can inspire the world to make a change for good.

Design takes the intangible and makes it concrete. Your job as the designer is to translate a company's abstract concepts into something everyone can understand. You create the experience. Design communicates by resonating with an audience—one that probably doesn't know it's being designed for. And that's the point. The best design is barely noticeable because it works seamlessly into its environment and for its audience.

WHY DESIGN RULES MATTER

Rules take on many forms, and we begin to learn rules the minute we comprehend language. Don't stick a fork in the electrical socket. Don't hit your brother. Color inside the lines. You have to eat your peas or you won't get dessert. Rules progress as we get older: Stop when the light turns red. Three strikes and you're out. Take out the trash if you want an allowance. And as adults, the rules just keep coming: Pay your taxes. Take out the recycling. Empty the dishwasher. Clean up the dog poop.

We need rules to function as a society. Without them we would have chaos. Some rules are firm: Stop when the light turns red or you may cause an accident. Some are more flexible: If I don't take out the trash tonight, I can do it next garbage day. Design has rules too. Some are firm, some more flexible—but all apply to the work we create every day.

Knowing the rules is particularly helpful when dealing with clients. It is helpful to rationalize a design decision by saying, "I realize that magenta may seem like an odd choice for a monster truck rally poster, but the high contrast of the magenta and black inks against the fluorescent green paper creates an electrifying visual that both stimulates the senses and stands out among the typical masculine posters," instead of just, "It looked cool."

Some may find the idea of design rules silly, so think of them as "truths" instead.

Some things ring true regardless of how they are presented. Blue complements orange. Helvetica is a sans serif. Vertical text is difficult for Western readers, as they are used to reading horizontal and left to right. Kerning makes words easier to read. Paper folds better with the grain than against it. Print will not die (as predicted), and the digital world will continue to advance at lightning speed. These and other rules have become standard in the design world as functions and elements of design. They provide the basic knowledge needed to produce effective, creative and well-executed work that satisfies the client. You won't go to jail if you don't follow the rules, but you can't break them if you don't know what they are.

Creative anarchy is about pushing not only your own boundaries and expectations, but those of the client as well.

WHY CREATIVE ANARCHY?

Not every project calls for a design that follows the rules. Some projects need to bend them a little—or a lot—to

01 ● The Common Table Cellar Beer Menu LPs

communicate the message. Other projects need to break the rules entirely. How can you tell when it's the right time to bend or break the rules? That's a tricky question. Design rules are more like guidelines, so the answer is *anytime*. Don't forget your client, though. You may want to incite creative anarchy, but you still need your client as a co-conspirator, willing to go along with your master plan to take over the creative world. Seriously though, design is meant to be pushed.

There are no new ideas

There is nothing new under the sun. All design ideas can be traced back to something in the past. Rays of the sun in the background of an image? Check out the war flag of the Imperial Japanese Army from 1870 or Russian Constructivist posters from 1919. Surely those cool modern hipster logos must be original. Think again. Go back to logos from the 1940s through the 1960s. The new Microsoft Windows logo? Just an evolution of the original from twenty years ago.

If everything has already been done, what can you bring to the table? Give an old idea a creative twist. Use established theory to redefine the design. Pull in bits and pieces of many ideas to form a new one. Make the concept yours.

The ability to push boundaries is a respected quality. It shows you are willing to go beyond the expected by demonstrating that you will invest time and creative strategy in a design concept. Boundary pushing proves that you are a thinker and a doer, not a follow-the-leader-er. There is a time and place for everything, though. The most successful designers embrace design innovation, while recognizing that not all designs should try to go outside the box. Some clients feel comfortable inside it, but it's up to you to figure out what the client wants and deliver it.

Which brings us back to the question: Why creative anarchy? Every design problem has multiple solutions. If you don't explore a variety of possible solutions, you're not doing your job. Exploring design means looking at the rules. Looking at the rules means investigating your options. Investigating your options means thinking about breaking the rules. Breaking rules calls for finesse. It can't be done willy-nilly. Breaking design rules means testing the limits of your creativity, challenging your strengths and strengthening your weaknesses.

HOW TO INCITE ANARCHY

There are no shortcuts to a great design concept. You must read, research, explore, innovate and create.

Start with design history

Every idea already exists. The Dada movement was the first to go crazy with type. David Carson did it again with *Ray Gun* magazine. The Constructivist movement used photo montages, angled images and bizarre juxtapositions. The Punk movement did it again with cut-outs and crudely arranged photocopies. The Arts and Crafts movement revolted against the cold, impersonal Industrial Revolution, just as the resurgence of hand lettering rebels against the cold, impersonal computer-driven typography of today. The past provides tremendous inspiration if you are willing to return to it.

Take risks

Breaking the rules is not for the meek designer or timid client. It takes guts to go against the industry norm. Fear breeds an attitude of, "Everybody else is doing it so I should probably do it too." But ask yourself: Is there a valid reason

02 ● *P. 1921*, 1921 (collage): Hausmann, Raoul (1886-1971). Dada movement.

why everyone is doing it, or is everyone doing it just because everyone else is doing it? The creative anarchist always questions why. Perfume advertising is a great example of this lemming-like attitude. A sullen, handsome, chisel-faced male looks longingly into the distance. A stunning girl comes to him. They embrace, almost kiss, and exchange smoldering looks while posing as beautifully as possible. That's it for 90 percent of perfume advertising. Creativity? Innovative concept? Too many industries do the same thing over and over again. But once in a blue moon, an advertiser dares to be different. Dari Marder, chief marketing officer of Iconix Group, Inc, turned the advertising world on its head when she suggested that the 1997 Candie's shoe advertising campaign feature Jenny McCarthy sitting on a toilet. With underwear around her ankles and Candie's shoes on her feet, McCarthy, and Marder, created a provocative, controversial and highly-successful ad campaign. The target audience girls loved it—the moms, not so much. Shoe advertising was never same again.

"Provocative" is music to the ears of the creative anarchist. Other great words and phrases include: *unexpected, infectious, viral, unusual, shocking, spectacular, double-take,*

03 ● F_ _ _ Paul Rand Invitation

visual surprise, "I want to hang it on my wall," and "I want to show everyone." In fact, try to make hearing those words your goal when pushing design boundaries.

Stay open

You have to learn the rules before you can break them. That's what the first half of this book is about. You may be tempted to skip to the second half. Resist that urge. Even Michelangelo said, "I am still learning." Design learning needs to continue whether you are still a student, fresh out of college or have been working for twenty years. I fall in the latter category and love learning new things. I haven't

read it all, seen it all or designed it all, so I keep myself open to discovery. Some days I learn a simple software trick from a student. Another day I may learn about a recently discovered archive of an entire design movement. Learning is exciting. There's nothing sadder than a person resistant to acquiring knowledge. Never stop learning, never stop exploring, never stop doing what you love, and always create the best design you can. Some client projects will be "stodgy and classic" and others will be "exciting and rebellious." Whatever the project, never declare it complete until you satisfy the creative anarchist in you.

LEARN THE RULES

Design is everything.
Everything! — PAUL RAND

MESSAGE IS COMMANDER

Communication is at the heart of it all: Brochures, logos, advertisements, posters, invitations, T-shirts, websites, apps, book covers, annual reports, magazines, guerrilla advertising, packaging and branding materials all relay information to an audience. Communication trumps everything, even aesthetics. It's absolutely part of our job to make things look good—we are designers after all—but looking good without offering substance doesn't serve the client. We must deliver the client's message. Whether big or little, the audience must understand the message. Communication is our number one priority.

SAY IT, SEE IT

Design is dominated by two types of communication, verbal and visual, working together to communicate the client's message. Verbal communication is both written and spoken. This part is generally left to marketers and copywriters, who develop information to present to the consumer in order to engage them with the product or service. Verbal communication is enhanced by the visual treatment but doesn't need it to work. Print, TV, radio and digital advertising are famous for their verbal communication prowess. Some slogans are so recognizable that you don't need any visual cues at all. People just know them from repeated exposure and catchy phrases: "I'm loving it!" from McDonald's; "The Breakfast of Champions" from Wheaties; "You're in good hands with Allstate." from Allstate Insurance; "What's in your wallet?" from Capital One.

Visual communication, both static and animated, is the domain of the designer. Visual impact has the power to sell a product, launch a brand and generate support by speaking to a wide audience. Catchy advertising slogans aside, visual communication is typically more memorable than verbal communication is. There's a reason why the often-quoted

04 ● "In the image, the plastic baby dolls were used as metaphors for the young children impacted by horrific attacks. The letterforms strewn out to each corner relates to the turmoil caused by the event. The interaction of the dolls seen through the type bars was intended to represent their fragility, defenselessness and vulnerability." —Lanny Sommese

aphorism is "Show, don't tell." The visual speaks to the audience faster than the verbal; a picture of a strawberry will be recognized more quickly than the word *strawberry*. Designers rely on the viewer's personal experiences and cultural background when creating visuals. The more recognizable, the faster the audience will get the message. This rule applies not just to imagery, but all elements—type choice, background, color and layout need to be recognized as well.

FORM FOLLOWS FUNCTION

The idea of form following function isn't new, but we credit the Bauhaus movement for pushing it to the forefront of design. Whether it is a chair, teapot or poster, the concept of putting functionality before design is the difference between design and fine art.

I love great commercials, especially the ones that go viral and are talked about nonstop for a few days. These commercials do a fantastic job of generating buzz, but they don't all function as well as they should. I watch the Super Bowl not for the football but for the commercials. The next day I have a class discussion about the commercials. Inevitably there will be a discussion about an incredibly memorable commercial that starts something like this:

> *"Did you see the awesome one where the dogs burst*
> *through the door?"*
> *"Oh yeah, it was so cool!"*
> *"What was that commercial for?"*

Sound of crickets fills the room. No one can remember anything except the "coolness" of the commercial. Form overwhelms function, and communication is lost.

05 ● A beautiful Bauhaus example of form following function.

Function gets the better of the form too. Plenty of perfectly functional websites look terrible. They communicate the client's basic needs but ignore user-friendly aesthetics. What about the Comic Sans-typed note reminding employees to empty the fridge each Friday? Does it matter if the fridge note looks "designed"? That, my friends, is the important question.

Function and form should work as balanced partners, neither one more important than the other, beginning with the concept. Your first priority is maximizing the client's message, which sets the tone for the concept. Next comes matching the message with the right design elements. The interplay of type, imagery, color and format visualize the

06 ● "I look at design as the vehicle for communication. Creativity is the fuel to get that vehicle moving. The process gets faster and easier if you practice and 'refuel' in fun new ways." —Kimberly Beyer

07 ● Smashing Iced Tea

concept. Does it attract and inform the viewer? If so, then congratulations: You have struck the right balance.

An emphasis on functionality doesn't mean a design can't be beautiful and vice versa. Smashing, a proposed brand of sparkling iced tea, has a design featuring a humorous Victorian theme with a modern twist. The lovely figure illustrations draw the viewer's eye down through the center of the label to the detailed ornamental frame. The ornamentation acts both as a decorative element and a bull's eye, directing the eye to the product name. The hierarchy and unity of the elements work together to build clear functionality in charming form.

HIERARCHY

Hierarchy refers to the creation of varying degrees of emphasis within a design. Hierarchy says to the viewer, "Look at me! Start here!" You control what the viewer sees and when she sees it through the size, position, visual weight and color of the content elements. The viewer needs direction about what information she should gather from the design. If everything has the same emphasis, or if the emphasis is in the wrong place, she will abandon the design before properly absorbing the information.

Help her by determining how much emphasis is needed for each piece of content. Once you figure out the hierarchy,

BREAK IT DOWN

Design projects are complex beasts. Smashing all the client's goals into one perfect concept is difficult and overwhelming. Learning to simplify the message makes it easier.

1. Grab your design brief and get ready to take notes. Read through the brief and write down all the client goals, communication points and other necessary information.
2. Review your notes. Eliminate any repetitive notations. Restate the objectives in two or three succinct sentences.
3. Now take that information and condense it into one sentence. What is the main message?
4. Now do it in three to five words. Simplify it.
5. Can you get it down to one word? Maybe two? This is your message. Conceptualize it.

you can determine placement and design attributes. A natural assumption is that the largest element on the page is the most important, and this is true for the majority of design solutions. However, emphasis can also arise from the element's visual attributes or positioning. The most important element could conceivably be the smallest one on the page.

Visual attributes refer to weight, color and size. Typography's main visual attributes track within a font's family. Black and extra bold create heavy visual weight; narrow, light and book weights connote lesser visual importance. The combination of the type weights also confers degrees of hierarchy. Dark, bold or vibrant colors tend to stand out more than soft, dull or pastel colors. Contrasting or complementary colors used together also control emphasis. As mentioned earlier, a large element produces more emphasis than a smaller one. Big, bold, vibrant illustrations will have more emphasis than a small, lightweight, pale headline. Different combinations of weight, color and size let you emphasize anything you want. A small, bold, vibrant illustration will have emphasis over a large, lightweight, pale headline.

LEGIBILITY AND READABILITY

Have you ever come across a design you love but can't figure out what it's for? The headline type is crazy, swirly, super-cool hand-done letters, but you don't know if it says "Swiss cheese" or "sweet jeans." Or the body copy overlays a photo and you can't see the type well enough to read it. Effective design relies on legibility and readability.

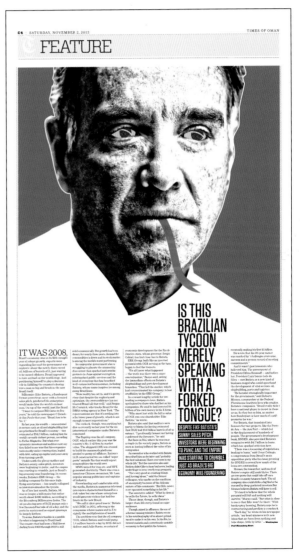

08 ● Clear hierarchy helps the reader navigate the page.

09 ● The experimental approach to this science museum poster pushes the boundaries of both legibility and readability.

Legibility refers to the viewer's ability to discern the words and imagery of the design, and is determined by the physical makeup of those elements. Does the "R" look like an R? Does the word "Event" look like the word Event? Does the photo of the horse look like a horse, or does cropping it distort it too much to recognize? The viewer should be able to easily discern the main message. Legibility also applies to concept. The audience must understand the message. An abstract conceptual design may be too obscure for most audiences, though you can push the boundaries. But you need to know when you have crossed that legibility line. Your audience should "get it" within a second or two. Any longer and the concept is not legible.

Readability depends on the arrangement of words and images: the size, weight, and font choice of the type; image placement; color of elements; and the overall detail of the design—meaning, is the design literally readable? A design can be legible without being readable, but you can't have readability without legibility. A common advertising technique is using a large photo for the background of a design. If the tonality of the image is too high contrast or colorful, text will get lost. The type itself may be legible but the background makes it unreadable. Experiment with changing the color of the type or background image to strike the best readability balance.

THE COMPUTER IS ONLY A TOOL

I suspect you spend way too much time staring at your screen. Stop it. Right now. Listen up and pay attention. I'm here to tell you that the electronic device you love so much is hindering your creativity. It keeps you from choosing the color you want, forces type decisions you don't love, and takes away your ability to think beyond a tri-fold format. Your computer and other electronic devices are brain-sucking creativity leeches that turn your ideas from grand to bland. A computer is a tool. It does not magically create awesome design, contrary to what your clients may think. A computer is no different from pencil and paper. The final execution may look better, but without the concept, the design fails.

IT'S ALL ABOUT THE CONCEPT

All effective design solutions begin with good ideas. As mentioned, if a design has no supporting idea, then the work is simply a pretty picture—nice to look at but doesn't tell us anything. Design needs a concept; the idea that supports a design's direction, purpose and reasoning. A concept is not, "I think I'll draw a purple box around the type and use a great big flower in the background." Type, color, layout, alignment, shapes, contrast and any other visual decision are components of aesthetics. A concept is, "I'm going to develop an analogy between the three Fates and the pitfalls of poor education." A visual may pop into your head along with the concept statement, but it's not the specific visuals that matter right now. It's the strength and validity of the idea.

It ain't easy

Generating concepts takes work. Some days you will be bursting with crazy ideas, other days you'll stare blankly at your notebook and listen to the crickets chirping

10 ● "This narrative icon series represents an interpretive story of The Tortoise and the Hare directly compared to life. Both the tortoise and the hare have skeletal bodies to represent mortality. The tortoise has a compass as a wheel to represent his slow navigation through the race while the hare has a clock as a wheel to represent his fast pace. This is directly compared to our challenge in life to navigate quickly but to navigate it correctly." —Nicholas Stover

inside your head. I wish I could tell you there is a creativity switch somewhere in your head—there isn't—but there are processes that can assist your concept development. Start by defining the problem. What is the product/service? What are the project goals? Who is the audience? These answers may be vague or specific. Sometimes the client doesn't know exactly what they need, but they know they need *something*.

Take matters into your own hands. Do your research with an objective eye. You shouldn't rely on only information generated by the client. Look at the industry and the competition. Delve into the client's product or service. What are the goals, products and positioning? What does it do? Who uses it and why? What separates it from the competition? What can you discover?

11 ● When the invitation is folded just right, the viewer can manually spin the record to play an "invitation song" recorded by the happy couple. The clear flexidisc record, foil stamping and revealing illustration are all contained in a groovy cover with a letterpressed band.

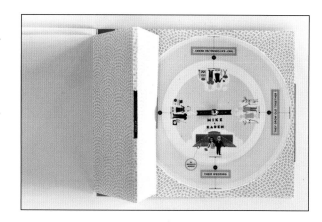

Pencil before mouse always! Starting off with a bit of paper and a pencil before I start designing anything on the computer was the best bit of advice I ever got. —SAM BARCLAY

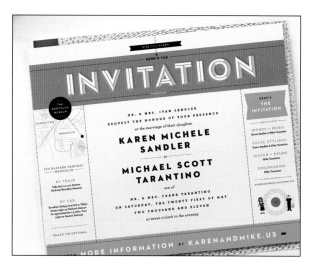

TITLE: Peanut Chews packaging
DESIGN FIRM: Bailey Brand Consulting
ART DIRECTORS: Dave Fiedler, Steve Perry
DESIGNER: Denise Bosler
CLIENT: Goldenberg Candy Company

Goldenberg's Candy Co. (now owned by Just Born, Inc.) of Philadephia was a small company with a big problem. Their product, Peanut Chews—a dark chocolate, caramel and peanut candy—hadn't changed since its creation in 1917, and the product packaging hadn't changed in more than eighty years. Goldenberg's needed to market to a younger audience.

The situation was dire. The little advertising the company did had no effect on sales. The dated red-and-brown packaging made the product recede on the shelf among the other more brightly colored candy. The younger generation had zero interest in trying "old people's" candy. With the help of Bailey Brand Consulting, Goldenberg's launched a rebranding initiative, starting with research. The results outlined several areas for improvement: The Peanut Chews product name was more important than the Goldenberg's brand name. Their desired younger audience was in favor of a milk chocolate version of the candy. Brighter colors for the packaging were needed. The need for an illustration of the candy came as a surprise.

The team at Bailey Brand Consulting went to work. Custom typography was created, adding a youthful playfulness. A large Peanut Chews product name also became the focus of the package. Red and brown was retained for brand recognition, but the colors were shifted to a more vibrant tone. A new blue band across the top of the package distinguished milk from dark chocolate. An illustration of the candy was added. Marketing tactics shifted. Goldenberg's began to advertise more aggressively. The changes worked. Goldenberg's saw an uptick in sales and created inroads with a younger audience, and all was right in the world of chocolate and peanuts once again.

WHERE DID I PUT THAT IDEA?

Problem defined; research complete. Now it's time for idea generation. There is no single tried-and-true process for generating a killer idea. I happen to get my best ideas while running. The left side of my brain is too focused on keeping my legs moving and can't spare the energy to interfere with my right-brained creativity. What works for me, however, might not work for you. And what works for one project may not work for another. It's good to have a repertoire of idea-generation techniques to create that winning concept.

First, let's discuss the rules of idea generation:

RULE ONE. Just go! Generate as many ideas as you possibly can.

RULE TWO. There are no bad ideas. It doesn't matter if you think the idea is off base or plain ol' silly. Record it anyway. Anything goes.

RULE THREE. That's it. Confused? Stuck? See Rules One and Two.

12 ⬤ "I used to take the train to go to work and noticed that the cabin tables were filled with empty coffee cups. This gave me the idea to turn coffee cups into business cards. I'd put these on the train tables whenever I had the chance. It displayed my name, artwork and a link to my online portfolio." —Hiredmonkeez

Seasoned designers and newbies alike tend to shoot something down before the idea-generation process is complete. This is a huge mistake. Don't edit yourself while brainstorming. You never know when a seemingly absurd or silly idea will generate something plausible and successful. Designers' brains work in unexpected ways. Make it a practice to turn off your inner editor.

who came before me?
its all around you
influences
inspiration - not just design
creativity — ideas - share
rethink ideas
dont settle
try new things
who are you?
find your voice
have fun
Creative Anarchy
push the limits
- rework it
be a scientist
experiment - rip it
cut it
get messy
get clean
make your best work
EXPLORE — no rules
learn first explore second)
do what you want
overthrow
revolution
listen to who?
make mistakes
break the rules
make new rules
learn to be bad
dont give up
no police
know the rules
- study the masters
history

Keep writing extensions until you've exhausted all ideas.

Write it down

Mind mapping is a popular idea-generation technique. A word is written in the center of a piece of paper, and ideas are extended from it like a spiderweb. The title of the design problem is typically written in the center. Lines drawn out from the center have subcategories attached, relating to the researched materials and goals of the client. Lines are extended from those subcategories, and so on. The result is an extensive spiderweb of ideas just waiting to be executed.

List generation is an organic flow of associative words and adjectives written in a long stream of consciousness. Each word launches from the last, filling the whole page (or pages). Associative connections are made between the words, and ideas are born. This can also be done round-robin style as a group session. One person starts by saying a word, with each person adding a word related to the last. You'll be surprised, and hopefully inspired, to see where this takes you. Just make sure you have a good note taker handy, or record the session with audio and/or video.

Get visual

Do you respond better to visuals than words? Not to worry. Mind mapping and list-generation techniques work well with sketches too. It may take a little longer to execute, but the results are the same.

Mood boards for visual concepting capture the essence of a project rather than concrete ideas. Many different methodologies exist for creating mood boards. The easiest method is to simply collect, sketch or cut out anything that inspires an idea for the project. It can tackle the mood (hence the name), feeling or essence that the project needs to project. An image of Beyoncé is chosen for a bold and flirty message. A picture of the sidewalk outside is a reminder that the final package must hold up to wear and tear.

Ideas can strike anytime, and you need to be prepared. Carry a small notebook, or slip a folded piece of paper into your wallet. Remember to keep a writing utensil handy. Markers, pens, crayons… It doesn't matter. Want something smaller? Snag a golf pencil. Smartphones and tablets are great for recording ideas. Tons of software options are available for taking notes, drawing sketches, recording audio and collecting references. If the idea is complex, call your office phone and leave a voice mail, or email it to yourself. Take pictures or video, remembering to document why.

A creative anarchy mood board should put you in the right mode for reading this book.

A clipping from a floral-print fabric is chosen for a tone of purple in the petals. Mood boards are collections of representations, not necessarily literal solutions.

Get up and out

It's inevitable that the ideas will stop flowing. No matter how hard you try, they just aren't there. You stare at the page, willing your pencil to keep moving, but there's just nothing. Of course, this usually happens when you're feeling the pressure of a deadline. Your brain works all day and all night to keep you going. It makes sure you breathe, sleep and move away from a hot burner. You push it to the max and expect it to always come through for you, but truth is, sometimes your brain needs a break.

Listen to your brain when you hit the creative wall. If you continue to push it to perform, it will respond with dribbles of forced and unimaginative thinking. Take a break, even if you don't think you have time. Get up and move away from the project. If you are really pressed for time, take a walk down the hall, go up and down a flight of steps or take a brisk walk around the building. Sometimes just changing positions from sitting down to standing up helps. If you have a little bit more time, get away from the office altogether. As mentioned, running works for me. Discover what works for you. Perhaps it's a walk in the woods or a trip to the gym. Try golf, ping-pong or yoga. If a group brainstorm session is stuck, stop and play a game. Musical chairs and chair races down the hall have an amazing effect

on creativity. It doesn't matter what you do as long as you get the blood flowing while not thinking about the task at hand. The brain responds amazingly to a short vacation.

Be inspired

I often find design students combing through design archives, looking for inspiration. This is not a bad technique. It's good to learn from others' design work, as long as you aren't directly copying someone else's design ideas. It's also good for designers of all skill levels to keep tabs on current design. There's amazing stuff out there. Just don't get stuck looking only at design work. The world is full of inspiration.

Nature is an excellent inspiration. Everything from the pattern on a caterpillar's back to the colors of the changing leaves can inspire. I once picked a color by examining the exact hue of a blue sky (not an easy task). Museums are also great places for inspiration. The history and beauty of fine art stimulates both eyes and brain. Color, texture, content, technique and creativity abound inside a museum. Impressionists' color palettes; Expressionism's alternative representation; the Renaissance's tone and mood; and Modern art's approach to movement and form are just begging to be interpreted as design concepts. If you don't have a museum or gallery nearby, most have their collections posted online for virtual tours.

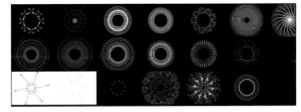

13 ● Kolam is an ancient folk art form that is still practiced daily on the floors of Hindu temples and on the doorsteps of homes by the women of South India. In this interactive installation, users generate real-time kolam-inspired art; a small component of a larger constantly changing piece.

TRY IT:

BUILD A REFERENCE LIBRARY

Surrounding yourself with reference materials is a great way to have an endless supply of inspiration at your fingertips.

1. **Books:** Books, books, magical books. Books are the epitome of a reference library. They are also expensive. Start small with this part of your library to ease the strain on your wallet. Choose a few books that speak to you. The subject matter could be design, but it can also be the content that inspires you. If the work of the De Stijl movement resonates with your design aesthetics, purchase a book about that artistic era. Purchase a current design annual, a book about butterflies or an old collection of 1940s children's stories. It's not the subject that matters; it's the inspiration it gives. Scour bargain bins, library sales, used bookstores and flea markets for books. You can score a complete set of early-century encyclopedias for practically nothing. Ask for books as gifts. Finally, allow yourself to splurge once in a while on a gorgeous book about your favorite design.

2. **Clippings:** Anytime you read or see something that sparks inspiration, rip it out. If it's part of an item you can't destroy, then photocopy, scan or take a picture of it. Write directly on the clipping why you chose it: color, illustration style, use of graphic elements, inspiring passage or a process that you want to try. Do not rely on your memory to recall the information at a later date.

3. **Digital media:** Similar to clippings, anytime you find something on the web that inspires you, bookmark it, download it or take a screenshot. Videos, photos, websites, blogs, and other pages provide endless sources of inspiration. Remember to indicate why you collected it.

4. **Cataloging:** Cataloging is the most important part of creating a reference library—and the most cumbersome—but there's no sense in creating a reference library if you can't find the reference when you need it.

Books are the simplest to catalog because the titles are on display. Consider how you want to organize them. The easiest way is by general content and, within that, specific subject matter. For instance, place all your design books together, then sort by branding books, creativity books, typography books, etc.

Clippings are a little tougher. It's easy to create a huge pile of awesome materials and never use them because you can't remember what you have. Binders help you stay organized. Categorize binders by subject matter, such as typography, color, cool techniques, inspirational articles and so on. Anything that can be hole-punched goes right into the binder. Page dividers let binders do double duty. For objects and clippings that are too small to hole-punch, pick up some protective sleeves or folder inserts at any office supply store. I like hole-punched folders with a Velcro closure. Ziploc bags work well if you need to do it on the cheap. Buy freezer bags for thicker, stronger plastic. Hole-punch the non-closure side to create a secure place to hold small items. Accordion folders are another great solution; just remember to label each divider, as it's harder to see the contents at a glance.

Digital media is the trickiest to organize. It's amazing how quickly data can get lost or forgotten. Work smart. Bookmarks function best if you organize them within folders, a utility found in all web browsers. It takes a few seconds longer to file, but it's so worth it to easily browse your archive. Be specific with the labeling system; don't just have a generic "design" bookmark folder. Break it down like the book and binder methods. Rename each link something you'll remember, and that will trigger why you bookmarked it in the first place. Online photo and file sites are wonderful for saving images. Remember to make sets/folders/boards to stay organized. Same goes for your hard drive. Organize, organize, organize!

REMEMBER THE BASICS

The best design derives from a structured approach. Concept development through final execution is a process, with each part building off the last. We would be amiss, then, to construct a design idea without its elemental backbone: line, shape, texture and value. These four basic elements have the ability to convey a message, lead the eye and shape a viewer's perception. Learn to love, use, embrace and explore them.

LINE

Let's start with the basic of basics—line. Lines are everywhere. They are the basis for every shape, letter and drawing. By definition, a line is a mark on a surface that goes from point A to point B. It can be short or long, fat or thin, or straight or wavy. A line can be made with a variety of tools, including pencil, charcoal, brush and computer. And a line can be static or in motion. The use of line dates back thousands of years ago to early man. The Lascaux cave paintings, and other paintings of the time, show early man's ability to connect lines together to form drawings that tell of prehistoric life. Lines continue through the centuries. Cuneiform marks pressed into clay. Roman lettering etched into marble. Illuminated manuscripts' elaborate images adorning biblical stories. The horrors of war communicated through battlefield etchings. Vintage advertisements touting a product's benefits. Infographics defining a business's process flow. Even nature is made up of lines—check out the veins on a leaf, the swirl of a snail shell or simply look to the horizon. Line is the design element that holds all other elements together.

The energy of line

Line communicates energy and emotion. A single horizontal line projects neutrality and calmness. Add another

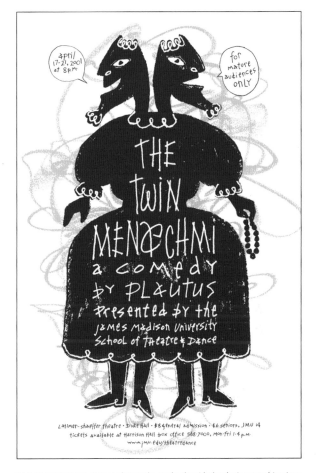

14 ● The expressive line quality works perfectly with the designer's objectives for the poster. "Menaechmi, an ancient play, was to be directed at the speed of a Howard Hawks screwball comedy. I wanted to capture some of that turbulence and chaos." —Wade Lough

vertical line through its middle and you've got motion and conflict. Increase the thickness of both lines and they become emboldened. Draw a series of diagonal lines and they're set in motion. Add diagonal lines going in the opposite direction and you've got tension. Lengthen the lines and create a journey. Add jagged angles to make it frenzied.

Smooth out those jagged angles and the line flows and becomes peaceful again. Draw the flowing line with charcoal and the line feels earthy and natural. Draw the jagged line with crayon and it projects naiveté. Every line is a statement. It's up to you to decide which one to make.

Line as a cattle dog

Lines keep design in order—herding type, corralling images, organizing content and fencing in pages. Sometimes they work out in the open, barking loudly at the viewer. Other times lines are invisible—silently working the content into its proper position. Visible lines create a physical barrier that keeps the viewer focused by leading the eye around the page. Magazines and other publications frequently utilize these lines to separate content and control the flow of information across a page. Visible lines keep type from "floating away." Borders are used to frame and organize design. A border is the designer's way of saying, "Look at everything I've put inside here. This is the important stuff."

Visible lines are also used as decorative elements. What better way to draw attention to something than to surround it with an attention-getting flourish of lines? It can be as simple as a line above and below a pull quote or as complex as an illustrative combination of lines highlighting the name of a product or company. Nature trails illustrate this quite well. Head to your local park and take a walk along a trail. Notice where the trail leads into the distance: The trail borders act as leading lines to focus your attention to the point at which the trail disappears—the trail not yet traveled—encouraging you to go on and explore.

Invisible lines are the guides and/or grid that create the structure for a design. These lines herd content silently, providing consistency within the layout. Content flows into columns, allowing separation with negative space. Invisible lines are the unsung heroes of organization.

SHAPE

The natural progression of line is to go from connecting points A and B to point C, and back to point A again, thus creating shape. Line is the building block of the design's surface; shape is the building block of the design's space. Line occurs in a single plane—it's only until we connect the lines that we have a sense of form and space. Shape isn't limited to the simple geometric forms you learned in grade school. Shape applies to complex images, including photographs and illustrations, and even to this paragraph of text, which may not have a solid area behind it but still forms a shape.

TRY IT:

EXPLORE LINE

Develop your line repertoire by trying a variety of image-making marks for your next project. Once complete, scan in and voilà: a distinctive line for a creative design. Experiment with different tools, like:

- Pencil
- Marker
- Pen
- Charcoal

- Pastel (chalk and oil)
- Crayon
- Brush pen
- Calligraphy pen

- Thread (hand sewn or sewing machine)
- String/yarn glued to paper

Try dipping the following items in ink or paint:

- Toothpick
- Cotton swab
- Feather (both ends)
- Twig
- Pine cone
- Evergreen sprig
- Acorn

- Leaf
- Crumpled paper towel
- Cotton ball
- Toothbrush
- Paper clip
- Pushpin
- Fork

- Spoon
- Knife
- Whisk
- Ice pick
- Edge of a coin

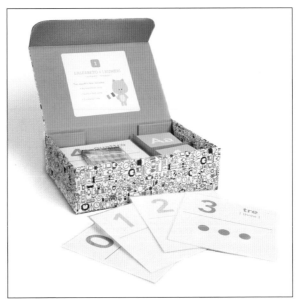

15 ● Simple shapes work perfectly for this children's language learning system.

Shapes defined

Geometric shapes like circles, ovals, squares, rectangles, triangles, rhomboids, hexagons, octagons and dodecahedrons, to name a few, are likely the first thing that pop into your mind. The Swiss, Bauhaus and Constructivist movements especially loved big, bold, simple geometric shapes, and their disciples used them everywhere—in the background, around type and through images. The Art Nouveau and Psychedelic Art movements' artists favored organic designs whose flowing edges and amoebic shapes created a natural feel. This type of shape encourages movement and fluidity within the confines of the rigid boundary of a poster or screen's edge. Nature has graciously filled our world with organic shapes: ivy, trees, flowers, ant hill burrows and winding rivers. Abstract shapes, on the other hand, are more contrived. Neither geometric nor organic, abstract shapes are designed to represent objects. Universal symbols are a good example: handicap access, men's and women's restrooms, baggage claim, and taxi pickup icons. Some steal from geometry while others sample nature.

Shapes highlight and organize information, but unlike line, they can also create the illusion of space. Overlapping

16 ● Rock concert poster for The Grateful Dead, The Doors and others at the Fillmore, San Francisco, 1966.

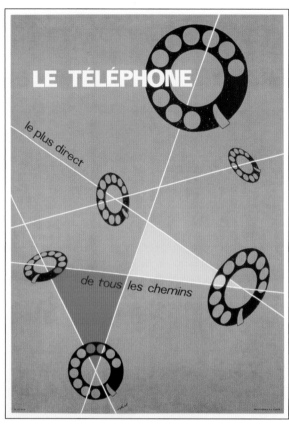

17 ● Advertisement for the telephone, c.1937 (colour litho).

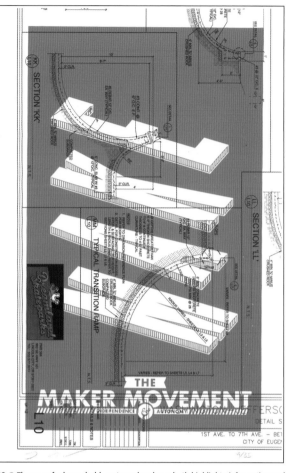

18 ● The use of a large, bold, rectangular shape both highlights information and provides a visual pop to draw in the viewer.

Shape type

two shapes suddenly gives dimension to a flat surface and becomes an active and engaging design. Lead the viewer's eye by using various shapes at different places on the page. A design with all circles and one triangle draws attention to the triangle. A giant arrow pointing to a small word em-

A large initial cap at the beginning of a paragraph is more than just a letter; it's a shape. *O* is geometric, *S* is organic and *K* is abstract. Illuminated manuscripts used the shape/ initial cap combination to give the viewer a visual cue to the beginning of a new story or chapter. Modern designers use the same technique, though not quite as decorative, in longer publications like annual reports, magazines and brochures. Paragraph text set in something other than a rectangle really grabs your attention. Page through a magazine and—*wham*—a paragraph in the shape of a circle, star, or tornado funnel surprises you, making the type instantly

"Challenge the expected. Design from the inside out. Challenge first, then channel. Don't get caught up in the weeds. Always deliver an idea in a simple yet captivating way. Be 'arty, smartsy'—artistic by nature, smart and strategic by design." —**GREG RICCIARDI**

phasizes the word, not the arrow sixteen times its size. Uncle Sam points straight out, putting the emphasis on *you*.

more interesting to read. The same trick works for photographs and illustrations too.

TRY IT:

EXPLORE SHAPE

Shake up your shapes by trying new ways to form them. Scan or photograph the results.

- Found object collage
- Masking tape
- Duct tape
- Cut paper
- Torn paper
- Cut/sewn fabric
- Silhouette
- Stencil (both positive and negative shapes)

- Potato/eraser stamp
- Tangrams
- Graph paper
- Clay
- Wood
- Paint-by-number style
- Reduced to only black & white
- Repeated elements (images or type)

- Origami/folded paper
- Stained glass
- "Snowflake" style
- Form a larger shape with a series of smaller shapes
- Use only geometric shapes
- Use only organic shapes
- Blown ink

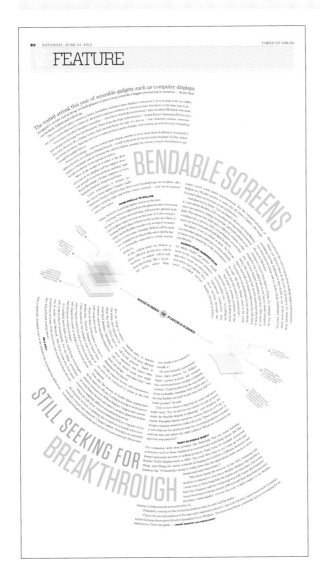

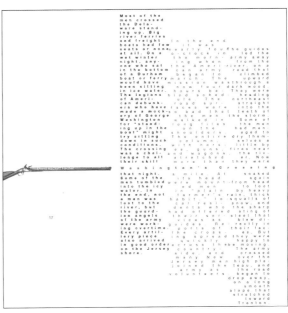

19 ⬤ (left) The format of the text works seamlessly with the context of the story.

20 ⬤ (above) "We think of army regiments as precise and orderly, but maintaining organization while the men were marching in the dark, in the sleet and snow, on icy rutted roads? Impossible. Some of his barefoot men left blood marks on the snow as they marched, and this typographic composition expresses the drama of the march." —Jan Conradi.

TEXTURE

Texture is the visual or physical quality of a design that gives it a tactile sense. It is a secondary element but still important. Texture adds a finish to a project, like the bow on a beautifully wrapped package.

Make the viewer say "ooooh"

Texture is the difference between bland and wow. It adds depth, interest and mood. Almost anything can be used as texture. Grunge oil smudges, a wrinkled paper bag, woven linen, a stucco wall, grit, TV static, canvas and glittery pixie dust are great examples. It's very important to remember that the texture must support the content. Texture for texture's sake is like adding food coloring to plain water. It looks pretty but serves no purpose. For a community picnic poster, you can use grass or a gingham tablecloth for texture. If you are designing a florist's business card, create a floral pattern as a border or backer for the card. Textures should fit the personality of the design.

Ogle it

Visual texture is texture that is applied or printed. Adding visual texture is a great way to introduce interest to a sterile white page. A common texture application is an overall background or overlay image. The texture is a supportive element to the overall design. Remember not to let the texture interfere with the text and other design elements. Texture doesn't have to be subtle. Lines, shapes and other design elements can be combined to form texture. Mask the textures to fill type or other shapes. Let texture be the design itself. Wrapping paper is a great example of pattern-based texture design.

Texture inspiration is easy to find. Look around you right now. Your jeans, a flower arrangement, a bowl of apples on the kitchen counter, lined notebook paper, a crumpled paper bag, the cardboard from the back of your notebook, a sofa pillow, dirt from the garden, the driveway and the sidewalk leading to your front door are textures immediately within your reach. Pop the texture onto a scanner

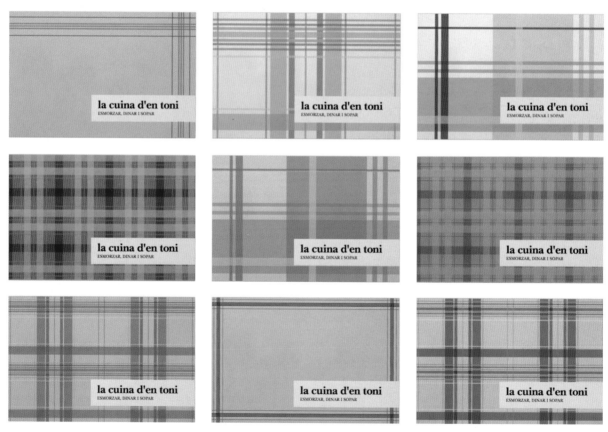

21 ● "La cuina d'en Toni is a flexible and dynamic identity for a restaurant located in Catalunya, Spain, that combines tradition and modernity. All the elements are based on the traditional tablecloth." —Dorian

22 ● The textural posters were designed in a World War II propaganda-poster-style.

TRY IT:

EXPLORE TEXTURE

Keep textures at your fingertips by creating a library of go-to textural elements.

Make a rubbing:

- Wall
- Tile
- Wood
- Brick

- Asphalt
- Cement block
- Grate

- Sneakers
- Lace
- Gravestone

Photograph it:

- Tree bark
- Sidewalk
- Pebbles
- Stones
- Rusted metal

- Grass
- Leaves
- Kitchen counter or cabinet
- Granite

- Marble
- Candy
- Fabric
- Clothing

D.I.Y. textures:

- Crumple paper and smooth it back out
- Flick paint with a toothbrush
- Dry-brush paint
- Watercolor wash

- Scribble
- Layer typography
- Paint a bike tire and ride across paper a few times

- Repeat a stamp to create a pattern
- Charcoal wash
- Shoe prints

23 ● Beautiful black on black printing creates an elegant and feminine card.

or photograph it. Create it yourself if you can't find the texture you want. Use the computer to create a classic stripe or dot pattern that's more "design-y" and clean. Use traditional media for a natural, hand-done look. Anything goes in visual texture.

You have permission to fondle

Tactile texture is just as powerful as visual texture. Have you ever held someone's business card and felt the need to run your fingers over it again and again because of the paper? I know I have. Physical texture is powerful because it combines the viewer's senses of sight and touch, a distinctive experience that can only occur in print design. Paper choice is the easiest way to create a tactile experience. A rough, uncoated paper and a smooth, coated one create two very different experiences. Paper choice enhances the design concept. A brochure for an organic vegan café will have more impact on uncoated stock than on a slick coated paper. The emotive feeling of organic vegan doesn't mesh well with glossy and sleek.

Tactile texture can also be added during the printing process. Die-cutting, foil stamping, embossing and debossing are additive processes that affect the surface of the paper. Die-cutting is a process in which a die is created to stamp out the paper into a specific shape, just like making cookies with a cookie cutter. A single die cut creates a textural surface, whereas layering die-cut paper over a non-die-cut paper creates a dimensional texture. Foil stamping uses heat to melt foil onto paper. It's usually a shiny metallic, but flat colors are also available. Foil stamping creates a smooth, raised surface on the paper. Embossing and debossing techniques are created with a non-cutting die. When pressed onto the paper, it creates a raised or lowered area in the shape of the die. The results resemble a topographic map with raised (embossed) and depressed (debossed) sections of paper. Braille is a great example of embossing.

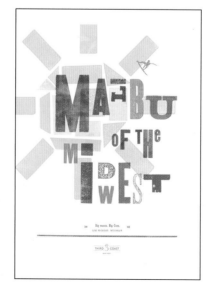

24 ● Wood shapes and type are playfully positioned in this expressive letterpress poster series.

25 ● Letterpress cards.

PRINT THE TEXTURE

Texture can be added through the printing method itself—letterpress and silk-screening, for example. In letterpress printing, the design is raised above the surface of a metal block or plastic plate so that when ink is applied and pressed into the paper, it prints and embosses at the same time. Silk-screen is a printing process in which a design is chemically adhered to a mesh screen, then ink is drawn across the surface. The design blocks off the mesh holes in the negative space of the design, allowing ink squeegeed across the screen to transfer the positive areas to the printed surface. Screen printing ink is thicker than other types of printing inks, and so it forms a raised surface as it dries. Silk-screen printing is not limited to a fixed position like other printing methods, which makes it possible to print on other materials such as wood, plastic or metal.

VALUE

Value and color are not the same thing. Color refers to the actual hue of an object, while value describes its overall lightness or darkness. Value is what provides the overall visual contrast within a design, and it is only partly dependent on color to do so. An effective design should work well regardless of color. If a design's communication is unclear, then it's a result of a poor design concept, layout or choice of design elements—not color. Color is too often a crutch.

Highs and lows

Make a photocopy of your design. Is there a value difference between elements? A stark difference means your design has high contrast. If there is little difference in tones, then your design is low contrast. All the elements of a page produce contrast. A light-colored square next to a dark square

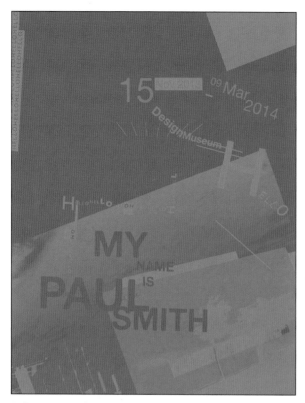

26 ● Low contrast and an unusual color palette introduce the famous fashion designer.

27 ● The stark contrast in color value, coupled with the strong graphic, creates a dynamic political statement.

has a high contrast/value difference. The same light-colored square next to a similarly light square has low contrast/value difference. Value is relative. Nature provides brilliant examples of high and low contrast within an environment. The high contrast of a bright yellow, pollen-laden stamen against a dark purple flower beckons bees and other insects. A green chameleon on a green branch evolved to be low contrast, allowing it to stalk prey without being seen. In both of these examples, the color is less important than the value contrast created by the color.

Value directs

Value provides more than just visual contrast, it's a key tool in directing a viewer's eye, because the eye is attracted to

high contrast. A dark background littered with objects of lighter value causes the viewer to see the lightest object first and then work around the page to the next darkest and so on. Value also produces the illusion of movement. A subtle progression of values set along a path will trick the eye into seeing motion, forcing the eye to follow it.

Value is moody

Different value contrasts elicit different emotional reactions. High-contrast values create energy, activity, zest, feistiness and playfulness. They jump up and down and say, "Look at me!" Low-contrast values create calm, soft, subdued, delicate and sophisticated feelings. They're design zen.

TYPE IS EVERYTHING

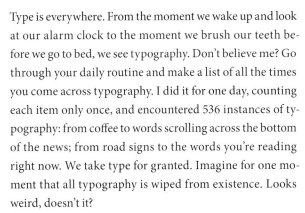

Type is everywhere. From the moment we wake up and look at our alarm clock to the moment we brush our teeth before we go to bed, we see typography. Don't believe me? Go through your daily routine and make a list of all the times you come across typography. I did it for one day, counting each item only once, and encountered 536 instances of typography: from coffee to words scrolling across the bottom of the news; from road signs to the words you're reading right now. We take type for granted. Imagine for one moment that all typography is wiped from existence. Looks weird, doesn't it?

Humans communicate through the written word. Typography is how we express ourselves, sell products, distinguish food from poison, separate one brand from another, understand instructions, stick to the speed limit, bake a

soufflé, help our kids fall into fairy tale-induced dreams… You get the idea. The easier it is to read and understand, the better. We rely on typography, so it is important to use it properly.

TYPE SPEAKS VOLUMES

Typography communicates beyond the words it spells. Typography is an expression of those words. It evokes a feeling from and connects with the viewer through the letters' aesthetics. Typography controls how words are perceived, which, in turn, controls how products, brands and businesses are perceived. It's a domino effect. A rigid-looking letterform will project a conservative feeling, whereas a loose, flowing one will feel organic or elegant. A distressed

29 ● Snask, a Swedish design agency, turned what to communicate into how to communicate by creating a visual identity and communication by hand.

30 ● The poster typography explores questions about gender theory and promotes the elimination of all gender label, proposed by singer Morrissey, through typographic and image exploration.

letterform will feel, well, distressed. Picking the right typeface is challenging, but when you do, the result is the perfect marriage of concept and design.

The late Steve Jobs, CEO of Apple Inc., understood this. In his commencement address to Stanford University graduates on June 12, 2005, he spoke of his realization of the importance of typography and that its expressive application could enhance a brand.

> "Reed College at that time offered perhaps the best calligraphy instruction in the country. Throughout the campus, every poster, every label on every drawer was beautifully hand calligraphed… I decided to take a calligraphy class to learn how to do this. I learned about serif and san serif typefaces, about varying the amount of space between dif-

ferent letter combinations, about what makes great typography great. It was beautiful, historical, artistically subtle in a way that science can't capture, and I found it fascinating.

> None of this had even a hope of any practical application in my life. But ten years later, when we were designing the first Macintosh computer, it all came back to me. And we designed it all into the Mac. It was the first computer with beautiful typography. If I had never dropped in on that single course in college, the Mac would have never had multiple typefaces or proportionally spaced fonts... and personal computers might not have the wonderful typography that they do." [1]

Choosing the right typeface makes a word sing; choosing the wrong typeface makes it whisper hoarsely, or worse yet, say something wrong. This is tricky stuff. One typeface's connotations to me may be very different for you. How do you choose? There are three steps. First, understand your client's needs. What style of typeface does the client view as professional or sophisticated or flirty or some other adjective that describes her business? Knowing that the client believes Comic Sans is an acceptable professional typeface is valuable information. You have the chance to figure out how to explain why your typeface choice is more appropriate than a comic-inspired font. The second step is to understand the audience. You can't interview everyone in your audience, but you can get an overall sense of their aesthetic by looking at all the other products and services marketed to them. Finally, and most important, is the message itself. A serious subject demands serious looking letterforms. A playful subject yearns for lively letters. Experimental letters can sometimes be the solution for the appropriate message.

So how do you choose the best typeface? The wrong answer is to sit in front of the computer and try out every single font in your software's library. This is time-consuming and rarely generates the perfect typeface. The right answer is to educate yourself in the who, why and what-for of typography and letterforms so you can choose a font that speaks your message with feeling.

[1][Stanford Report. 'You've got to find what you love,' Jobs says. Stanford University. http://news.stanford.edu/news/2005/june15/jobs-061505. html. Published June 14, 2005. Accessed August 8, 2013.]

TYPE IS EVERYTHING

Serif and sans serif

Serif letters have structural extensions that come off the strokes of a letterform. Serifs come in many shapes and sizes: fat, thin, tall, short, pointed, curved, squared, cupped, prominent or barely visible.

Sans serif letters have no extensions and instead end in a terminal. Terminals can take on many forms, including blunt, curved, cupped or pointed. *Sans* is a French word meaning "without," hence the phrase *sans serif* means "without serif."

Creative Anarchy

Creative Anarchy

Creative Anarchy

Creative Anarchy

Creative Anarchy

Letter parts

Other than serifs, the parts of each letter are the same for both serif and sans serif fonts. Analyzing and learning about these parts helps you understand what makes type-faces different from one another, which allows you to determine the best choice for your design.

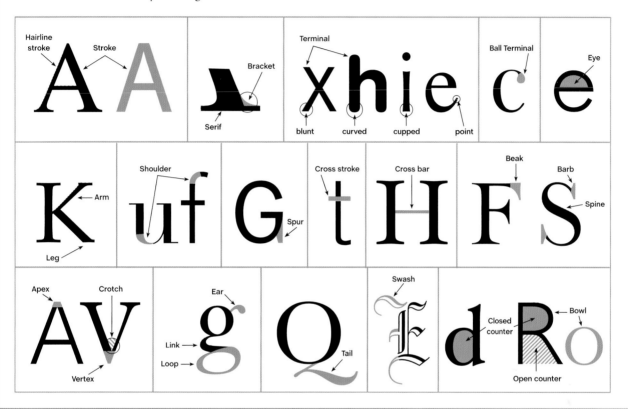

Basic classifications

OLD STYLE

Influenced by ancient Roman lettering, Old Style typefaces were originally created as metal type for early printing processes. They are characterized by letters with serifs that run straight or cupped along the edge, with noticeable brackets. The ends of the serif range from straight to rounded. The counters have a biased stress, and there is low contrast between the main and hairline strokes. Letters feel somewhat heavy and the x-height tends to be tall in relation to the cap height. Ball terminals are shaped like teardrops, and the ascenders tend to be taller than the cap height.

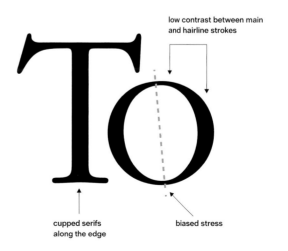

TRANSITIONAL

Transitional typefaces originated in the late eighteenth century and serve as a transition between Old Style and Modern lettering. These letters have a straighter and sharper serif, with smaller brackets. The letterforms have slightly biased or vertical stress and medium contrast between the main and hairline strokes—more contrast than Old Style. Like Old Style, the x-height tends to be tall in relation to the cap height and the ascenders can be taller than the cap height.

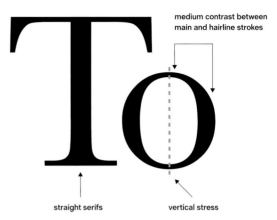

medium contrast between main and hairline strokes

straight serifs

vertical stress

MODERN

Modern typefaces are from the late eighteenth and early nineteenth centuries and are the result of further improvements in printing processes. The serifs are straight along the edge, with tiny or no brackets. The letterforms have vertical stress and high contrast between the main and hairline strokes. The x-height tends to be medium to tall in relation to the cap height.

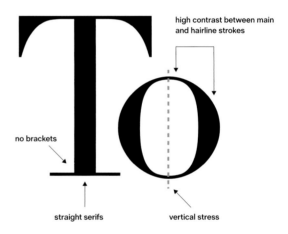

high contrast between main and hairline strokes

no brackets

straight serifs

vertical stress

SLAB SERIF

Commercial demand for bolder, heavier fonts led to the creation of Slab Serif typefaces. Also called Egyptian, these typefaces have thick, heavy serifs (slabs) that are straight across the edge, with small or no brackets. Usually the serif is the same thickness as the main stroke, giving the font a monoline look. The letterforms have vertical stress and little to no contrast between the main and hairline strokes. The x-height tends to be medium to tall in relation to the cap height.

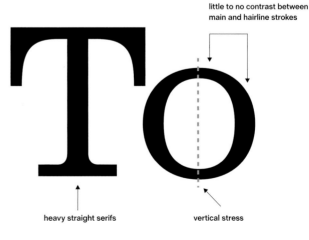

little to no contrast between main and hairline strokes

heavy straight serifs

vertical stress

SANS SERIF

Sans Serif letterforms are derived from ancient informal Roman lettering, which had no serifs. The strokes end in terminals. The letters generally have a vertical stress and no contrast in the strokes, giving it a monoline look. The x-height tends to be tall in relation to the cap height.

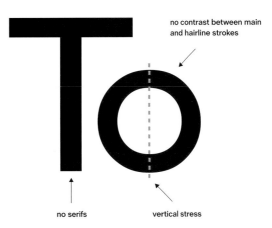

no contrast between main and hairline strokes

no serifs

vertical stress

BLACKLETTER

Blackletter is based upon European script lettering and dates back to medieval times. Drawn with a flat pen or nib held at an angle, the letters are created using sharp vertical, horizontal and angled strokes. The letterforms have vertical stress and extreme contrast between the main and hairline strokes. The x-height tends to be tall in relation to the cap height.

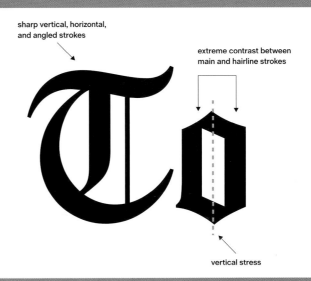

sharp vertical, horizontal, and angled strokes

extreme contrast between main and hairline strokes

vertical stress

DINGBATS

Dingbats are strictly illustrative elements that can be typed out on a keyboard. Some Dingbats are fun little illustrations that can be used as clip art; others are more decorative and ornate. Dingbats serve as enhancements to a type design, though they cannot be read as letterforms.

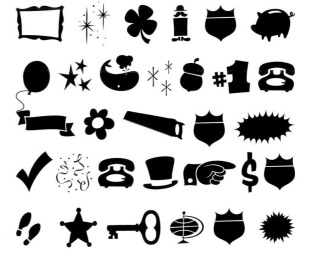

Ed Bengbats

SCRIPT

Script has its origins in handwriting and calligraphy. Script typefaces generally have a fluid, cursive feel. Swashes run the gamut from minimal to elaborate. These typefaces tend to read better when used sparingly. They are virtually impossible to read when used all in caps.

Fluid and cursive-like

Typography

TYPOGRAPHY

All caps are impossible to read

DISPLAY

Display typefaces tend to read well at larger sizes but are illegible when smaller or when used in long line lengths of text. They are generally used for headlines, initials and logos and can include experimental, distressed and hand-written elements. Use restraint: Reserve Display typefaces for emphasis only.

ITALIC AND OBLIQUE

An Italic is an angled version of a typeface. It is redrawn so the architecture of the letters remains consistent but the overall look is more script-like. Obliques are letters that angle with little or no change to the letterforms.

Roman
Italic

Roman
Oblique

Regular
Condensed

CONDENSED AND EXTENDED

Condensed letters are designed to be a narrower version of a regular typeface. Extended letters are designed to be a wider version of a regular typeface.

Regular
Extended

TYPE IS EVERYTHING

OLD STYLE NUMBERS

Old Style numbers are designed to have varying heights within ascenders and descenders. The *1*, *2* and *0* align with the x-height, the *6* and *8* have ascenders, and the *3*, *4*, *5* and *7* have descenders.

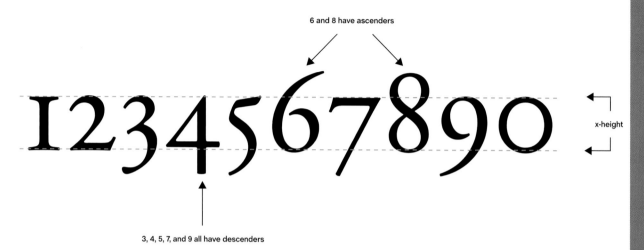

6 and 8 have ascenders

x-height

3, 4, 5, 7, and 9 all have descenders

LINING NUMBERS

Lining numbers all line up along the cap height. Lining numbers are far more common than Old Style numbers and are associated more with everyday use because they aren't as "fancy."

1234567890

x-height

Why stick to just one typeface? Why not use two, or three, or four or—what the heck—a different typeface for every line? Variety in design is great, but using too many typefaces confuses the viewer and distracts from the hierarchy.

On the other hand, using a single typeface makes the design dull and hard to navigate. Therefore, the general rule of thumb is to use two typefaces—three if something really special needs attention.

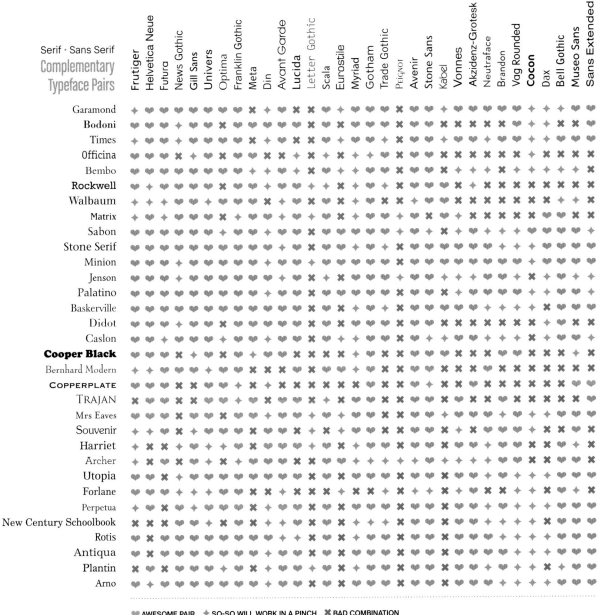

Serif · Sans Serif
Complementary Typeface Pairs

💜 AWESOME PAIR   ✦ SO-SO WILL WORK IN A PINCH   ✖ BAD COMBINATION

The first of two giant "cheat-sheet" charts for complementary type pairs. You'll never be without the perfect pair again!

Why two?

Using two typefaces gives the viewer variety to look at and provides you with a variety of options. They can play off each other to form a harmonious or contrasting complement. For instance, if the headline and subheads are a sans serif and the body text is serif, the viewer can easily distinguish them from each other. Further visual difference is achieved through style and weight. The best choice of complements is two typefaces of different styles. Serif and Sans Serif, Sans Serif and Script, or Display and Serif, to name a few.

One of the biggest challenges is finding typefaces that complement each other. Fonts that are too similar don't provide the contrast needed, and fonts that are too different will clash on the page. A couple of guidelines make finding complementary pairs easier: Look for similar qualities—x-height, weight, width, height, bias, counter sizes—and consider using fonts from the same historic period or same designer. In the end, it all comes down to a gut reaction—do they complement each other or not?

Script · Display · Serif · Sans Serif — Complementary Typeface Pairs

	Vonnes	Akzidenz-Grotesk	Neutraface	Brandon	Vag Rounded	Cocon	Dax	Bell Gothic	Museo Sans	Sans Extended	Harriet	Archer	Utopia	Forlane	Perpetua	New Century Schoolbook	Rotis	Antiqua	Plantin	Arno
Carolyna	✕	✕	✕	+	♥	✕	+	✕	♥	✕	+	♥	+	♥	♥	♥	+	♥	✕	✕
Ed	♥	♥	♥	+	♥	♥	+	+	♥	♥	+	♥	+	+	♥	♥	♥	♥	+	+
Shelley	♥	♥	♥	✕	✕	✕	✕	+	+	♥	✕	+	♥	♥	♥	♥	♥	♥	+	♥
Snell Roundhand	♥	+	♥	+	✕	✕	+	+	+	♥	♥	+	♥	♥	♥	+	♥	♥	✕	♥
Embassy	+	✕	♥	+	♥	✕	+	✕	+	✕	♥	♥	♥	✕	✕	♥	✕	+	♥	✕
Berthold Script	✕	✕	✕	+	✕	✕	♥	♥	✕	+	♥	+	+	+	♥	♥	+	♥	✕	✕
Montague Script	✕	✕	✕	✕	+	✕	♥	♥	✕	+	+	+	+	+	+	♥	+	♥	✕	✕
Boulevard	✕	✕	✕	✕	✕	✕	✕	✕	+	✕	♥	✕	✕	+	✕	+	+	✕	✕	✕
Ribbon	✕	✕	+	♥	✕	✕	✕	✕	+	✕	+	✕	♥	♥	✕	♥	♥	✕	✕	✕
Kuenstler Script	✕	✕	✕	✕	✕	+	✕	+	+	+	+	♥	♥	+	✕	+	♥	+	♥	♥
ED IINTER LOCK	♥	♥	✕	✕	+	✕	✕	✕	+	✕	+	♥	✕	♥	✕	✕	✕	✕	✕	✕
Bodoni Poster	♥	♥	✕	+	♥	+	✕	✕	+	✕	+	+	♥	✕	✕	✕	✕	✕	♥	✕
DINER	+	+	+	✕	✕	+	✕	+	+	+	+	✕	♥	♥	+	✕	✕	+	+	✕
TIKI	+	♥	✕	✕	✕	♥	✕	+	✕	+	✕	✕	+	✕	+	✕	✕	+	✕	✕
ROSEWOOD	+	+	✕	✕	✕	✕	+	✕	+	+	✕	✕	✕	✕	✕	✕	✕	✕	✕	✕
Madrone	+	+	✕	✕	✕	✕	✕	✕	+	♥	♥	✕	✕	+	✕	+	✕	+	✕	✕
Girard Slab	♥	✕	✕	♥	+	+	+	✕	+	♥	✕	♥	✕	+	♥	♥	✕	♥	✕	♥
Miehle	✕	✕	+	✕	✕	✕	✕	✕	+	♥	✕	✕	+	✕	+	♥	♥	✕	+	✕
KINGPIN	+	+	♥	♥	♥	+	+	✕	+	+	+	♥	✕	✕	✕	✕	✕	✕	✕	✕
Spookhouse	+	+	✕	♥	✕	✕	✕	♥	+	+	✕	✕	✕	✕	✕	✕	✕	✕	✕	✕

♥ AWESOME PAIR   ✦ SO-SO WILL WORK IN A PINCH   ✕ BAD COMBINATION

MAKE YOUR OWN TYPE CHART

Using the same set of typefaces again and again makes your work predictable and less creative. Save time and keep your work fresh by creating a customized complementary typeface chart of your own.

1. Pick out ten serif and ten sans serif typefaces. Choose your favorites and mix in some classics too.
2. Type each out as a headline (24 pt) and text (9 pt).
3. Compare each serif with each sans serif. Look for similar qualities and make note of which work well together.
4. Create your chart and keep it near your workstation for quick access.
5. Add to your chart as you acquire new typefaces.

IT'S THE LITTLE THINGS THAT MATTER

Design is in the details. Paying attention to them shows that you care about your work. Finessing the details means you take the time to polish every design 100 percent. 98.5 percent is not good enough. You're under a deadline, the client is emailing every five minutes, and you have to get the job out the door right now! It's awfully easy to tell yourself the design is acceptable and to send it out. The client will never notice, right? Wrong. As a professional, you need to step up, making certain that every last little detail has been attended to. Attention to detail is the difference between a good designer and a spectacular one. Not convinced? If your car is being repaired, do you want the mechanic to fix the issue perfectly or is "good enough" good enough? What about a hair stylist who doesn't bother to check the cut's evenness all the way around your head? Is it OK if the left side is slightly longer than the right—not dramatically, but just enough so you notice? Of course not. Complacency shouldn't be good enough for your client either. Show her you care about her business just as much as she does by attending to every detail.

Kerning

Consistent spacing between letters means good readability. Two letters either too close together or too far apart result in halted words and unintended messages. These gaps between letters also break the visual flow. Kerning, the manual adjustment of the space between two letters, resolves these issues. A font should have kerning pairs—sets of two letters whose spacing has been modified from the normal preset space—already incorporated to eliminate problematic let-

> *"Creativity is messy—I expect things to change and evolve until the project is delivered. Sometimes good ideas come at the beginning, sometimes at the end, sometimes not at all. Sometimes clients are a breeze, and sometimes they're a challenge. If you can remember that the process is messy from the get-go, it makes the process a little more endurable. My philosophy: Embrace the mess."* —TONY LEONE, LEONE DESIGN

ter spacing. Not all fonts are created equally, though, and even fonts with kerning pairs sometimes need tweaking.

Sometimes you just need to kern one pair of letters, while other times you will need to kern a whole word or multiple words. Remember that kerning a pair of letters only affects those two letters, and only in that particular word. The font itself remains unaffected. You may have to kern the same set of letters multiple times. Particular attention should be paid to larger type because size exaggerates poor kerning pairs. The larger the size, the bigger the space. Even if you have no time for other detailing before a job must go out the door, at least take five minutes to kern.

Kerning Kerning
Kerning Kerning
Kerning Kerning

Note how the spacing between the letters becomes more uniform with each step. Practice makes perfect.

Tracking Tight

Tracking Regular

T r a c k i n g Loose

Loose, regular and tight tracking.

Kerning makes the words easier to read, and it shows you care about doing a good job.

Tracking

Tracking is the spacing between all the letters in a word or sentence, versus just a pair of letters in kerning. Tracking influences readability. People read by recognizing the shapes of the letters. Spacing around each letter helps the viewer distinguish one letter from the next. Too-tight tracking interferes with letter recognition because the letters are too close together. Conversely, very loose tracking pushes letters so far apart that a viewer has trouble telling where one word ends and the next begins. The goal is to strike just the right balance to maximize readability. Sometimes, different tracking can be used to enhance a design, such as a logo. Overly tight or loose tracking can create emphasis and mood. In addition, wide or extended fonts sometimes benefit from tighter tracking so the letters don't feel like they are drifting apart. Thin or condensed fonts can also benefit from looser tracking so the letterforms can be read

Widow

"A lot of time you might think that there's not enough
time to finish your work, while actually you have
"too much" time on your hands... Its really easy to get
distracted by social media, TV etc, to lose focus on
your projects, so its best to avoid these during your
work."

-Edmundo Moi-Thuk-Shung, HiredMonkeez

Widows break the flow of text and must be addressed even in the shortest document.

Fixed

"A lot of time you might think that there's not enough
time to finish your work, while actually you have "too
much" time on your hands... Its really easy to get
distracted by social media, TV etc, to lose focus on your
projects, so its best to avoid these during your work."

-Edmundo Moi-Thuk-Shung, HiredMonkeez

Orphan

I am inspired by design pioneers, who went into
fresh markets to push the discipline forward. I
started my company, Name&Name with the aim
of using creativity to effectively lift clients projects,
be it branding, packaging or advertising–in both
developing and developed markets, to make things
the best they can be in any culture. I am interested
in how design connects with varied cultures–from
elegant european modernism, to bold impactful
American humour, to humanist Asian cuteness. I
like to put the same effort into big or small projects,
so whether it's an international advertising campaign
seen by millions, or a small project seen by a few
thousand–the quality is always high, and people can

appreciate it.
-Edmundo Moi-Thuk-Shung, HiredMonkeez

Fixed

I am inspired by design pioneers, who went into
fresh markets to push the discipline forward. I
started my company, Name&Name with the aim
of using creativity to effectively lift clients projects,
be it branding, packaging or advertising–in both
developing and developed markets, to make things
the best they can be in any culture. I am interested
in how design connects with varied cultures–from
elegant european modernism, to bold impactful
American humour, to humanist Asian cuteness. I
like to put the same effort into big or small projects,
so whether it's an international advertising campaign
seen by millions, or a small project seen by a few
thousand–the quality is always high, and people can
appreciate it.

-Edmundo Moi-Thuk-Shung, HiredMonkeez

An orphan can falsely indicate that a sentence or sentences belong to the next paragraph or next column.

---

separately, because they already sit tightly together. No two
fonts are created alike, so track each font independently.

Widows

A widow is a line at the end of a paragraph that is one-third
the line length or less. It's often just one or two lonely words.
These castoff words break the flow of text from one paragraph to the next—syncopation in the typographical sym-
phony. It happens in both print and digital formats. The
fixes vary, with the easiest being to adjust the tracking of
the paragraph. Be careful not to add or subtract too much
tracking though, or the paragraph will look out of place.
Another fix is to adjust the width of the paragraph ever so
slightly. Type size can also be adjusted as long as it doesn't
break consistency with surrounding text. The text width
can be adjusted, but be warned: Manually "squishing" or
stretching type will destroy the integrity of the original letterforms. Do not adjust more than 2 percent. Better yet,

choose a condensed typeface instead. The last resort is ed-
iting the text, but only with the client's permission.

Orphans

An orphan is either the last one or two lines of a paragraph
stranded at the top of the next column of text, or the opening line or two of text stuck at the bottom of one column
while the rest is in the next. Like widows, orphans break the
flow of text and create readability issues. The fixes for orphans are the same as for widows, with the added option of
lengthening the paragraph's column at the bottom or top to
allow the words to rejoin the original paragraph.

Dashes

It comes as a surprise to many people, designers included, that there are three types of dashes in written communication. Designers may be equally surprised to find that
they are indeed responsible for knowing and using all three

Mother In-Law

February–April

I do the heavy lifting—she takes care of the details.

Hyphen, en dash and em dash, respectively.

correctly. Design is in the details. A client may neglect proper usage, but that doesn't mean you can too.

- **HYPHEN:** shortest dash; used for words that break at the end of a sentence and for compound words such as *mother-in-law* or *good-natured*
- **EN DASH:** medium-length dash; indicates a range of items or the passage of time (Examples include: 2–3 P.M., February–April, or listing pages 17–23. An en dash's length is equal to the width of the font's lowercase *n*.)
- **EM DASH:** longest dash; indicates a change of thought or emphasis (The em dash's length is equal to the width of the font's lowercase *m*. In a sentence with an independent clause, it can be used in place of a colon or a semi-colon. It also can replace a coordinating conjunction such as *and, so, nor, for, but,* or *yet*. Here's an example: "I do the heavy lifting—she takes care of the details." In a sentence with a dependent clause, it can be used in place of two commas or parentheses, like this: "Choosing the right typeface—even more than choosing the perfect color palette—can make or break a design." People will frequently use two hyphens in a row to indicate an em dash.)

Make sure to proofread the text thoroughly and fix any misused dashes.

After a period

The space before and after every character on typewriter keys is exactly the same, whether it is a *T, c, b,* period or question mark. This is called *monospacing.* The small metal plate holding the letter is slightly larger and wider than the actual letter. To adjust for the monospacing, it became the practice to add an extra space after a period in order to more easily distinguish sentences from each other. Thanks to the computer, kerning pairs and adjustable spacing are built into fonts, so that the type fits together properly—no more monospacing. Because type is now appropriately and evenly spaced, we no longer need two spaces after a period. It is still an ingrained habit for many people, so be sure to double-check the text for these extra spaces before you finalize the design.

Quotes: smart vs. prime

Smart quotes (or curly quotes) are quotation marks that curl or angle toward the text in your typography. These are often confused with prime marks (or dumb quotes), which denote inches and feet. Prime marks look like quotation marks, but instead of angling or curling toward the type, they are straight up and down. Typing prime marks is easily avoidable because most design and layout software inserts smart quotes automatically. But issues can arise when importing text. Dumb quotes are found in abundance in

"Anarchist"

"Anarchist"

Prime vs. Smart quotes.

ch ct ck it ip sp st tt
ff fi fj fl ft fü ffi ffl

Æ Æ Œ MP Æ HE MD
UP MB TY VH CT TT

Ligature examples.

Non-Hanging

"Commit to rigorous and unrelenting work habits. Never settle."
-Craig Welsh, Go Welsh

Hanging

"Commit to rigorous and unrelenting work habits. Never settle."
-Craig Welsh, Go Welsh

Shifting the punctuation to hang outside of the alignment creates better visual flow through and around the text.

---

word processing documents and on the web, so be sure to read through text carefully if you receive it from an outside source. Issues also arise when you actually do need a prime mark for an inch or foot measurement—the mark must be inserted manually.

Ligatures

Simply put, ligatures are two or more letters that touch. The most common ligature combinations are *fi*, *fl*, *ffi* and *ffl*, though any combination of letters can become a ligature. Some letters create awkward shapes when appearing next to each other. In the case of *f* and *i*, the dot over the *i* interferes visually with the overhanging ball terminal of the *f*. Well-designed typefaces incorporate special ligature characters—single characters that replace the original two letters—in the font. In the case of the *f-i* ligature, the dot becomes part of the *f*'s ball terminal, thus improving the word's readability. It's a subtle difference compared to a separated *f* and *i*, but it is an important one, especially in larger type found in headlines, subheads and logos.

Specialized letter combinations or too many ligatures can impair readability, so be careful. Be cautious with loose tracking as well. A tightly kerned ligature looks odd if its spacing doesn't match the rest of the word.

Hanging punctuation

In left-aligned text that begins with a quotation mark, the quotation mark causes the first line to appear indented, creating poor optical alignment. "Pull" the whole line to the left, so that the punctuation "hangs" over the edge of the block of text. Do this by inserting a negative left indent or using the automated optical alignment functions found in design software. Hanging punctuation is necessary for quotation marks, question marks, hyphens, commas, periods and exclamation points. Hanging punctuation is normally used just for large type, but if a design has only one or two text paragraphs, some choose to hang the punctuation in the smaller text as well. Most designers don't bother if the design has multiple paragraphs or pages of paragraphs.

COLOR MATTERS

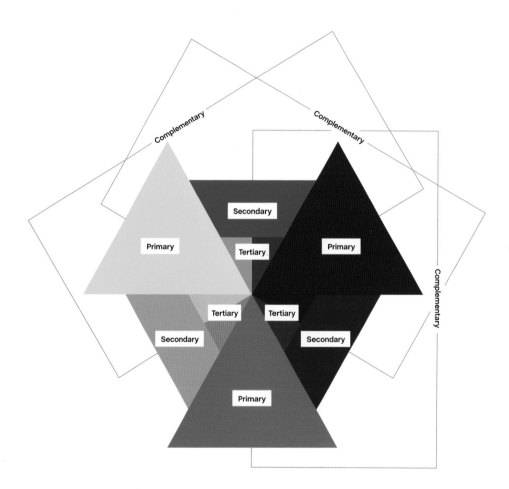

Designers certainly don't fear color. Full rainbows everywhere! Throw in some blue here and a little red there and voilà—it's a successful design. Or not. Color plays a vital role in a viewer's perception of a design. The wrong color alienates—or worse, bores—the person you're trying to reach. The right color delights the senses. It connects emotionally and psychologically. It makes a boring subject interesting and an interesting subject superbly exciting.

Before we can choose the right color for a design, we must review color basics. You know, the ones we learned in grade school. There's the primary color wheel, secondary colors, tertiary colors and complementary colors. There are also Pantone colors, Toyo colors and a whole gamut of other color systems from which to choose. We need to talk about hue, tone and saturation. We also need to have a serious discussion about connotation.

THE BASICS

As children we were taught the three primary colors: red, yellow and blue (RYB). Our art teachers showed us how to mix them together to produce the secondary colors: orange,

31 ● Cyan, magenta and yellow help to reinvent a Venn diagram.

32 ● Intricately woven color creates a subtle, yet vibrant ad for books.

green and violet. Then it got fun. Mixing primary and secondary colors together created the tertiary colors: red-orange, yellow-orange, yellow-green, green-blue, blue-violet and red-violet. Then we got to use them as finger paints. Even more fun, but we had to be careful. Swirl them together too much and it created a mud-brown mess. What an eye-opener for a six-year-old. That was the most disappointing and, at the same time, the most educational aspect of learning about colors. The finger painting lesson teaches us early on that we need to be careful about our color choices or else a design will look like mud.

Let's go back to those basics for a moment. Growing up, we discover two more sets of primary colors: cyan, magenta, yellow and black (CMYK) for printed materials; and red, green and blue (RGB) in the visible light spectrum and digital media. CMYK is very similar to the original RYB primary colors. In combination, CMYK can produce 100 million ($100 \times 100 \times 100 \times 100$) different colors. By comparison, RGB creates only 16,777,216 ($256 \times 256 \times 256$) colors. Realistically we need to focus on the 16.7 million RGB colors because those are the only ones our eyes and brains can process. It may sound disappointing, but there are still a lot of colors available for designing. This demonstrates the incredible importance of examining all the possibilities for any given project.

Let's talk complements

"You're a brilliant designer."

"You picked the perfect colors!"

"How could I live without your fabulous design skills?"

These are great compliments and I love to hear them, but we really need to talk about a different kind of complement. Complementary colors bring visual interest to a design. One color can look great, but adding a complement can really make it pop.

Complementary colors are the ones opposite each other on the color wheel: orange and blue, violet and yellow, and red and green. The list grows as tertiary colors are added. As a rule, complementary colors set each other off and create a vibrant duo. Another way to choose complementary colors is by breaking free of the color wheel and matching cool colors (blues, greens, purples) with warm ones (reds, oranges, yellows). A rule of thumb: Complementary colors look great

33 ● Prim and proper imagery with cool blue and green undertones alters the mood and color temperature of this chocolate bar series.

"Designers have a prestigious role in society. As tastemakers, we have a responsibility to use our creativity to find ways to add color when the world is in gray scale. We must live and breathe design in order to be prepared for the next idea that changes one life or millions. If you want to make an arrest, you better be in uniform." —RYAN MEYER

side by side but tend to vibrate when placed on top of each other. Using complementary colors to create contrast within the design is a surefire way to grab the viewer's attention.

Harmonious colors are those that are similar in color. These are colors that sit next to or near each other on a color wheel. Blue and green are harmonious. Orange and yellow-orange are harmonious. They work well with each other and we intuitively sense a relationship, as they are derived from the same color base. This type of color pairing is good for creating design elements requiring unity.

Taking color's temperature

First, let's get a few terms out of the way:

- **HUE** is the name of a color. Blue, yellow and pinkish-purple are all hues.
- **TINT** is the range of lightness within a color. Think of it as adding white to a color.
- **SHADE** is the range of a color that comes from adding black to it.
- **SATURATION** is the range of intensity from full to dull. The pure hue has the greatest saturation. Once the color is tinted or shaded, the saturation level drops.

Now that we have that out of the way, let's talk temperature. Colors are described as hot, cold, warm and cool. Temperature is an important design consideration because the eye naturally causes warm colors to advance and cool colors to recede. Understanding this mechanism lets you control how a viewer sees your design. Need a headline to pop off a page? Use red. Want a background to recede? Make it blue.

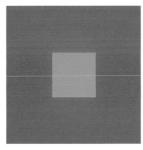

Color temperature

Need a poster to really jump off the wall? Try complementary hues of a warm and cool color together.

We're not done yet. You can break the color thermometer to create a subtle or blatant temperature shift in the opposite direction. Tone, shade and saturation all contribute to a color's tendency toward a particular temperature, which can be shifted. Shifting a color's temperature also depends a lot on its environment. For instance, small amounts of pale pink added to a dominantly blue snowy scene will take on a coolness. The cool blue overwhelms the eye and the lighter color, pale pink, no longer appears warm. On the opposite side of the color wheel, letting cool lime green go to its maximum saturation intensity creates a bright fluorescent color that is hot and electrifying when paired with magenta.

Other color systems

CMYK has limitations, which is why there are plenty of colors beyond the 100 million CMYK combinations specifically created for use in printed materials. Although CMYK can produce just about any color, some of them—particularly secondary colors—can't get the same saturation intensity as primary colors. Oranges in particular never seem to get as intense or as bright as magenta using CMYK. Proprietary color systems such as Pantone, Toyo, Trumatch and Focoltone are used to create specific inks and colors for printing presses. Pantone Matching System (PMS) 485 is a bright pure red, more intense than can be achieved through

COLOR ME HUNGRY

Psychologists have long known that color influences us at many levels. But did you know that the color of your food and even the color of your surroundings can influence how and what you eat? Research has proven that warm colors such as reds, oranges and yellows stimulate the appetite. Think about the major fast food chains: McDonald's, Burger King, Arby's and Wendy's all use deep, rich, warm, inviting colors for their logos, food wrappers, advertisements and interior design. This shouldn't be a surprise, as these colors evoke feelings of intimacy, energy, happiness and passion. What better colors to use to invite hungry customers into a restaurant?

Associations are made early on between color and food. Red juicy apples, luscious orange oranges, salty yellow potato chips, healthy green spinach. This "earthy" color range becomes the acceptable color range for food. One color rarely seen in association with food is blue. Save for blueberries and blue corn tortilla chips, blue pretty much shuts down the appetite. Along with black and purple, blue is nature's way of saying the food is toxic or moldy. This primitive reaction has persisted. Today, dietitians recommend blue plates or blue painted kitchens to help a client lose weight. Some go to the extreme of recommending blue food dye be added to a meal to limit the dieter's desire for a food. I don't know about you, but I find the idea of eating blue spaghetti nauseating. It turns out the sight of food is more important than its texture or smell. This is what makes blue such a powerful appetite suppressant.

Of course, there are exceptions to every rule. Children's foods tend to be more adventurous in color because children don't have deep-seated biases about color. Blue M&M's, blue gummy bears, blue cotton candy and blue raspberry snow cones rank among children's favorites, especially when they turn the tongue blue too.

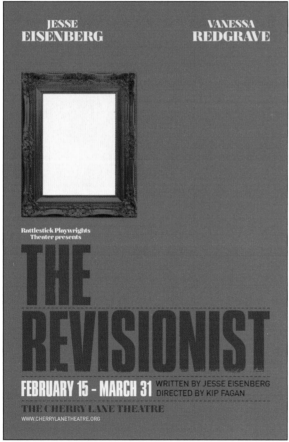

34 + 35 ● Peace and a tenuous relationship are both forged in red. Connotation of color is all in the context.

CMYK. These colors are specially formulated by the company and distributed for use on printing presses. Because of this, a job printed in the United States on one press and another printed on a press in China will have an identical color match. This is not always true for CMYK colors, as inks may run "heavy" or "light" on a press, affecting the final CMYK output. Another advantage to colors from a proprietary color system is their ability to formulate metallic, pearlescent and true fluorescent colors. These ink colors have properties not present in CMYK.

COLOR SPEAKS

Color speaks differently to each person. For instance, when I say the word *green*, your brain immediately pictures a certain hue. The likelihood that it's the same green I'm picturing is slim. Our experiences and environment affect what we see. The same person will even envision different greens at different times. You may picture an electric lime green while busy at work with the day's tasks, and a deep forest green while at home relaxing on the weekend. In addition, when I say "green," you may also feel something different than I do. We can even be looking at the exact same color green and it will still evoke different reactions. Mine may be a feeling of peace and calm, while yours may be strength and power. The perception of a color can also change through a person's life. A small child may perceive the color green as a jovial color associated with the outdoors, but the same person in later life may associate green with sickness and longing.

Color affects and reflects what a person feels. Understanding this psychology is a huge advantage for designers because it's another way to control the audience's perception of the presented design. The trick is using this emotional association to strengthen a design, because while the wrong color can bring it down fast, the right color can skyrocket a design to new levels.

Color emotes

Here are some of the universal meanings, created by both psychological and emotional connections, associated with common colors. This is not an exhaustive list, but it begins to make the process of choosing the correct color a little easier. Many colors in this list have opposite meanings included, because changes in meaning occur when changes are made to the hue, tint, shade and saturation of the overall color category. When choosing colors, consider the response you want to elicit. Choose colors from those main categories and then expand your search to find the exact hue to express your message.

- **RED:** passionate, romantic, loving, powerful, dangerous, attention-seeking, aggressive, rebellious
- **ORANGE:** active, energetic, playful, stimulating, appetizing, hot, spicy
- **YELLOW:** optimistic, confident, cheerful, bright, warm, cowardly, acidic, sickly
- **GREEN:** healthy, natural, verdant, fresh, balanced, wealthy, greedy, envious
- **BLUE:** powerful, strong, trusting, peaceful, tranquil, frigid, weak, depressed
- **VIOLET:** royal, sophisticated, spiritual, creative, fantastical, immature, arrogant
- **GRAY:** conservative, reliable, dignified, luxurious, calm, neutral, drab, indifferent
- **BLACK:** strong, sophisticated, mysterious, powerful, evil, negative, sad
- **WHITE:** pure, innocent, perfect, clean, new, stark, isolated, empty

TRY IT·

EMOTIVE COLOR PALETTES

Choosing colors can be agonizing. Create a library of color palettes to make the process less painful.

1. Start with the basics. Choose five to ten hues for each color of the rainbow. Pick a range from light to dark and make sure the hues vary. For example, the blues can range from cyan to navy to teal.
2. Select a variety of emotive adjectives. Here are a few to get you started: energetic, quality, corporate, caring, natural, serene, fresh, empowered, intelligent, delightful and festive.
3. Put together palettes that express the chosen adjectives. Pick three to five colors for each palette. Choose colors that work well together and "feel" like the adjective. Don't necessarily pick expected colors. Throw in a pop color here and there.
4. Try to create three or more palettes for each emotive quality.
5. Name the palettes for easy reference.
6. Use the palettes as is, or as a jumping off point for your next project. Continue developing palettes with each new design.

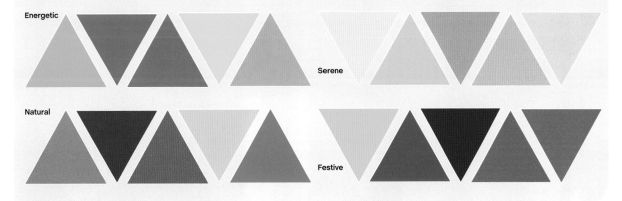

Energetic

Serene

Natural

Festive

RULE **6**

IT'S HIP TO BE SQUARE

The size and shape of your page is just as important as the design on the page. Format is the physical manifestation of a design. This book is an 8.25" × 10.875", multiple-page paperback book; a gig poster is typically on 18" × 24" heavyweight paper; and the last website I designed was 1024 × 768 pixels. Format is like a grid system. It should be natural, practically invisible and let the content do the talking. Awkward sizes, cumbersome shapes, unstable binding and clumsy folds come between the viewer and the content. Format doesn't have to be boring, but it does need serious consideration so as not to distract from the content.

Assume nothing

You have 30 seconds to grab a piece of paper and fold it into a brochure. Ready. Set. Go! Raise your hand if you grabbed a letter-sized paper and folded it into a tri-fold brochure? It's OK, you can admit it. Ninety-nine percent of us did the same thing. Format is fraught with assumptions. Designers (and clients) assume a brochure is an 8.5" × 11" (or A4) tri-fold, a poster is 11" × 17" or 18" × 24", a website is 1024 × 768 pixels, and soup belongs in a can. All those formats work, but they aren't the only way to go. All the creative anarchist needs is a bit of inventiveness and experimentation.

Client directives

A client will want an 8.5" × 11" (or A4) sheet for his letterhead. It runs easily through a printer and fits into a standard business envelope. This is not an unreasonable request. Designers adhere to format constraints by clients all the time. After all, the package needs to work with the filling machinery and a direct mail piece needs to stay within a postage budget. Sometimes format restrictions are intended to save money by using up supplies of already purchased materials, or matching current materials. You won't always be able to choose the format, but the trick is learning to work within the constraints, figuring out how to be creative and practical at the same time. For instance, if you're stuck using 8.5" × 11" for a letterhead, try other ways to modify the paper.

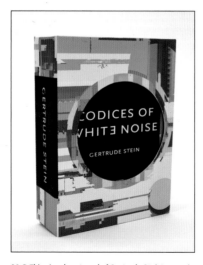

36 ● This visual portrayal of Gertrude Stein's experimentation with the linear form of language fragments the anthology into four codices that progress in visual complexity.

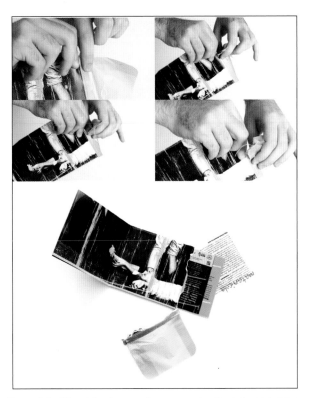

37 ● 8 postcards depicting sketches by the show's costume and set designer, Max Allen, and short bios of the choreographers are sewn together to form a creative after-performance keepsake for Israeli-Italian, Berlin-based, choreographer duo Matanicola.

Choose one with a different texture, finish or weight from what the company generally uses. Propose a different color or a recycled paper. Be creative with your suggestions. If a direct mail piece needs to fit a 6" × 9" envelope, consider ways the envelope can be eliminated in favor of a format that doubles as a self-mailer. The price difference between eliminating an envelope and printing on a larger sheet of paper may offset each other. Few clients would balk at a solution that reduces waste and printing costs.

Remember that design ends up in the hands of the client's audience, who will:

- file it away
- place it in a drawer
- hang it on the wall
- stick it to the fridge
- pop it into a wallet
- buy it from a grocery store
- shelve it in a kitchen cabinet
- view it on a phone or
- look at it once and then throw it away

The final design destination determines the choice of format. A business card made of thin, easily torn paper will

38 ● "The idea was to create an engaging, but not overly elaborate or expensive piece. It was a piece that's base purpose was to ask for money, but also to educate students about the true impact they can have early with philanthropic support and the importance it has played in the 180 year history of Wake Forest. Functionally, we wanted the piece to be a fresh structure compared to traditional solicitation materials. We thought of a structure that while pocket size, could open into a full sized poster." —Hayes Henderson

39 ● A fun small-scale party for creative people in London deserves an equally fun small-scale invitation. "The matchbox with 'partying matches' concept made sense to show a party in a small space. The event name was mostly written in a custom font—3pix, a 3 pixel high font—the smallest size grid we could use to make a font." —Ian Perkins

40 ● "Once we found out that the annual Mentor Iowa Tidrick Honors Auction was scheduled for May 1, we knew the party should carry a whimsical May Day theme. More than an invitation that looked like a basket, we wanted the invitation to be a basket. We worked with the printer to create an invitation that fit into an envelope to help with mailing costs. Once assembled, the basket could hold small candies or prizes." —Saturday Mfg.

never withstand long-term storage in a wallet, and a direct mail piece using polystyrene will anger an audience who

An invitation that's tall and skinny, or square, instead of the traditional rectangular A2 or A7 has the wow-factor because of its unexpected size. A website designed with responsive formatting—programming a design to fit every possible viewing device, often with significant changes from one device to anoth-

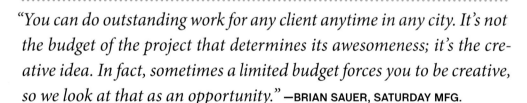

"You can do outstanding work for any client anytime in any city. It's not the budget of the project that determines its awesomeness; it's the creative idea. In fact, sometimes a limited budget forces you to be creative, so we look at that as an opportunity." —BRIAN SAUER, SATURDAY MFG.

recycles. Long-lasting designs demand format and materials that will withstand the elements. Shorter-term designs should use sustainable materials and processes whenever possible, as they will end up recycled or in a landfill.

Size surprises

If you need to make a huge impact, make the format literally huge. Create a brochure that folds out to a poster, or just send a poster. Perhaps you'd rather be subtle and cute. How about a small booklet with charming pop-ups? Format doesn't have to go to extremes to make an impact.

er—will wow when pushed to its minimum or maximum size as it changes from the standard web view.

Cut it out

Die-cutting provides tremendous impact at nominal cost. Just as changing size grabs attention, so does changing the shape. Rectangle is the most common shape in printing. Brochures, business cards, posters and boxes are all rectangles. Small nuances in shape work just as well as dramatic ones. Rounded corners in a sea of squared-off ones will stand out, as will a square among endless rectangles.

41 ● (above) The book has a die cut that runs throughout, adding a dimension of interactivity for the reader.

42 ● (below) "Band names for this collaborative experimental rock album were present only in the negative space of the die cut letterforms. The inside digipak was as bold and colorful as possible to contrast with the plain white die cut paper of the sleeve. The band kept the outer sleeves in their van while they were on tour. They said that there were so many punched out letters in the bottom of their van that it looked like a crate of alphabet soup had exploded." —Doe Eyed Design & Illustration

43 ● (above) "This business card 'artifact' is scored and perforated so the recipient can build a chair. It's a card, it's a chair, it's a conversation starter." —Jamie Runnells

44 ● (below) The simple and sophisticated square format card is a perfect fit for a high end home accessories designer.

Printers keep a variety of die shapes on hand. Give a call to see what's available for your project. It could lead to a solution you hadn't considered. Using already formed dies keeps the cost down as well—a benefit for you and your client, which your client is sure to appreciate.

Die-cutting isn't limited to the outer edges. Push Pin Studios drilled a hole through the center of their *Push Pin Graphic* No. 54 titled "The South, 1967." The issue served as a political statement against racism and the tragic inequities of white-on-black crime. Images of black victims were arranged with idyllic images from the "white" South. The victims' images were positioned so the hole pierced their heads like a bullet. That hole amplified the impact of the message immensely. Concept goes beyond images; format can be conceptual too.

Industry regulations

No matter how cool an idea for a format, it still needs to be functional. Do not overlook postal regulations. Watch what can happen: You design an awesome square format invitation piece. You've convinced the client to use a beautiful special order paper, a quadruple foldout, silver foil stamping and embossing. It looks amazing. It had better, because it pushed the budget to the max. You drop the mailers off at the post office and discover that the unusual shape incurs a 40 percent postage increase. Mailing costs are up several thousand dollars, which eliminates your profit margin and freaks out the client. This is all your fault. Properly researching your project would have alerted you to the need to economize somewhere, either by creating a standard envelope-sized invitation or cutting back on a special technique.

The post office wants to work with you. Create a mock-up of your design and take it to them. They will review the piece for postal standards and offer suggestions to fix any problems.

The printer has standards too. Designing a crazy format without first consulting them leads to up-charges and headaches. It's devastating to discover that a cool diagonal crease can't be machine-folded

45 ● Poster origami at its best.

and instead has to be done by hand. Or a life-size poster can't be printed on the in-house press because it's larger than the maximum sheet size. And that amazing custom circular box only gets one print per press sheet, which means buying more paper and generating six times the waste of a simpler design. On top of that, the circular box doesn't fit well on a shelf (squared boxes fit side by side better than round boxes) so the client needs to pony up more money for increased shelf space. These issues demolish your bottom line and the client's faith in your capabilities. Work with the post office and printer to create solutions that maximize effectiveness and minimize the waste of materials, time and money.

Bend and fold it

Kids are wizards at paper folding. I used to create origami birds, cootie catchers and paper footballs all the time. It was fun, and the medium made it easy. Paper yearns to be folded. Problem is, we forget how much fun we can have with paper. We stick to the same old tri-fold format and wonder why it's boring. Instead of folding the edges of a typical tri-fold toward the middle, fold the paper into a Z-fold, or accordion, instead. It still fits inside a business envelope and opens more quickly for the viewer. Or fold the paper lengthwise in half for a booklet fold that fits a No. 6 envelope. Take that folded paper and fold it in half again. It's called a French fold, and it fits an A2 announcement envelope. Now cut it along the top edge and you have a little booklet. Looking to add oomph to something larger? Use legal-sized paper (8.5" × 14"). The extra length creates more folding options:

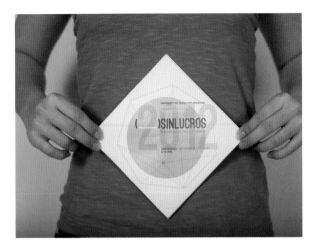
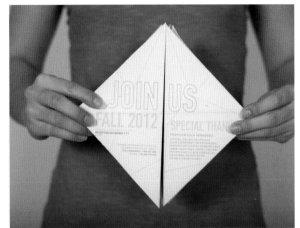
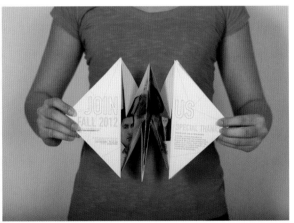

46 ● "The element of surprise is what made this design successful. Every person who opens the invite for the first time is simply fascinated by the folds." —University of Texas-Pan American

TRY IT:

FOLDING LIBRARY

Re-create each of the folds diagrammed in the section "Bend and Fold It." Bring them out each time you need to work on a design that requires a folding format. Handling, folding and unfolding physical samples helps to visualize the final concept. Consider all the ways information can be arranged on the different panels, and choose the best fold for the job.

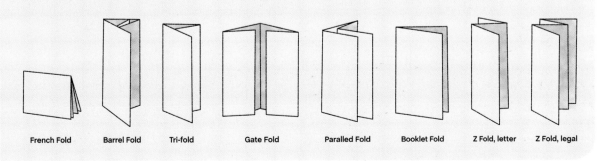

French Fold   Barrel Fold   Tri-fold   Gate Fold   Paralled Fold   Booklet Fold   Z Fold, letter   Z Fold, legal

COMMON PAPER TERMS

WEIGHT: A paper's weight is defined as the weight of five hundred sheets expressed in pounds (lb or #; 20lb and 20# are both used).

TEXT: This is the type of paper typically used for letterheads and interior pages of documents. Text weights range from 20# to 80#.

COVER: This is typically used for folders, posters, business cards, postcards, greeting cards and other items that need to be thicker or heavier. Cover weights typically range from 80# to 220#.

COATED: The paper is treated, producing a glossy finish varying from matte (most dull) to high gloss. Ink remains on the surface of coated papers instead of sinking in, resulting in more vibrant colors.

UNCOATED: This is the term for untreated paper that feels soft or rough to the touch. Inks absorbed by the paper make the printing look a bit duller and less crisp than on coated paper. Uncoated paper connotes warmth and friendliness, and it also works well for screen printing and letterpress.

COTTON: This is a high-quality paper made from cotton fibers. It's found mainly as text weight and is commonly used for higher-end letterheads.

VELLUM FINISH: This is a smooth surface finish for uncoated paper, not to be confused with vellum paper that is translucent.

LINEN FINISH: This is an uncoated finish that simulates the appearance of the horizontal and vertical weaving of linen cloth. It's commonly used for letterheads, business cards and covers.

LAID FINISH: This is an uncoated finish that has a pattern of parallel lines (horizontal or vertical) running through it. The lines are created during the paper-making process through the use of a special roller. It's commonly used for letterheads and business cards.

BOND PAPER: This is a cheap text-weight paper used for photocopiers and desktop printers.

RECYCLED PAPER: This is reconstituted paper made from paper and other material waste. One hundred percent post-consumer recycled paper is most desired because it's an eco-friendly, sustainable product. Bits of foreign matter tend to dot the paper—an indication that it is truly recycled.

parallel, gatefold and barrel. An 11" × 17" (tabloid or A3) piece of paper offers even more creative folds that still fit in a standard envelope, and even work as a self-mailer.

WE INTERRUPT YOUR REGULARLY SCHEDULED READING with this important information about self-mailers. The post office does not sort mail by hand. Mail flows through a chute-like machine that uses optical character recognition (OCR) to decipher the address on the envelope. In order for your mail to make it through this process, the main fold needs to be at the bottom edge of the finished, folded piece, and the lead front corner must be a closed folded corner. An open edge or open corner gets caught in the machinery and leads to OCR sorter rejection. The rejected piece is then hand sorted, risking delays in delivery. If a significant number of your mailing pieces are rejected, the post office

has the right to send all of them back to you as undeliverable. Take the initiative to bring a mock-up of the finished self-mailing design to the post office and ask if it will work correctly with the machinery. It's much better to know this before final printing.

Books and other publications

Book format refers to anything with four or more pages. A *booklet* is a short to medium length paper-covered document. A *book* is a longer volume with a paper or hard cover, with no limit on size or shape. Interior pages are called *signatures*, a group of pages combined and printed front and back on a larger sheet of paper. The number of pages grouped together depends on the final sheet size. The arrangement of the pages on the sheet, both front and back, is

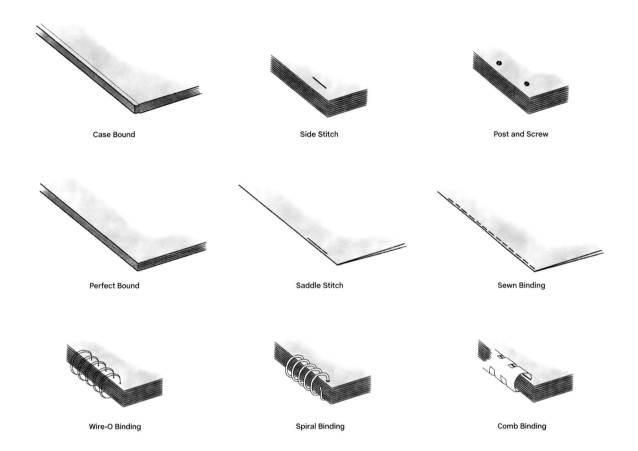

Case Bound

Side Stitch

Post and Screw

Perfect Bound

Saddle Stitch

Sewn Binding

Wire-O Binding

Spiral Binding

Comb Binding

called *imposition*. These pages are upside down, right side up, and in a different order than they appear in the book. After the paper is printed, folded, cut and trimmed, the pages appear in the correct order. Understanding imposition allows you to experiment with interactions between pages and spreads.

Bind it

Multiple page formats need something to hold the pages together. Binding considerations, like post office regulations, tend to be left until the end of the design process. Like mailing issues, binding can create unexpected headaches, so it's important to understand your available options.

- **CASE BOUND:** This is the binding used for hard-cover books. Signatures are sewn together in small sections. The sections are then placed side by side and glued to end papers, which are, in turn, glued into the hard-cover's spine.
- **SIDE STITCH:** Wire is punched from front page to back page (instead of through the spine) and folded over.

Decorative tape or a secondary cover is often added to hide the stitching.

- **POST AND SCREW:** Holes are punched or drilled through the front cover along the spine. A post is inserted through the back and a screw is put through the front into the post and tightened. Post and screw is a common binding for swatch books and photo albums.
- **PERFECT BOUND:** Signatures are aligned side by side at the edge of the spine. The spine ends of the signatures are trimmed off, the paper is roughened for better adhesion, and the pages are glued together. A cover is then wrapped around to hold it all together. Paperback books are perfect bound.
- **SADDLE STITCH:** This is the most common and economical binding. Metal wire or a staple is punched through the outer edge (spine) of the document and folded over on the inside center to bind the pages together. Be aware that the more pages you saddle stitch together, the more the inner pages will stick out farther than the outer pages. This is called *creep*, and it occurs because the thickness of the paper builds up in the area

47 ● Resizing from a tablet to a phone isn't as simple as a reduction in size. All of the elements need to be rearranged to maximize the available screen space.

of the spine. This makes the innermost pages narrower than the outer pages when the document is trimmed flush. Lay out your design accordingly.

- **SEWN BINDING:** This is a very expensive stitch binding in which the entire spine edge of the document is sewn with thread.
- **WIRE-O BINDING:** Exactly like comb binding except the comb is made of wire. The durable binding allows the pages to lay flat when opened.
- **SPIRAL BINDING:** A corkscrew-shaped wire is twisted through a series of holes punched into the document. The ends of the wire are trimmed to size and crimped to prevent the wire from slipping back out. This too allows the document to lay flat.
- **COMB BINDING:** This is an inexpensive binding for documents that need to lay flat when opened. A series of rectangular holes are punched though the document and a plastic comb is fed through. The comb rings curl around so the page edges are hidden by the binding.

Screen it

If you think choosing the right format for paper is tough, try deciding on the proper screen resolution size for digital projects. Technology changes so fast that a standard size today could be outdated tomorrow. Literally. Digital projects are based upon the devices used for viewing—smartphones, tablets, laptops and desktop computers. Each of these devices come in many different sizes from dozens of companies. Trying to design for every single screen resolution will only result in your head banging against a wall. The minute you think you have them all covered, a company will announce the next greatest device… which is a different size than everything else on the market. So how do you decide on a format for a website or an app?

Think about the audience, the content and the anticipated viewing device. For a website, a good rule of thumb is to start with one size for each type of device. For example, try 1366 × 768 pixels for a computer, 1024 × 768 for a tablet and 320 × 480 for a smartphone. This will narrow your design decisions and help the programmer create the code for you.

Top 10 Screen Resolution Sizes

RESOLUTION SIZES (PIXELS)	% IN USE WORLDWIDE (AUG 2014)
320 x 480	2.9%
1024 x 768 (horizontal and vertical)	11.6%
1200 x 800	6.0%
1280 x 1024	5.0%
1366 x 768	19.3%
1440 x 900	4.7%
1680 x 1050	4.1%
1600 x 900	4.4%
1920 x 1200	6.9%
Other resolutions	29.6%

Source: http://www.w3counter.com/globalstats.php?year=2014&month=7

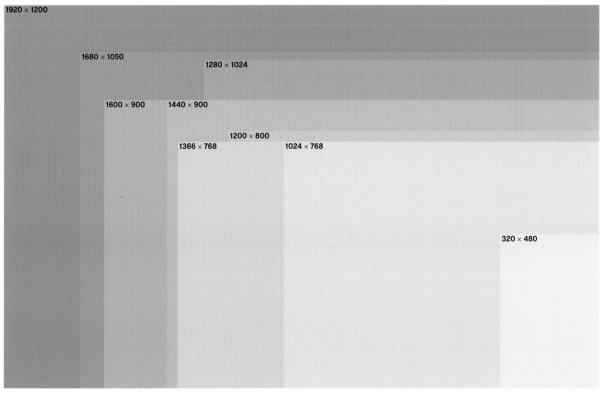

It's impossible to design for every screen size out there. Pick a few to work with.

USE A GRID

I once polled an Intro to Design class about their issues with grids after noticing a strong resistance to using them. I was surprised by the answer; I thought my lecture on grids went quite well. Turns out my young designers had developed a misconception that grids are rigid devices that sap all creativity and flexibility. They were afraid of being trapped in a design. This fear is understandable, but unnecessary. A grid gives structure to both print and digital pages, providing order, alignment and consistency to elements of the design. The structure offered by a grid also streamlines the design process. It's a frame, not a cage.

SERIOUSLY, A GRID HELPS

A grid is a lattice of horizontal and vertical lines that creates an invisible underlying structure, which helps bring order and consistency to a design. It needs to be used properly to be effective, which means you need to know how to build a grid. The parts of a grid are always the same: margins, columns, alleys, gutters, rows and modules. The arrangement and relative sizes of these elements are what give grids their personality. Let's review.

MARGINS are the spaces around the edge of the page. They keep content away from the edge so that nothing is inadvertently cut off when the paper is trimmed after printing. Margins also provide resting space for the eye outside the content area and leave space for important header and footer information. The outside left and right margins are also called **THUMB SPACE**, because that's where the viewer typically holds the page. Be sure to leave ample thumb space to avoid obscuring important content.

COLUMNS are vertical spaces between the margins that typically hold most of the content, both text and imagery. You

48 ● This poster was constructed with the focus on Sinaloa, a typeface designed by Tissi. The strong geometric forms lend themselves to an angled grid system.

can have anywhere from one to sixteen or more of them. Columns can also be different widths on the same page.

The small vertical space separating columns is called an **ALLEY**. The alley prevents content in each column from interfering with that in adjacent ones. (Note that some design software also uses the term **GUTTERS** to refer to alleys.)

On multipage designs, the inner margins where a left and right page meet are called **GUTTERS**. This area is obscured by the binding, so avoid placing important content there. Gutter sizes vary depending on the type of binding.

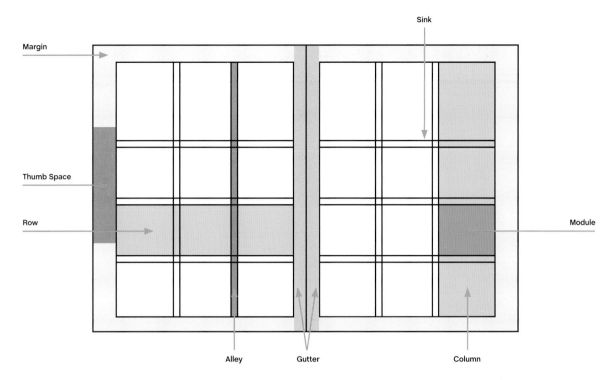

A grid is made up of a group of standard elements: margins, columns, alleys, gutters, rows and modules.

ROWS are secondary organizational elements that run horizontally across columns. They are most helpful for aligning content across columns. Like columns, rows can vary in size. Many longer documents have a row placed a specific distance down from the top of a page, called a *sink*, which acts as the starting point for each page and provides consistency across multiple pages.

A **MODULE** is the space created by the crossing of a column and a row. The more modules in a grid, the more options you have available to place content. A grid doesn't have to use modules, but they do allow more creative options for the design layout.

DEFINE YOUR GRID

You know your parts, now choose a style. There are a number of variables: page size, volume of content (text and imagery), number of pages in the total design, target audience and overall design concept. Some of your grid options include manuscript, column, modular, hierarchical and nontraditional.

Manuscript grid

A manuscript grid, the simplest of all, is used for a continuous flow of text such as a book or long essay. It contains margins and a single column. The gutter tends to be wide, to account for a heftier book binding. The biggest challenge with a manuscript grid is determining the proper width for the column, which should make the text line length comfortable to read over many pages. Thumb space is of particular importance

Experiment with margin width to create different visual connotation.

because a longer document will be in a viewer's hands for a significant amount of time. Be sure to leave enough space in the upper and lower margins for other information such as chapter headings and page numbers. Wider margins along the outer edges ensure that the thumb space is clear while keeping text at optimal reading length.

Column grid

A column grid is great for content that contains both type and imagery, such as posters, business cards, magazines, annual reports, newspapers and corporate brochures. The number and width of columns depends on the page size and the amount of text, imagery and other information

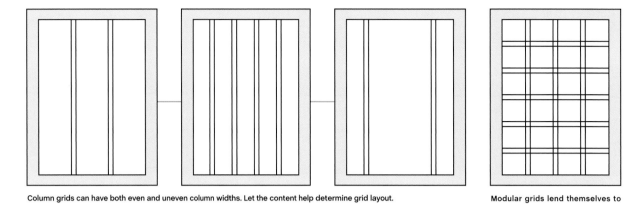

Column grids can have both even and uneven column widths. Let the content help determine grid layout.

Modular grids lend themselves to great variety within the layout.

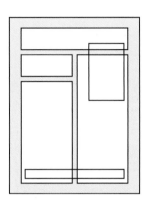
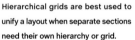
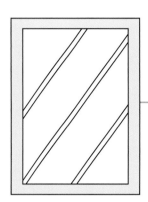

Hierarchical grids are best used to unify a layout when separate sections need their own hierarchy or grid.

Non-traditional grids work well to surprise the viewer.

49 ● Traditional column usage is complemented by strong bold imagery and generous negative space.

that needs to be included. As with a manuscript grid, column width needs to be optimized for readability. In the optimal column arrangement, the text flows smoothly from one column to the next and is easily followed by the reader's eye. Inexperienced designers mistakenly believe that columns must be exactly the same fixed width. Not true. Column widths may vary greatly even on a single page. A three-column grid can have any combination of wide and narrow columns, including three equal columns or three completely uneven columns.

Columns can be combined to create a compound column, which allows text and imagery to span more than one column. If you have a four-column grid, the content may flow in each column independently or across all four columns without nullifying the design of the original grid. See how much flexibility you can have with a column grid? But wait, there's more. The Rule of Halves dictates that columns can be divided in half, allowing content to flow from half column to half column, or half column to full column. Talk about flexibility—now you know why a column grid is so popular among designers.

Modular grid

A modular grid is a grid with both columns and rows, which work together to create modules. This grid is extremely flexible; however that flexibility can quickly create more confusion than clarity if not used well. A modular grid is best for designs with large amounts of complex content, or for a design with two or more separated content areas. Compound columns and the Rule of Halves also work with modular

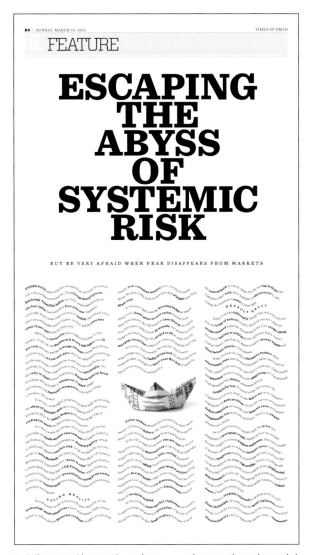

50 ● The use of modules can be obvious or subtle. Let the content guide the usage. Designer Adonis Durado took the word *transition* literally and fashioned the flow of the text as if readers are using the stairs—moving from point A to point B.

51 ● The wave grid communicates the content and engages the readers to challenge their reading habit.

grids, and you can form compound modules by combining modules horizontally, vertically or both. This gives modular grids nearly infinite possibilities for content layout. But you have to be careful. It's all too easy for a modular grid to become chaotic. You must have a strong conceptual and visual plan for the design when using a modular grid.

Nontraditional grid

Want to experiment with layout without feeling constrained by columns, rows and modules? A nontraditional grid may be for you. Diagonals, curves and shapes are used in place of traditional parts of a grid. Although the nonconformist attitude and free spirit of this style is incredibly appealing, it must be used with caution. Content layout is much more

difficult with a nontraditional grid, and it can be very tiring to view for a long time. Think about it. Would you want to read an 128-page brochure containing all diagonal columns? I wouldn't. Stick to using a nontraditional grid for single pages or short documents. Although nontraditional grids are powerful, interesting and supercool, you need to give serious consideration to their appropriateness for the message.

Hierarchical grid

Hierarchical grids are used in the digital world when different sections of information need to be viewed independently of one another. Unlike in other kinds of design, the content dictates the grid. In digital design, navigation and the content of complex websites or other apps is typically

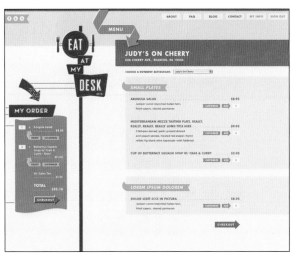

52 ● Hierarchy within navigation and text areas works together with "the simplicity of the color palette, offset edges, and textures of the text and shapes to give the website an authentic, vintage diner feel." —Sean Costik

distinguished through different grid placement and treatment. The result is often an irregular pattern of columns and rows, which allows for a more organic flow of information while still keeping it organized.

BREAKING THE GRID

There are times when an established grid isn't quite flexible enough for your content. Sometimes a grid system doesn't work at all and the only solution is to break the grid. (Pause here for audible gasp from grid enforcers.) Let me explain. Breaking the grid does not mean throwing it out the window. It means, on occasion, purposely extending elements beyond the confines of the vertical and horizontal guidelines.

Breaking the grid is done to create a dynamic visual statement. It can be done to draw the viewer's eye to a focal point. Sometimes the breakage is a happy accident: Content

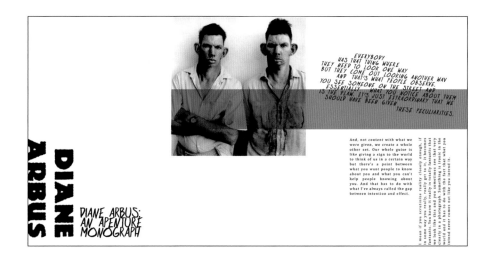

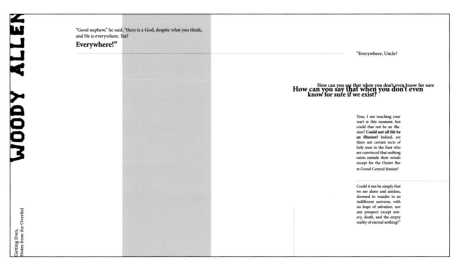

53 ● Using typography and an irregular grid, the layouts communicate each presented artists' personal madness and creativity.

is inadvertently placed outside a grid only to have it land in a spot that creates either contrast or good hierarchy. Sometimes the content's placement "just feels right" even though it's outside the grid. Always remember that breaking the grid requires effective communication and achievement of client goals. Relinquishing either of these—no matter how awesome the design looks—results in failure.

HOW DO I CHOOSE A GRID?

Deciding on a final grid can be as painful as choosing the best typeface. It's tough, but not impossible. Here is some advice for establishing the best possible grid for your content and design direction:

- Monotony leads to bored viewers. Make sure your grid is complex enough to be interesting but simple enough to avoid confusion.
- The smallest piece of your content should define the size of the modules (and therefore of columns and rows).
- Allow enough white space to accommodate flexibility, grid breakage and eye flow.
- Don't forget compound columns and the Rule of Halves to enhance the design.
- The more content you have, the more flexibility you need.
- Grids should work with the content, not fight against it.
- A grid is merely the underlying structure. It cannot bring the design to life. That is your job.

USE THE SPACE

The negative space of a design is just as, if not more, important than the content. Negative space controls the viewer's eye flow around the content, provides a resting place for the

55 ● Beautiful use of negative space. Need I say more?

TRY IT:

MAKE A GRID LIBRARY

Grids take time to create, and it's easy to fall into a rut using the standard two- or three-column grid over and over again. Put time back on your side by developing a grid library.

1. Start on paper. Sketch as many grids as you can think of. Start with a one-column manuscript and move up through multicolumnar modular.
2. Tip: Be methodical in your approach. For example, for a three-column grid, try:

   a. three equal columns

   b. two wide, one narrow

   c. one wide, two narrow

   d. one narrow, one wide, one narrow

   e. And so on. Do this process up to, at least, six columns.

3. Start adding rows to the columnar grid to form modules. At this point, you should have at least fifty or so grids. Throw in a few nontraditional grids too.
4. Digitize them. Use your preferred layout software to make templates of your grids. Do them in a size you commonly use. If you do a lot of standard-size annual reports, for example, make the pages 8.5" x 11". Don't forget spreads. The template could change from left to right.
5. Put them in a folder labeled "grid templates." Remember to give each file a descriptive name so you can easily find the one you need.
6. The next time you work on a project, pull out those sketches while brainstorming and utilize the templates when you start your computer work.

"Never give up, especially for students. Put yourself out there and take risks. Create. Have Fun. Read comics. Smile." —NICK HOWLAND

eye, and helps the viewer distinguish between different sections of content. Inexperienced designers tend to fill every inch of space, resulting in a crowded design with little readability and much confusion. The eye needs room to breathe and a good hierarchy to navigate the contents of a design.

Here is some advice for maximizing negative space and using it well:

- Use the largest possible margins and keep them clear of content.
- Open the alleys to keep columns of text from running together.
- The open space around an image should be equal to the width of the alley.
- Indent or use extra space to indicate paragraph breaks.
- Eliminate all unnecessary elements (defined as anything that does not enhance a design).
- Don't let the background interfere with readability.
- Resist the urge to completely fill the page.
- Eliminate *rivers*, which is the term for white space that runs vertically through the text.
- Use left-aligned text instead of justified, which fills columns completely and makes the column look fuller.
- Avoid content placement that leaves oddly shaped or trapped negative spaces. If you have awkward space, try to push it above, below or outside other page elements.
- Closely analyze hierarchy to maximize communication.

MAKE THINGS THE SAME–OR DIFFERENT

Good communication comes from layout and design elements that work well together. Arranging these elements to create maximum impact on the viewer is key to optimizing communication. Learning how elements associate with each other in a design puts you in charge of how a viewer will react and respond to your design.

DESIGNS UNITE

Purposefully arranging design elements to create a cohesive look is what keeps your design from looking like a jumbled mess. Consistency and unity of design, the visual relationship between all elements, supports the concept. A consumer wants to know what a package contains; a poster should advertise only one event. The viewer also needs to know they are still in the same document when they turn the page or navigate to another area of a website. The Gestalt principles of proximity, similarity, continuity, closure and figure/ground are used to create a better design through unity.

Gestalt, a field of psychology that focuses on cognitive behaviors, subscribes to the theory that the whole is greater than the sum of its parts. A design isn't complete until all the parts are in place. The header, navigation, logo, headline, image, text and contact information isn't a website until everything is integrated into a pixel document. Unity describes the quality that makes those elements part of a cohesive concept. Consistency in layout and visual relationships enhance unity and communication.

PROXIMITY refers to two or more elements placed close together or touching. Elements in close proximity form a relationship. The closer they get to each other, the stronger the relationship.

56 ● Overlapping objects and grouping text creates strong proximity.

Proximity is a great tool for designs with more than one set of informational content. Grouping related elements together using proximity gives the design organization and clear communication.

"Become well versed in the formal aspects and theory of visual design. This will provide range in how one can approach a multitude of design problems as well as really push or break 'the rules.'" —HANS SCHELLHAS

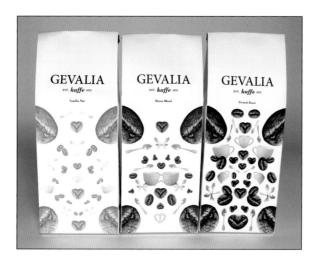

SIMILARITY refers to the principle that shared visual characteristics form relationships. It is based upon factors other than the form of the element. Similarity is achieved through color, size, shape, subject and arrangement. For instance, a design with a purple headline and a purple image creates a similarity-based unity. They don't need proximity to form a relationship; the color acts as the unifier. A magazine design that uses the same typeface for all its department page headlines creates unity (and consistency) throughout the multiple-page document. The similarity is stronger if the type is also the same color, size and position on each of the pages on which it appears.

CONTINUITY dictates that once the eye begins to follow something, it will continue traveling in that direction until it encounters another object. Continuity is a powerful tool for directing the viewer's eye around a page. Directional arrows are the best example of this. The eye will follow the arrow wherever it goes. Other elements can be used to create paths: a series of images placed in close proximity, a number of red dots leading down the page, or even an illustration of a person gazing in a certain direction. Think of all the fun you can have with this principle.

CLOSURE is what asks the brain to fill in the blanks. This principle states that, given enough information, a viewer

58 ● The playful ribbon winds around, leading the viewer to the comedic vision of Shakespeare.

59 ● This book cover lets the viewer complete the architect's face.

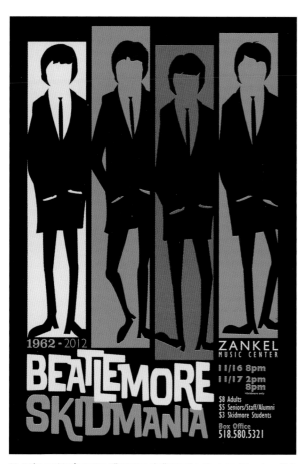

will spontaneously supply the missing parts. This works best if the element is easily recognizable or iconic. If the element is too complicated, the viewer may have trouble figuring out the remainder of the element. It can be tricky to find the right balance. Show too much, and the element no longer needs closure. For instance, do you really need to show Dorothy, Toto, the Tin Man, the Cowardly Lion and the Scarecrow for a poster advertising *The Wizard of Oz*, or can a viewer figure it out if the image shows a close-up of a girl's feet wearing ruby-red shoes instead? Finding the balance is a study in reduction. Remove elements from the design one by one until the message is lost. Then slowly add them back until you've struck the proper balance between communication and imagination.

The Gestalt principle of **FIGURE/GROUND** refers to the relationship between an element and its surrounding space. This principle gives the design a sense of depth. The moment two elements overlap, a figure/ground relationship begins. Experimenting with figure/ground is a great way to develop interesting visuals. Keep the viewer guessing as to which is figure and which is ground. M.C. Escher was a master at this. The relationship doesn't have to be as complex as his drawings to have an impact. A great example is the FedEx logo. The letters read as the words but also contain an

60 ● The positive/negative silhouettes challenge the viewer to determine which is figure and which is ground.

61 ● "Chilling as it may seem, the real problem wasn't those who had died. It was those they had left behind. The families of the deceased, over a million starving women, children and elderly people, with no source of income. The government took steps to prevent more suicides, but it was a case of too little, too late. And the rest of the country either did not know enough about the issue, or care enough. The awareness campaign began with an exhibition. 12 portraits of dead farmers were created from dry, burnt hay, displayed and auctioned. The very cause of their undoing proved to be a beacon of hope for them. Photographs of the hay portraits were replicated in print ads and posters and used to drive traffic to the exhibition held in Mumbai." —Taproot India

 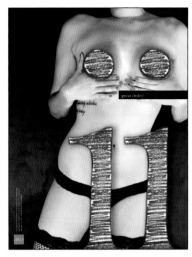 

62 ● This poster series has fun with sexually charged typographic terms. The type and imagery need each other to be successful.

arrow shape between the *E* and *x*. Depending on how you view the logo, the letters are the ground and the arrow is the figure, or vice versa.

VISUAL-VERBAL SYNERGY is essentially a restatement of Gestalt's "the whole is greater than the sum of its parts," but told specifically though the text and imagery. A headline and image may each work well enough on their own, but they pale in comparison to how they work together. Visual-verbal synergy is most noticeable in advertising. A brilliant example is a series of ads created for *The Times of India* by Taproot in Mumbai, India. Portraits of twelve deceased farmers were created using real hay. The portraits were then overlaid with the text, "Hang me again." The agency produced the portraits to bring attention to the almost 300,000 famers who committed suicide because of crop failure, drought and debt. The advertisements offered the originals for sale, with proceeds going to help the families. Without the visual, the headline means nothing, and without the headline, the visual isn't nearly as powerful. Visual-verbal synergy is a way to bring clever into a design. Not "haha" clever, but sophisticated clever. It's the aha moment a viewer gets when he views the design. The "Oh, now I get it!" kind of reaction. Visual-verbal synergy is easy to test. View the ad without the headline, and then view it without the image. Does the ad work with either one alone? If not, then it has visual-verbal synergy.

BALANCE: SYMMETRY AND ASYMMETRY

Humans are drawn to **SYMMETRICAL BALANCE**: a central axis with two halves of the same visual weight. It projects

63 ● Meticulously arranged ingredients lend balance to the overall layout.

the feeling of orderliness and tidiness. Our bodies are symmetrical, left reflecting right. Although symmetry is frequently found in nature, the two sides are never identical. This works the same way in design around an axis, whether that axis runs horizontally, vertically or diagonally. The two halves don't have to be identical, but the visual weight of one element must be equal to the visual weight of the other. For instance, a large image in one half that is the same visual weight as a bold headline in the other half has symmetrical balance.

On the other hand, **ASYMMETRICAL BALANCE**—a central axis, but with unequal visual weight—feels spirited, edgy and expressive. Asymmetrical balance must be carefully planned so that the content intermingles with no obvious effort at maintaining balance on either half. Alternately, elements can be arranged to purposely create tension by severely throwing off the balance. For instance, grouping the headline, imagery and body text all on the left side of the page and leaving the right side blank makes the page feel heavily weighted on the left. Asymmetrical balance is best used for dramatic visual effect.

Other types of balance

Symmetry and asymmetry are the most common forms of balance, but there are other options if you want something a little different. Elements in **RADIAL BALANCE** flow out from a central point instead of from a horizontal or vertical axis—symmetrically if the point is centered, asymmetrically if the point is off-center. Radial balance is found in many designs, the most common being layouts based upon sun rays or other similar elements. The radial design can also spiral out from the center, or be made of concentric circles.

RANDOM BALANCE is symmetrical or asymmetrical in overall feel but more arbitrary in appearance. This form of balance is not based upon any axis or point. It's more of an overall balance of the whole. It can be likened to the arrangement of a room: Many items of different weights and sizes fill the room. The inhabitants move around, sit on different furniture, and interact with different things, but there is still a focal point to the room. Let the viewer settle in, get comfortable and then show them around. Hierarchy still needs to be maintained, even though the design never sets out to purposefully be symmetrical or asymmetrical.

DOING THE TANGO

MOVEMENT is the result of proximity, similarity, continuity, closure and figure/ground—all the principles that influence tracking of the viewer's eye. The eye will follow the continuity of small elements to larger ones, and from one proximity grouping to another. Movement ties the page together through flow and organization.

REPETITION uses the Gestalt principles through organized replication of design elements to create continuity. Repeated elements enhance consistency within a design. Repetition can be accomplished on a small scale by having several elements repeat across a page section or on a larger scale by repeating elements across several pages. Be careful, though; repetition is boring when overused.

64 ● The combination and arrangement of type with imagery creates an overall random balance.

65 ● Typography treatments create rhythm throughout the CD booklet.

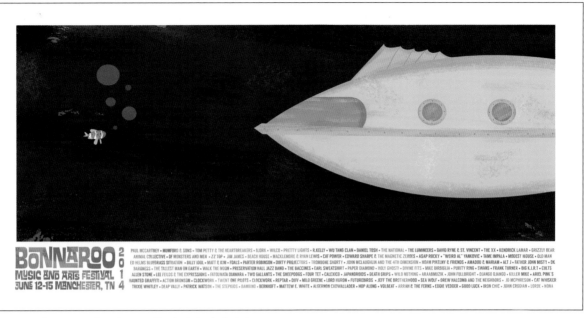

66 ● Extreme size contrast reflects the types of bands playing the festival.

RHYTHM is what creates the flow through a page. Envision a favorite song as shapes moving across a page. The highs and lows within the tune generate a rhythm that is repeated over and over. This effect can be replicated with design elements. For instance, using a varying-sized pattern (type, images, shapes, textures) across a section of a page and repeating it again elsewhere will create a rhythmic flow. The more repetitions of the pattern, the more rhythm on the page. Longer publications use the grid to create rhythm; design elements are placed in the same positions from page to page.

CONTRAST

Contrast creates interest and emphasis and is achieved through the use of differences in size, color, texture, type, alignment and other design elements. Without sufficient contrast, a design is monotonous and unexciting. The greater the difference, the greater the contrast. A large image and a small headline, or vice versa, use contrasting sizes to create visual interest. Complementary type pairs, opposites on the color wheel, two different paper types—these are other great ways to generate contrast. The differences must be obvious, but not so much that the viewer's eye bounces back and forth between too many elements with nowhere to focus.

LEAVE YOUR EGO AT THE DOOR

We designers pour ourselves into our creations. Designs are our babies, sprung from the deep creative recesses of our brains and brought forth with love and nurturing. We caress the type, tell stories with pictures, and mold our designs into greatness. And when a creative director, client or fellow designer takes issue with our design, it isn't merely an objection to the aesthetics; it's a personal attack on us. How could they not love it? We all feel this way about our work. We work hard, and the designs we create should all be praised, right? Wrong. The work we do isn't meant to bring us personal glory; it is created to serve the needs of the client. The client hired *you* to create work for *them*. The mark of a good designer is not leaving a mark. Design is anonymous. It isn't signed by the artist. Even if a design is recognized as having been created by a famous designer, it's likely another designer who noticed it, not the general public. There is no room for ego in design.

THE CLIENT IS ALWAYS RIGHT, SOMETIMES

Designers have a love/hate relationship with their clients. We love them for the work (i.e., money) they provide, and we enjoy solving their design problems. On the other hand, we hate the way they ruin our work by insisting on a much-too-large logo, providing secretary-drawn napkin sketches, and demanding Papyrus for the headline. Either way, we have to learn to work with them.

The client loves and nurtures her business, and she enjoys watching it flourish. She knows its ins and outs, its strengths and weaknesses, its capabilities and its history. The client deserves respect from you because she is the one who knows her product or service best. You should defer to the client about all business matters. After all, you are being hired to communicate this information to the client's

67 ● "MixMax Brasil is an exhibition for children aged 6 to 13 years at Tropenmuseum Junior. This do!-exhibition focuses on the mixed-culture in the northeastern Pernambuco region of Brazil. The campaign combines photos and materials such as Cordel booklets (woodcuts), murals and a football shirt. On top of this composite image lays a white sheet of paper with die-cut flip flops—the national footwear—and text. The image is alienating: do I look at flipflops on which a face is printed, or do I look through the paper to the underlying image? This is exactly what happens at the exhibition: nothing is what it seems, Mix is what it is!" —Autobahn

68 ● "Optimistactic" is a theme for a second year of Design It Yourself, an annual series of design events. The stylistic poster series invited small communities, business, and academics related to design to share their stories, ideas and inspirations.

audience. This doesn't mean you can't contribute. Be proactive; research the client's business. Investigate the competition, find out more about the services your client offers, and examine any materials the client may give you. Do your best to understand the business, because the more you immerse yourself in it, the more educated your design response will be.

Don't forget the design experience that you bring to the table. You understand connotative typographic meanings, color association and layout hierarchy. Just as you should learn about your client's business, you need to educate your client. Talk your client through the design process. For each design decision you make, offer a reason for it. This is your chance to offer solutions the client may not have thought of otherwise. Just remember that if you stray from a client's original directives, your reasoning must be sound. Design for design's sake still means nothing without a concept. When you show your clients that you are willing to partner with them, you will gain clients who are more apt to listen to your ideas. They may still demand Papyrus, but at least you know you did everything you could to create a quality design.

Difficult clients

Working directly with clients is an adjustment. Some are easy to work with and become lifelong friends; others will just make your job difficult. There are no tricks to working with clients, but you must remain professional at all times. Don't worry too much. Over time, you will gain confidence as you learn from each client.

I once worked for a client whose sibling partners frequently bickered during our meetings. I pretended to read my notes and patiently waited to continue until they were finished with their argument. I was not about to let their unprofessional family spat rattle my professional image. Fortunately they never directly involved me or got out of control. If they had, I would have had to find a way to address the situation.

Difficult clients are, well... difficult. We've all run across them in our careers. One of my most difficult client moments came when I hired an agreed-upon illustrator to create an illustration for a client-supplied product. The illustrator knocked it out of the park. I presented the illustration to the client, marveling at the incredible work. The client looked at the illustration for exactly 1.7 seconds and declared that he hated it. I was stunned. I could easily have taken the comment as a personal attack on my abilities as an art director. I didn't. I very calmly asked a series of questions. What did he think of the overall color? He said it was spot on to the original product. I asked what he thought of the detailing in the smaller components. They looked good too. He even complimented the illustrator for her accuracy.

I asked a few more questions. Everything was fine. Why did he hate the image? Stumped, I asked one last question about a small element that extended out from the product. This, he declared, was the wrong color and the shape was inaccurate. After we got over that one minor detail, the rest of the meeting went swimmingly. I learned an important lesson about client relationships: You have to be willing to talk through issues. Sometimes an abject declaration of hatred is nothing more than a dislike of one small element in an otherwise fantastic design.

Someday you will have a client who will be worse than all the others. He will make you want to bang your head against a wall. He will fill you with dread when he calls. He will make you do thirty-seven rounds of design and end up back at the first design for the final. He will bully you into using his design preferences even though you know it's the wrong decision. He'll be condescending and unprofessional. There will also come a time in your career when you must cut the cord. It's OK. You know why? For every terrible client out there, there are thirty great ones. Learn to say "no" when necessary and be a happier designer for it.

THE ROLE OF PERSONAL STYLE

While there is no room for ego in design, there is certainly room for personal style. Many great designers become known for it. Want gorgeous retro-vintage hand-done typography for a packaging label? Hire Louise Fili. Need a

69 ● Scotty Reifsnyder has made a career of his retro modern style.

70 ● This Starbucks mural series attempts to develop a more personal and memorable relationship between patrons and their cup of coffee. The murals communicate Starbucks' brand values through aesthetic suggestion, as the mid-century inspired typography utilized in these images inspires a collective nostalgia of "small business values" like customer service, quality and pride.

bold poster in a gig-style design? Call The Heads of State. Looking for an incredibly clever, analogy-driven design for a play poster? Bring in Luba Lukova. Want the very best book cover design to go with a potential best-selling novel? Run to Chip Kidd. Designers build careers on personal style: Stefan Sagmeister, David Carson, Paula Scher, Seymour Chwast, Aaron Draplin, Armin Vit, Jessica Hische… I could go on and on. You can become one of them. How? By working hard for tons of clients. They honed their skills with each job until they became masters.

Your personal style can be part of your design, *but—* and this is a *huge but*—it must be appropriate for the cli-

"Do the work that makes you happy. If you don't do that, then why do it?" —JAKE BURKE

ent. If a client comes to you because of your personal style, then it is perfectly acceptable to work that into the design. Forcing your personal style onto a job where it's neither appropriate nor desired is not acceptable. There will be plenty other opportunities to make it happen. Although the designers listed above are known for a style, they also create just as much work that bears no resemblance to their better-known stuff. If your personal style doesn't work for a client, don't use it. Remember, the client chose *you* to create work for *him*. He should be confident that you will provide him with the best possible design solution, whether or not it includes your personal style.

Get style

Research, practice and intuition are required to develop a personal style. Start by getting out of your design bubble.

Know your history. Look at what's happening in the world of design. Draw inspiration from the Art Deco, Art Nouveau, Bauhaus, Russian Constructivism, Expressionism, Psychedelic and Web 2.0 movements. Resist the urge to develop a style around whatever is trending now. Design follows the same cyclical pattern as fashion. What's old is new and what's new becomes old. What you think is trendy now won't be in a year or two. Develop something uniquely your own.

Design is a skill that needs to be practiced. You get better at it the more you do it. Check out your work from five years ago compared to now. You should notice improvement. You develop new design skills with each job you do. You will discover strengths and weaknesses. Over time you will develop your own design aesthetic.

PUT IT ALL TOGETHER

Visual concept is the marriage of style and the client's needs. Think of it as a game plan for the design. Making decisions before executing the work greatly simplifies the process. A visual concept can be abstract, literal, symbolic, classical, playful, chaotic or stark. It must work

71 ● Surabaya's Urban Knowledge Dynamics is a platform that aims to collect, organize and disseminate the rich dynamics of urban experience and knowledge. Its organic set of visual identity, icon and typeface has an easy going attitude that can easily be translated in a wide array of mediums.

with the client's goals, type, images, layout, grid, hierarchy, communication, readability and design style. You also need consistency, but don't confuse that with being boring. There is plenty of room for variation as long as the overall design remains cohesive. For instance, in a multipage document, the pages shouldn't all look like identical twins, as the design will become dull very quickly. But you don't want them looking like fourth cousins twice removed either. The balance between uniformity and surprise is what keeps the audience's attention.

BREAK A RULE OR TWO

There comes a time in your career when you question whether you learned enough and tried hard enough, and if you are giving your clients everything you can. You research, brainstorm and sketch. You refine your ideas, generate well-kerned typography and arrange optimal hierarchical communication. The design looks great. It fills each of the client's needs. But somewhere deep in your gut, it's not enough. You want more creative exploration. You want to break free. You want to create something bigger, badder and better. You want to ignite spectacular creative anarchy.

These feelings are natural from a creative mind. Unfortunately, it's not always appropriate to express them to a client. Before your inner creative anarchist gets the better of you, consider how much creativity your client can handle. Is he literal and straightforward, with little tolerance for creative freedom, or is she open-minded, with a high creative tolerance? Rate your client on a scale of one to ten, with ten being highly tolerant of creativity and one being not at all tolerant. If you say two or above, you have an opportunity to break a rule and create something that pushes the client's (and your) design boundaries. For some, it means using a sans serif instead of a serif; for others it may mean half-legible typography on a fluorescent-green patterned background with a purple unicorn flying through the middle, printed on stainless steel. You will need to experiment to find out where your client's boundaries lie.

TESTING THE BOUNDARIES

Don't second-guess your client. Explore his level of creative tolerance by asking him questions. Use the opportunity to dig deeper into your client's thoughts about his business. Discover what design elements he likes and dislikes. The dislikes are more telling than the likes—now you know what to avoid. If you have ideas early on, work them into

72 ● Calexico's was made with the ambition to take Mexican food to Stockholm's dining rooms. The hand-painted type is inspired by Mexican street taqueria signs, and the pastel and copper color palette creates a luxurious feel. It's a mix of street taqueria and luxury with a hint of sweaty margaritas and sangria on the rocks.

the conversation to see how the client reacts. Once you have a grasp of the client's creative tolerance, you can present varying degrees of creativity during the initial design phase. Present the highest tolerance design you can without offending your client or completely abandoning his communication and conceptual needs. Here are the four degrees of design options:

1. **SAFE:** These options make the client feel comfortable; they are conceptually solid and serve the client well if selected.
2. **MODERATE-SAFE:** These options push the concept a little further but stick to the client's tastes. Stretch the client's design boundaries through color, typography, grid, layout, etc. The client may be a little

pronto'za

The Texican
pizza

Popeye Pesto
pizza

Crabcake
pizza

Chicken Toscana
pizza

Meat-Zilla
pizza

Great Scott
pizza

Monkey Mango
pizza

Schrooms Gone Wild
pizza

Malibu Chicken
pizza

73 ● Upshift veered far from the old-world Italian clichés and created a fresh logo that embodies the unique pizzas the restaurant makes. To many in the U.S., *pronto* means fast—so why not a running piece of pizza? Versions of the main logo character to represent every one of their specialty pizzas were also created.

uncomfortable with these options but should still be open to the ideas.

3. **MODERATE-EXPERIMENTAL:** These are options that propel your concepts outside the client's comfort zone. Explore different image-making marks, materials, experimental typography and nontraditional grids. Go outside the box and show your client the potential of "riskier" design, always remembering to keep his communication goals in mind. You will have to educate the client about your reasoning and address any fears he may have about venturing into something a little different. It will be a struggle for some clients to accept these options. Present justification for your choices to help the client see the design's validity.

4. **ANARCHIST:** These options go for it all and demolish the boundaries. Of course, the idea still needs to be justified to the client—it is her money, after all—but if you can sell the idea, have at it.

WHAT RULE DO I BREAK?

Before breaking any rules, you first have to ask why. Why do you need thirteen fonts on a page? Why a horizontally scrolling website? Why is a flying purple unicorn appropriate for this client? If the answer is "because it looks cool,"

74 ● This traditional collage and ink film festival poster depicts revolution eating his own children.

I look cool.

design isn't about your ego or the cool things you can do; it's about the client's needs. Start by developing the concept for a rule-following design first, even if it's only in sketch form. This initial concept sketch will help define hierarchy, content and basic elements needed for the design. Carefully consider your research and decide what makes the most sense. If the client's logo is great but the color mimics the competition, then do something different with color. If everyone in the category uses corporate blue, choose lime green or tangerine orange. If the client's current materials use a conservative three-column grid, try a modular grid system with text overlaying angled images. If a website uses the standard 1024 × 768 pixels, consider designing a continuous page that's 9000 × 768 pixels and have the viewer scroll horizontally to reveal the rest of the information.

then stop right now. Go back and reread all the rules again. You're clearly not ready for creative anarchy. However, if you believe the broken rule will enhance the design, if you have sound reasoning behind your decision *and* if you have a client who is conducive to rule-breaking design options, then you are ready.

Which rule do you break? You can't break all of them at once. That would result in a chaotic mess. Remember that the

Are they really rules or just guidelines?

Because you won't get your knuckles smacked for breaking a grid or using too many fonts, aren't the rules more like guidelines? Good design practices start from a solid knowledge base. The more you are educated about design, the more informed your design decisions. Anyone can jump

75 ● Yes, it's a concrete business card.

on the computer and create a poster. Does that make him a designer, or just someone who knows how to type, add a picture and hit print? A designer understands the difference between a Modern and Slab Serif font, why color makes people react the way they do, how designs benefit from an organized grid, which typefaces will attract the target audience, and how proper hierarchy controls the viewer. A designer educated in the history of design understands that her idea has been done before, but also that she has the opportunity to make the idea her own. Design rules are the designer's toolbox. It's up to you to decide whether a rule-based design is appropriate or if breaking a rule better serves the client.

DESIGNERS NEED ETHICS

Ethics are moral principles that govern a person's behavior. The most talked about design ethic is *copyright*. Copyright is the legal right to one's own work—to perform, film, record and design original material—and maintain the right to sell or distribute it. In simple terms, what you create is

yours. Except if you work for a design firm; then it's theirs. Everything created on your work computer legally belongs to the company. Sometimes the copyright belongs to the client. To eliminate confusion, the legalities of who owns what should be spelled out in the design contract.

You have an ethical responsibility to treat your client with respect. You should be professional and honest in your business dealings. Any communication between you and the client is confidential unless specifically noted otherwise. The client's strategies, future plans, product design and other relevant information need to be kept quiet. This means not talking to your spouse, significant other, parent or best friend about confidential work. Such discussions could be overheard by a competitor, with potentially dire consequences.

Don't copy

Don't copy someone else's work. No excuses. Don't do it. Ever. It's your job to create one-of-a-kind work for your client. It is disastrous both ethically and financially to produce work that resembles another company's design, especially within the same business category. It should go without saying that you should not steal other people's ideas and pass them off as your own. Designer Shepard Fairey learned this the hard way in 2008, when he produced a poster for the Obama presidential campaign tilted "Hope" in an effort to support the future president. The poster became hugely popular during the campaign and was quite lucrative for Fairey until an AP photographer named Mannie Garcia took issue with it. He claimed that Fairey's image was a replication of a photo he took of Obama. After initially denying the charges, Fairey admitted that he copied Garcia's photograph. The court ruled that Fairey infringed upon Garcia's copyright and owed retribution to Garcia. In addition, Fairey was sentenced to two years' probation, three hundred hours of community service and a $25,000 fine.

TRENDS AND CREATIVITY

I love trends, but by their very definition, trends have short-lived popularity. Design is chock full of trends—some good, some bad. They appear, disappear and reappear years later. A company launches an "innovative" design and everyone jumps on the design bandwagon. Humans like change. We are always looking for something newer, better, faster and cooler. Trendy design is a way to fulfill this desire, but it's not always a wise solution. If the design is meant to be short-lived, such as advertisements, then being on trend is perfectly acceptable. More likely than not, the design will die out with the trend anyway. The majority of clients, however, want their product or service to stick around for a long time. Therefore longevity is much more important than trendiness. Look at the Coca-Cola logo. It hasn't changed significantly since the early 1900s. Sure, little modifications were made here and there, but it's essentially the same logo. It is a truly classic design. Good design should withstand the test of time.

THE CREATIVE ANARCHIST'S AGREEMENT

I will listen to the client's goals.

I will diligently research the project.

I will generate unrestricted brainstorming ideas.

I will investigate both "safe" and "anarchist" concepts.

I will never expect a computer to magically create ideas.

I will experiment with line, shape, texture, type, color, format, grid, Gestalt principles and balance.

I will never break a rule just for the sake of looking cool.

I will not let my ego interfere with creating the best possible design solution.

I will constantly question.

I will assume nothing.

I will try everything.

Signed: _____

Date:_____

IMAGES

INTRODUCTION

01 ● **TITLE:** The Common Table Cellar Beer Menu LPs
DESIGN FIRM: Caliber Creative/ Dallas Texas
ART DIRECTORS: Brandon Murphy, Bret Sano
DESIGNERS: Bret Sano, Brandon Murphy, Justin King, Maxim Barkhatov, Bryan Gleghorn, Kaitlyn Canfield
WEBSITE: www.calibercreative.com
CLIENT: The Common Table
Caliber Creative—Dallas TX © 2014

02 ● "P. 1921", 1921 (collage) Hausmann, Raoul (1886-1971) / Hamburger Kunsthalle, Hamburg, Germany / Bridgeman Images

03 ● **TITLE:** F Paul Rand Invitation
UNIVERSITY: Corcoran College of Art and Design — Senior Class
PROFESSOR: Neal Ashby
STUDENT: Jason E. Sunde
WEB: jasonsundedesign.com

RULE 1:
LEARN THE RULES

04 ● **TITLE:** Stop Child Abuse
DESIGN FIRM: Sommese Design
CREATIVE DIRECTOR: Lanny Sommese
DESIGNER: Lanny Sommese
WEB: graphicdesign.psu.edu
CLIENT: Institute for Art and Humanistic Studies at Penn State

05 ● Tea Infuser and strainer, made by the Bauhaus Metal Workshop, Weimar, 1924 (silverwith ebony, Brandt, Marianne (1893-1983) Private Collection / Photo © The Fine Art Society, London, UK / Bridgeman Images

06 ● **TITLE:** Banned Books
UNIVERSITY: Kutztown University
PROFESSOR: Elaine Cunfer
DESIGNER: Kimberly Beyer
WEB: kimberlybeyer.com

07 ● **TITLE:** Smashing Iced Tea

UNIVERSITY: Moore College of Art & Design
PROFESSOR: Keith Fledderman
DESIGNER: Megan Rhodes
WEB: megrhodes.com

08 ● **TITLE:** Speaking with a forked tongue
DESIGN FIRM: Times of Oman
DESIGNER: Adonis Durado
WEB: timesofoman
© 2013 Adonis Durado

09 ● **TITLE:** The 5 Senses: Water
UNIVERSITY: Moore College of Art + Design
PROFESSOR: Dorothy Funderwhite
DESIGNER: Christy Dishman
WEB: moore.edu

RULE 2:
THE COMPUTER IS ONLY A TOOL

10 ● **TITLE:** Tricon Series
UNIVERSITY: Kutztown University
PROFESSOR: Vicki Meloney
DESIGNER: Nicholas Stover
WEB: nicholasstover.com
Nicholas Stover © 2014

11 ● **TITLE:** Paper Record Player
DESIGNER: Kelli Anderson
WEB: kellianderson.com
Kelli Anderson © 2014

12 ● **TITLE:** Mokkaccino crafts
DESIGNER: Hired Monkeez
WEB: behance.net/Hiredmonkeez

13 ● **TITLE:** Art of Indian Kolam: Traditional Design & New Media
DESIGNER: John Miller in collaboration with Bruce Wall
WEB: kolamncc.com

RULE 3:
REMEMBER THE BASICS

14 ● **TITLE:** The Twin Menaechmi
DESIGN FIRM: Red Shoes Studio
DESIGNER: Wade Lough

CLIENT: James Madison University Department of Theatre and Dance

15 ● **TITLE:** Little Lingo
UNIVERSITY: Philadelphia University
PROFESSOR: Gavin Cooper
DESIGNER: Christina Minopoli
WEB: minopolidesign.com

16 ● Rock concert poster for The Grateful Dead, The Doors and others at the Fillmore, San Francisco, 1966 Wilson, Wes (b.1937) / Private Collection / Bridgeman Images

17 ● Advertisement for the telephone, c.1937 (colour litho) Chol (fl.1930s) / Private Collection / DaTo Images / Bridgeman Images

18 ● **TITLE:** MAKE Posters
DESIGNER: Jeremy Tinianow
WEB: jtinianow.com

19 ● **TITLE:** Bendable screens
DESIGN FIRM: Times of Oman
ART DIRECTOR: Adonis Durado
DESIGNER: Adonis Durado
WEB: timesofoman.com
© 2013 Adonis Durado

20 ● **TITLE:** Washington's Crossing
UNIVERSITY: Rowan University
PROFESSOR: Jan Conradi
STUDENT: Stuart Lopez

21 ● **TITLE:** La cuina d'en Toni
DESIGN FIRM: Dorian
DESIGNER: Gabriel Morales
WEB: estudiodorian.com
CLIENT: La cuina d'en Toni

22 ● **TITLE:** Ride Till You Die
UNIVERSITY: Moore College of Art & Design
PROFESSOR: Gigi McGee
DESIGNER: Brittany Slopey
WEB: cargocollective.com/brittanyslopey

23 ● **TITLE:** Sandra Lovisco Hair & MakeUp

52 ● **TITLE OF WORK**: Eat at My Desk website
DESIGN FIRM: Projekt, Inc.
DESIGNER: Sean M. Costik
WEB DEVELOPERS: Dustin Caruso, Dave Moylan
WEB: projektinc.com
CLIENT: Eat at My Desk

53 ● **TITLE**: Creative Madness
UNIVERSITY: James Madison University
PROFESSOR: JUN BUM SHIN
DESIGNER: Camisha Matthews
WEB: educ.jmu.edu/~shinjb

54 ● **TITLE**: Me Without You
UNIVERSITY: Mississippi State University
PROFESSOR: Jamie Runnells
DESIGNER: Jonathan Prudhomme
WEB: jamierunnells.com
CLIENT: Me Without You

55 ● **TITLE**: Creating more space for masterpieces
DESIGN FIRM: Times of Oman
ART DIRECTOR: Adonis Durado
DESIGNER: Adonis Durado
WEB: timesofoman.com
© 2013 Adonis Durado

RULE 8:
MAKE THINGS THE SAME—OR DIFFERENT

56 ● **TITLE**: Andrea Zittel Lecture Poster
UNIVERSITY: Moore College of Art & Design
PROFESSOR: Gigi McGee
DESIGNER: Lauren Ladner
WEB: moore.edu

57 ● **TITLE**: Gevalia Redesign
UNIVERSITY: Kansas City Art Institute
PROFESSOR: Tyler Galloway
DESIGNER: Alexandra Khoder
WEB: behance.net/andrakhoder

58 ● **TITLE**: Celebrating the Comedies of William Shakespeare
DESIGN FIRM: Sommese Design
CREATIVE DIRECTOR: Lanny Sommese
DESIGNER: Lanny Sommese
WEB: graphicdesign.psu.edu
CLIENT: Penn State Dept of English

59 ● **TITLE**: Le Corbusier
DESIGN FIRM: FILUM
CREATIVE DIRECTOR: Slobodan Stetic
DESIGNER: Bojana Pasajlic
CLIENT: FILUM

60 ● **TITLE**: Beatlemore Skidmania

UNIVERSITY: Skidmore College
PROFESSOR: Deb Hall
DESIGNER: Joe Klockowski
WEB: joeklockowski.wix.com/jklockowski

61 ● **TITLE**: Farmer's Suicide
DESIGN FIRM: Taproot India
DESIGNERS: Santosh Padhi and Anant Nanvake with Paul Chakaravarti
WEB: taprootindia.co.in
CLIENT: The Times of India

62 ● **TITLE**: Typography Posters
UNIVERSITY: Kutztown University
PROFESSOR: Elaine Cunfer
DESIGNER: Laura Dubbs
WEB: behance.net/lauradubbs

63 ● **TITLE**: Oregon Chai Redesign
UNIVERSITY: Kansas City Art Institute
PROFESSOR: Tyler Galloway
DESIGNER: Wendy Vong
WEB: wendyvong.com

64 ● **TITLE**: Fighting Racism
UNIVERSITY: Isfahan Art University
PROFESSOR: Ladan Rezae
DESIGNER: Elham Hemmat

65 ● **TITLE**: The Page
UNIVERSITY: University of Georgia
PROFESSOR: Julie Spivey
DESIGNER: Samira Khoshnood
WEB: juliespivey.com

66 ● **TITLE**: Bonnaroo
UNIVERSITY: Kutztown University
PROFESSOR: Ann Lemon
DESIGNER: Nathan Hurst
WEB: nathanhurstart.tumblr.com

RULE 9:
LEAVE YOUR EGO AT THE DOOR

67 ● **TITLE**: MixMax Brasil
DESIGN FIRM: Autobahn
ART DIRECTORS: Maarten Dullemeijer, Rob Stolte
DESIGNERS: Maarten Dullemeijer, Rob Stolte
WEBSITE: www.autobahn.nl
CLIENT: Dutch Royal Institute for the Tropics

68 ● **TITLE**: DIY Optimistactic
DESIGN FIRM: butawarna
DESIGNER: Andriew Budiman
MOTION GRAPHER: Motionanthem
WEB: butawarna.in
CLIENT: C2O Library and Collabtive

69 ● **TITLE**: Young at Heart series
DESIGNER: Scotty Reifsnyder
WEB: seescotty.com

70 ● **TITLE**: Starbucks Typographic Mural
DESIGNER: Jaymie McAmmond
WEB: jaymiemcammond.com
CLIENT: Starbucks

71 ● **TITLE**: AYOREK-Urban Knowledge Dynamics platform
DESIGN FIRM: butawarna
ART DIRECTOR: Andriew Budiman
DESIGNERS: Andriew Budiman,C2O Library and Collabtive, Chimp Chomp, Graphichapter
WEB: butawarna.in
CLIENT: Various communities and NGO

RULE 10:
BREAK A RULE OR TWO

72 ● **TITLE**: Calexico's mexican restaurant branding
DESIGN FIRM: Snask
CREATIVE DIRECTOR: Fredrik Öst
DESIGNER: Magdalena Czarnecki, Jens Nilsson
WEB: snask.com
CLIENT: Debaser

73 ● **TITLE**: Pronto 'Za Logo
DESIGN FIRM: UpShift Creative Group
CREATIVE DIRECTOR: Nick Staal
DESIGNERS: Nicholas Staal, Grant Steiner, Chrissy DiNello
WEB: upshiftcreative.com
CLIENT: Pronto 'Za Pizza Restaurant

74 ● **TITLE**: Revolutions
DESIGN FIRM: Atelier Cédric Gatillon
DESIGNER: Cédric Gatillon
WEB: cedricgatillon.com
CLIENT: Cinéma L'Écran Saint-Denis

75 ● **TITLE**: Concrete business cards
DESIGN FIRM: MURMURE
DESIGNERS: Julien Alirol, Paul Ressencourt
WEB: murmure.me
CLIENT: MURMURE Self promotion
© 2014 Murmure

76 ● **TITLE**: Hemslojden exhibition poster
DESIGN FIRM: Snask
ART DIRECTOR: Fredrik Öst
DESIGNERS: Magdalena Czarnecki, Jens Nilsson
WEB: snask.com
CLIENT: Liljevalchs Art Gallery

INDEX

CREATIVE ANARCHY

CREATIVE ANARCHY

HOW TO BREAK THE RULES
OF GRAPHIC DESIGN
FOR CREATIVE SUCCESS

Denise Bosler

HOW BOOKS
Cincinnati, Ohio
www.howdesign.com

DEDICATION

To my former and current students—you are my inspiration.

ACKNOWLEDGMENTS

This book could not have been completed without the kind help and support of many people. My deepest sincere thanks to Dr. Lucy Hornstein, who went above and beyond with her investment of time and wonderful advice, and who helped me say exactly what I wanted to say… again.

I extend my warmest thanks to all of the very talented designers who graciously allowed me to use their work in this book. I am excited to share your work with the design community.

Special thanks to Nick, Arren, Roger, Tracy and Barb for their encouragement, and contributions to the content, imagery and my sanity.

I extended my deepest gratitude to the faculty and staff of the Kutztown University Communication Design Department for their guidance over the years.

Thank you to Scott Francis for his belief in both me and this book, and Claudean Wheeler for helping to visualize my idea.

And last but not least, I can never express enough appreciation to my family, for their generous offer of time, assistance and support so I could see this anarchic vision through to completion.

AUTHOR BIO

Denise Bosler is an award-winning graphic designer, illustrator, author and professor of communication design at Kutztown University in Pennsylvania. She is the principal of Bosler, a design firm that focuses on illustration for the licensing and surface design industry, print collateral, packaging, logos and brand identity. Denise survives in creative anarchy mode most of her days, but her mantra remains simple—kern well and design great. She is the author of Mastering Type: The Essential Guide to Typography for Print and Web Design (HOW Books 2012) and this fabulous book. As a professor, she is known for her obsession with the proper treatment of type and is frequently heard admonishing her students when they fail to kern accurately. She has also been known to make a student start over when a concept goes missing.

BREAK THE RULES

CONTENTS

BREAK THE RULES

"Art is like masturbation. It is selfish and introverted and done for you and you alone. Design is like sex. There is someone else involved, their needs are just as important as your own, and if everything goes right, both parties are happy in the end." —COLIN WRIGHT

CHAPTER 1

ADVERTISING

Advertising has been around as long as people have been selling things—albeit not in any form we would recognize today. It's hard to pinpoint the very first advertisement, but it likely dates back to papyrus scraps found in ancient Greek and Roman ruins. Due to the low literacy rates of the era, town criers announced the availability of wares and services. Tradesmen hung iconic signs outside their homes and businesses. Advertising began its inexorable march.

Moving on, the first print advertisement in a newspaper appeared in 1704 for an estate sale on Long Island. Around the same time, Benjamin Franklin began including an advertisement section in his Philadelphia newspapers. Franklin was also responsible for magazine advertisements, including them in his *General Magazine* in 1742. Capitalizing on this phenomenon, Volney Palmer opened the first advertising agency in Philadelphia in 1841. The next step in the growth of advertising occurred in 1941 when television aired its first advertisement: It was for Bulova watches. Radio advertising took a step forward in 1956 with the advent of prerecorded commercials. Fast forward, and advertising has infiltrated pretty much everywhere: television, radio, internet, newspapers, magazines, direct mail, packaging and transit signs and billboards. You can't get away from it, which is a dream for those in the advertising industry.

START WITH THE MESSAGE

When we think of innovation, we typically think of technology, gadgetry and other stuff like that. Innovative advertising has more to do with the message than the medium. An advertising message is comprised of words and imagery, which must have visual-verbal synergy. Like all design, advertising needs to communicate a great idea. The

01 ● Taproot India developed a festival campaign that was specific to Mumbai. They used every single thing they could think of from the area: buildings, monuments, bridges, cabs, signals, people and more.

distinction is that advertising's explicit purpose is to sell something—an idea, a product or a service. Even corporate advertising—advertising created specifically to enhance a company's reputation, tout innovation or build goodwill—is selling something: the company itself.

Good messages have a strong conceptual base. They surprise, invite, entertain, provoke; they are mysterious and they have fun. The best messages are supported by an ad

02 ● For a month, cutting, folding, gluing and modeling became everyday tasks at Snask, including objects that would be reproduced in gigantic scale in cardboard and taken to the streets of Malmö.

that is strongly executed and beautifully designed. Hierarchy, clarity, brand consistency, typography, color, image use and legibility matter—all the more so, as an advertisement intrudes on the viewer's daily life.

The audience is engaged, sort of

Advertising is an up-close-and-personal medium. Flip through a magazine, and printed advertisements are just a few inches from your face. Pop onto the web, and advertising shares space with the content you want to read. Turn on the radio; it's there again between songs. Try to watch television; it interrupts your favorite shows. Annoying? Sometimes. Necessary? Afraid so. How else will you get your client in front of your audience? But here's a problem to consider: Is the audience actually paying attention?

The audience may be engaged with the advertising environment but not necessarily with the advertising itself. I may page through a magazine, but it's rare for me to stop and look at an ad. If I do, I'm either blown away by the design or I was looking for the advertised product to begin with. An advertising designer's biggest challenge is to pull the viewer away from the content to look at the advertising. It has to be special. It has to be amazing. It has to keep you in front of the TV instead of heading for the kitchen.

PRINT

Print advertising, referring to ads in magazines and newspapers, is what typically comes to mind when you hear the word *advertising*. There hasn't really been any changes in the layout formula for print advertising in the last fifty years: Imagery plus headline equals a print ad. Innovation comes from the visual-verbal synergy created by the image and headline. Clever copywriting will take an ad far. Excellent visual-verbal synergy will take it farther. The unexpected will get noticed. Do something the audience isn't ready for. Use different points of view, analogies, metaphors, humor, heartstrings, exaggeration, subtlety, fear and personal association to connect to the audience. Figure out what will get that message stuck in someone's head.

HONESTY IS THE BEST POLICY

People have a love/hate relationship with advertising, and for good reason. Before the advent of federal regulations, advertising was a bit shady. Ad agencies used to falsify the presentation of food products to make them look simply amazing. Food stylists used a variety of tricks to enhance the appearance of the food, like putting glass in the bottom of a soup bowl to force noodles and vegetables to have the appearance of floating at the top, using red lipstick to paint a strawberry just the perfect shade, and using colored shortening that wouldn't melt under the hot photography lights instead of ice cream. Once there were enough complaints about the disparities between the advertisement and reality, legislation was enacted. Eventually, all false advertising was declared illegal. But what about stretching the truth or omitting some of it? There are some exceptions. If an ad is for strawberry ice cream, the ice cream itself must be real, but the strawberries, mint or other items placed around the base of the bowl can be enhanced by any means desired.

 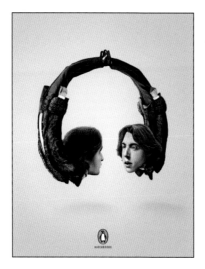 

03 ● "The client, Penguin, approached McCann Worldgroup India with the task of making their audiobooks exciting. They wanted to convey to the consumer that now they could hear the story straight from the author's mouth. Hence the life-like 3-D illustrations of famous authors (bent like headphones) whispering into the imaginary listener's ears."

The greater the impact on the viewer, the more likely the ad will succeed and result in a purchase, a donation or just some self-reflection.

If the budget allows, try something physical. Paper insertions can include embossing, debossing, foil stamping, die-cutting and any other print technique. Use a *tip-in*, the method of gluing a foreign object to a page, to give a sample of a product. The first non-beauty tip-in I ever saw was a 1997 Fruit of the Loom advertisement in *Rolling Stone* magazine: a tiny pair of men's underwear attached to the advertisement. (It was only included for those 1.25 million people who had a subscription.) After all these years I still have those tiny briefs. I also have an old print advertisement from Citibank that depicts a bulldog chewing on a smiling mouth chew toy. It hangs above my desk because it makes me smile every time I look at it. That is the sign of good advertising.

DIRECT MAIL

That glorious envelope or package in the mail—the simple act of retrieving it from the mailbox already puts it into your audience's hand. Will he open it? You wait with bated breath. What are the odds he will open the thing—the direct mail piece that you designed? Statistics show that the direct mail open rate hovers around 3 to 5 percent. If your mailing list goes to a specialized audience such as business-to-business direct mail, then the open rate increases a few more percentage points. Fact is, direct mail is a tough format. It just means you have to work harder to make an impact. If the message or image presented doesn't hit the mark, your piece will be labeled "junk," torn up and pitched. As with any other form of advertising, you need to grab the viewer's attention, either through the message, image, color or format of the direct mail piece.

Don't be coy. Tell them what's inside and why they want to open it. Now is not the time to be subtle. Something as simple as not using the typical #10 envelope increases your chances of an open. An unusual size, format, material or fold generates curiosity. Work directly with your printer to find out what they can do. See what dies are in stock. You can always reuse a die from someone else's job. Maximize the press sheet. Think about how folds interact with each other. What can be die-cut, popped out, interacted with? Give the viewer a visual, verbal or physical surprise. Include something useful within the design. Ask him to build it or write on it—do something that makes him want to keep it on his desk. Above all, make sure that every aspect of the direct mail piece communicates your message. That way if he does keep it around, you get to keep advertising to him.

OUTDOOR AND TRANSIT

Outdoor advertising has no more than a fraction of a second to get your attention. Driving a car or motorcycle is not exactly conducive to looking at advertising. Billboards that vie for your attention as you concentrate on driving, traffic and the guy riding your tail won't work if they are too complicated. You need a short message, as the audience doesn't have enough time to take in all the information.

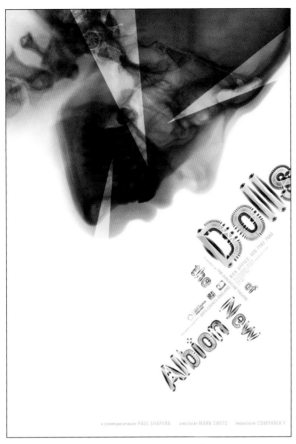

04 ● Subtle messaging stands a chance in outdoor transit advertising.

Even simple things like phone numbers and website URLs are forgotten a few miles down the road. Advertising on public transit (on and in buses, trains, subways, stops and stations) allows for more complexity than what's seen on billboards. Transit advertising has whatever amount of time it takes until the bus or train arrives or to get to the next stop—sometimes up to an hour or more. The viewer is literally trapped with your advertisement for the duration of their journey. Subtle or longer messages have a shot here. Take advantage of it. Be clever, be humorous, drive a point home and make it easy for the transit rider to access the information.

DIGITAL

Raise your hand if you regularly click on digital ads that pop up on a website or app. Me neither. Digital advertising is really tough to crack. Typical digital advertising appears as banner ads or little boxes on the edge of websites. The average user ignores them completely or finds them incredibly annoying. I don't recall ever clicking on a banner ad on purpose. Ever. This doesn't mean I haven't clicked on them accidentally, especially those that take over the screen and make the Close button difficult to find. What's a designer

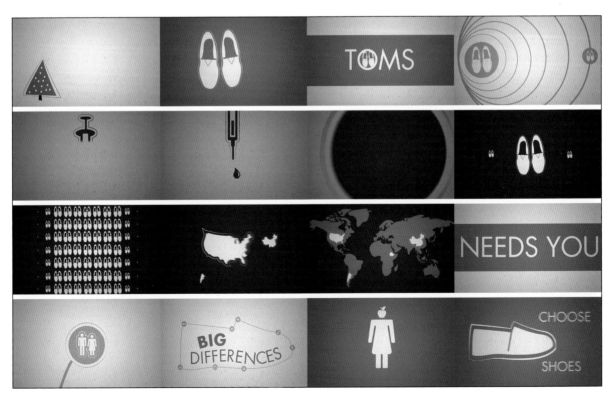

05 ● "Less is more" for this digital advertisement for Tom's Shoes. The easier it is for the viewer to follow the story, the easier he will grasp the concept.

06 ● "New Jersey Art Director's Club needed a breakthrough, sharable campaign that captures the interest of creative people in ad agencies throughout the Mid-Atlantic region. We wanted an idea that would get art directors, writers and creative directors to post it on their physical and virtual walls, nod their heads in recognition, and perhaps chuckle a bit." —Ann Lemon

to do? How do you get your message across without antagonizing the viewer? That is the million-dollar question. If I had the answer, I would be rich beyond the dreams of avarice, lounging on an island in Tahiti. There is no secret. Due diligence: plenty of research, knowing your audience and, most importantly, advertising on the sites (and in apps) that will give you the biggest return on your investment. There's no sense advertising high-end fashion on a motor parts website, right?

Some recent digital advertising success has come from an adaptation of traditional TV commercial techniques. The best advertising gets talked about. Combine that with motion-based advertising and you have the formula for viral success. *Viral* means the advertisement spreads rapidly across the digital universe just as a virus spreads through a body. Viral videos tend to be of cats, people's personal adventures, dogs, babies, and more cats. The best are short and sweet. They make the viewer laugh, cry or gasp. Super Bowl ads are now released prior to the big night in hopes of creating viral buzz. Some companies go further and create mini movies, seemingly unlinked to their company, to advertise more subtly. Chipotle created an animated mini movie called "The

Scarecrow," a haunting look at the overuse of antibiotics in animals, pesticides on food, and cruel conditions for animals. The message—"cultivate a better world"—focuses on fresh, farm-grown ingredients. The only connection to the advertiser is a simple logo at the very end. The video then directs a user to a game app that can be downloaded to a computer or phone. The simple and effective campaign, with virtually no advertiser presence, generated more than 7 million hits in less than three months. The media buzz generated was better than that from any print or TV ad campaign. With expenses limited to the animation and app creation, Chipotle

essentially created free advertising by uploading the video online. Advertising doesn't have to cost a fortune.

One of the best viral advertisements of 2013 was Volvo's Van Damme video that achieved 48 million views in eleven days. 48 MILLION! That certainly qualifies as successful viral advertising. However, the video touted the handling of Volvo's commercial vehicles, not cars or trucks for the average consumer. Despite its viral success, it's not yet clear how many average consumers were swayed enough by the video to seek out a Volvo for their next vehicle. In those terms, is the advertisement successful? Time will tell.

GALLERY

Òptic

CREATIVE ANARCHY: Obscured visuals, Extreme size

"The identity redesign turned the accent of the O into a lens. The simple and elegant imagery, the camera and consumer's view, is blocked by a large opaque logo." **— DORIAN**

TITLE: Òptic
DESIGN FIRM: Dorian
DESIGNERS: Gabriel Morales
WEB: estudiodorian.com
CLIENT: Òptic

TITLE: #MFEAirGuitars
DESIGN FIRM: Go Welsh
ART DIRECTOR: Craig Welsh
DESIGNER: Scott Marz
WEB: gowelsh.com
CLIENT: Music For Everyone

#MFEAirGuitars

CREATIVE ANARCHY: Guerilla advertising

"The goal of this campaign was to raise money for music education initiatives by convincing people on the streets of Lancaster, Pennsylvania, to play air guitar. Four sponsors agreed to donate funds for every photo that was shared via social media with the hashtag #MFEAirGuitars.

A guitar stand doesn't have much presence on its own—a guitar is needed for most people to even realize what they're viewing. It quickly became apparent that in order to get people to play air guitar, we needed a visual stage to be part of the project's sidewalk space.

Cardboard boxes proved to be the right material. The boxes were able to collapse flat when not in use and were zip-tied together in groups of six to help drive down the assembly time needed. Four air guitar stations were built and placed in Lancaster City during the city's 'Music Friday' events. The goal was to have as many people as possible play air guitar within a two-hour window of time. We had 483 people play air guitar in just two hours, and the project raised nearly $2,000 for music education initiatives." **—CRAIG WELSH**

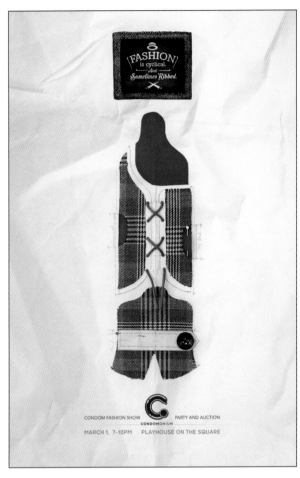

Condomonium

CREATIVE ANARCHY: Unexpected visuals

"Our primary goal was to promote a fund-raising condom fashion show and auction for a nonprofit reproductive health clinic. The event featured clothing made from condoms by some of the area's top designers. The ads used elements of clothing design for playful handmade condom fashions complemented by humorous headlines written on clothing tags. We were able to make provocative and memorable posters." **—KONG WEE PANG**

TITLE: Condomonium 2014
DESIGN FIRM: archer>malmo
DESIGNER: Kong Wee Pang
WEB: kongweepang.com
CLIENT: Choices—Memphis Center for Reproductive Health

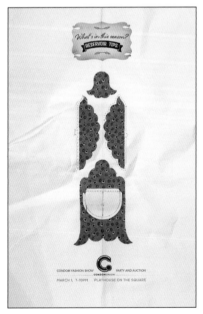

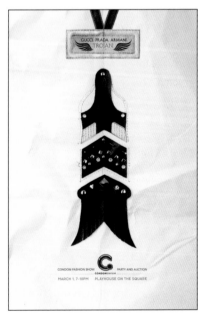

My First Agency - GRiT Student Seminar Poster

CREATIVE ANARCHY: Dual-purpose advertising, Historic influence

"The GRiT Student Seminar is an annual event hosted by the Des Moines chapter of the American Advertising Federation. We were tasked with promoting this event to local college students by creating posters to hang in schools. Our goal was to cut through the clutter typically found on college bulletin boards. Because the students were going to be touring agencies, meeting with ad people and working on a campaign as a team, we positioned the seminar as a way for them to 'play agency for day.'

Once we had the idea of a box design for the poster, we took it a step further to make the poster fold into a 3-D box. We wanted the deluxe play set to look as authentic as possible, with an ad agency twist. We used vintage toys bought on eBay and tweaked the inside with props and [Adobe] Photoshop. We added Addy Awards to the creative director's office, placed a TV on the wall in the brainstorming room, and even added some street art on the outside wall of the agency." —SATURDAY MFG.

TITLE: My First Agency - GRiT Student Seminar Poster
DESIGN FIRM: Saturday Mfg.
DESIGNER: Brian Sauer
WEB: saturdaymfg.com
CLIENT: American Advertising Federation: Des Moines Chapter

Mayhem in the Mable

CREATIVE ANARCHY: Collage, Humor in the absurd

"As we were planning our anniversary flapjack-themed party, we stumbled upon a debate about what brand of syrup to serve. Mrs. Butterworth's? Or Aunt Jemima? We were a camp divided and so we pitted the two syrup powerhouses against each other in a boxing match for the ages—Mayhem in the Maple.

The design was based on vintage boxing posters, but with a tongue-and-cheek modern twist. We used French Dur-O-Tone Butcher Orange [paper] with black ink to make sure the campaign was affordable. Throughout the evening, people could be heard debating the merits of one brand over another. Judging from the empty syrup containers at the end of the night, Mrs. Butterworth's was victorious."

—SATURDAY MFG.

TITLE OF WORK: Mayhem in the Mable
DESIGN FIRM: Saturday Mfg.
ART DIRECTOR: Brian Sauer
DESIGNERS: Brian Sauer, Annie Furhman
PLUS: Gina Adam, Scott Lewellen
WEB: saturdaymfg.com

TITLE: Guerrilla Street Ad - Eggo
UNIVERSITY: Montana State University
PROFESSOR: Meta Newhouse
DESIGNERS: Samantha Delvo, Krystle Horton
WEB: metanewhouse.com

Guerrilla Street Ad - Crest & Eggo

CREATIVE ANARCHY: Guerilla advertising,
Twist on the familiar

"As a class assignment, students were asked to go out and observe their surroundings and develop ads using only chalk and their ingenuity. The ads had be completed within a three-hour concept-to-production window.

David and Bret discovered a pothole on a shady street and felt that it was a great visual metaphor for a cavity in a tooth. The consumer visually connects the nuisance of a pothole caused by unmaintained roads, to the nuisance of a cavity.

Samantha and Krystle discovered a manhole cover and felt that it was a great visual substitution for a waffle. When you have the opportunity to incorporate a bit of serendipity into your design, you have to 'go for it.' The manhole cover substitutes in for an Eggo waffle, and the result is memorable and funny." —**META NEWHOUSE**

TITLE: Guerrilla Street Ad - Crest
UNIVERSITY: Montana State University
PROFESSOR: Meta Newhouse
DESIGNERS: Bret Sander, David Runia
WEB: metanewhouse.com

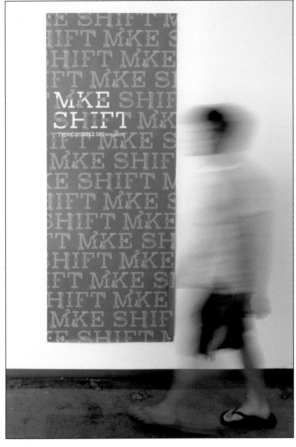

TypeCon 2012 Identity

CREATIVE ANARCHY: Traditional materials made modern

"We needed to create an original identity system for TypeCon 2012, the annual conference of the Society of Typographic Aficionados, that related to both Milwaukee's history and the history of wood type, since the Hamilton Wood Type & Printing Museum was an event partner. The 'MKE SHIFT' theme played off the local airport code and the fact the conference was being held in Milwaukee.

The students aimed to harmoniously capture the juxtapositions of old and new found both in wood type and in Milwaukee's heritage as an industrial hub. The solution incorporates multiple layers of meaning without being visually complicated. This work is all the more impressive because the students were tackling this project outside of their already heavy studio course load." —JULIE SPIVEY

TITLE: TypeCon 2012 Identity
UNIVERSITY: University of Georgia
PROFESSOR: Julie Spivey
DESIGNERS: Liz Minch, Blake Helman, Alli Treen, Mary Rabun, Kory Gabriel & Kaitlyn O'connor
WEB: juliespivey.com
CLIENT: Society of Typographic Aficionados

Grotesque

CREATIVE ANARCHY: Twist on the familiar,
Creative copywriting

"The objective was to create something specifically for fashionistas. There are so many fashion magazines out there, which speak highly (without criticism) about certain brands and trends, but there aren't any that say, 'Hey, that so-called trend isn't too flattering.' This zine does just that. The advertising for the zine is a guerrilla marketing campaign that displays the QR code as a usable code, and doubles as a curse word." **—SASHA MARIANO**

TITLE: Grotesque
UNIVERSITY: Kean University
PROFESSOR: Robin Landa
DESIGNER: Sasha Mariano
WEBSITE: sashamariano.com

+Glas/s

CREATIVE ANARCHY: Unexpected substrate

"We designed a logo and flyer for the glass department at the Rietveld Academy. In order to recruit more students, we printed a flyer on transparent PVC with a spot UV gloss varnish to give the effect of etched glass." **—AUTOBAHN**

TITLE: +Glas/s
DESIGN FIRM: Autobahn
DESIGNERS: Maarten Dullemeijer, Rob Stolte
WEB: autobahn.nl
CLIENT: Rietveld Academy

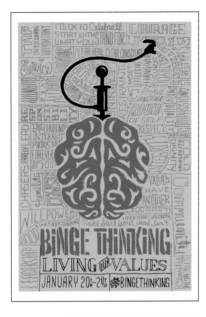

TITLE: Wake Forest University Binge Thinking Campaign
DESIGN FIRM: Wake Forest Communications
ART DIRECTION/DESIGN/ILLUSTRATION: Hayes Henderson
WRITER: Bart Rippin
CLIENT: Wake Forest University Campus Life

Binge Thinking

CREATIVE ANARCHY: Twist on the familiar, Visual and verbal risk-taking

"'Binge Thinking' was launched to bring into focus the hazards of overdoing it, the importance of common sense, the options students have, and the importance of self-respect at a time of great peer pressure. Posters, tent cards for cafeteria tables, and laptop stickers were distributed across campus; social media was utilized promoting events and awareness; the student paper covered the efforts; and an interactive installation was set up in a high-traffic area of the student center. The installation was made from materials all people could identify as an icon of the party environment—red solo cups. From a language standpoint, the tone was somewhat snarky and aligned overdoing it with things not cool or lacking in experience or control.

The initiative was a test in trying to say something fresh where it seems everything has been said. All of the warnings around underage drinking are well worn and generally overlooked either out of familiarity or a detached, institutional tone. We tried to reengage and turn the shop-worn phrases on themselves—by doing so, we captured people's attention as well as some respect from our audience for giving it an honest pass." **—HAYES HENDERSON, WAKE FOREST COMMUNICATIONS**

TITLE: Région Basse Normandie
DESIGN FIRM: MURMURE
DESIGNERS: Julien Alirol, Paul Ressencourt
WEB: murmure.me
CLIENT: The Lower Normandy region

Région Basse-Normandie

CREATIVE ANARCHY: Daring to let a pattern be the dominant visual

"The Lower Normandy region asked us to create a communication campaign for its cultural sector. The design is deliberately abstract. The success of the project was a two-stage discovery. First is a strong pattern graphic visual; second is the slogan. Together (slogan + visual), the message becomes clear." —MURMURE

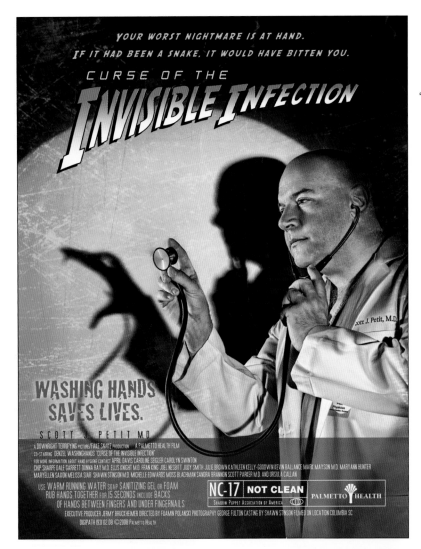

Hand Hygiene Movie Posters

CREATIVE ANARCHY: Twist on the familiar, Surprising imagery

"The objective was to improve the practice of hand hygiene at Palmetto Health, the largest health care system in South Carolina. Our hand hygiene scores were about the same as other hospitals across the nation at that time—a pitiful average of 35 percent. We knew we could improve and quickly needed the full attention of the staff. The concept used shadows to tell the story. People either loved or hated the posters, but it caused folks to talk. Over a nine-month period, our hand hygiene scores climbed from 35 percent to 85 percent. The amazing result is that mortality also dropped as a direct correlation. The impact of the posters had a part in actually saving lives." **—TIM FLOYD**

TITLE: Hand Hygiene movie posters
DESIGN FIRM: Palmetto Health Marketing and Communications
CREATIVE DIRECTOR: Tim Floyd
DESIGNER: Liz Phillips
WEB: Palmettohealth.org
CLIENT: Palmetto Health

Eat Play Laugh

CREATIVE ANARCHY: Juxtaposition of hand-rendered and photographic imagery

"Eat Play Laugh is a kid festival arranged by C2O library. The event series features a cookie-decorating workshop, hypnotic storytelling, a puppet theatre, a movie screening and more. Working on a tight budget, we drew playful illustrations to complement a flexible visual system. The tote bag merchandise, featuring three different words, can be (dis)assembled, functioning both on its own and as a whole. Strung together, they can also serve as a welcome signage. Child portraits from an orphanage, a collaboration organization with the program, were combined with playful illustrations and typography to convey their imaginative worlds and activities." —**ANDRIEW BUDIMAN**

TITLE: Eat Play Laugh
DESIGN FIRM: Butawarna
DESIGNER: Andriew Budiman
WEB: butawarna.in
CLIENT: C2O Library and Collabtive

EXERCISES

NOTES ABOUT
THE CREATIVE ANARCHY
AND CREATIVITY EXERCISES
FOUND IN THIS BOOK:

There are no rules to creative exercises.
Interpret, add, remove, alter and restructure
the exercises to fit your needs.

There are no boundaries. You have complete
freedom with your ideas. No one is judging you.

Document everything.
All ideas are relevant.

CREATIVE ANARCHY EXERCISE:

ROLE PLAY

RULE: Speak to the audience.
CREATE ANARCHY: Let the audience do the speaking.
RESULT: Create a different perspective from which to sell the product or service.

Advertising does a good job talking at the consumer. Buy this; go here; do that. But what if someone unexpected or unusual were telling you do it? Someone you never thought would be speaking to you. Verbal surprise is a surefire way to get an ad noticed.

 Let's do this

Grab an ad you're working on or have done recently. If you don't have one, look around your desk for something interesting to advertise. I happen to have my favorite Mont Blanc pen sitting next to me so I will use that.

Create a list of anyone you can think of who uses the product, including fictional characters. What would they say about the product? Start with broad ideas, then flesh out the concepts with further brainstorming.

Forget about the company for a moment and focus on the product itself. We know what the company would say; it's a great product, can't live without it, yadda, yadda, yadda. But what might someone else say?

Following is a list of people to help you get started:

- Optimist
- Boss
- Devil's advocate
- Fast food worker
- Mom
- Realtor
- Grandfather
- Lawyer

- Punk rock girl
- Alien
- Nanny
- Circus clown
- Caveman
- Napoleon
- Golf pro

- Angel
- Nosy neighbor
- Fireman
- Cleopatra
- Student
- Bill Clinton
- Toddler

- Thor
- Dog
- Airline pilot
- Buddha
- Masochist
- George Washington
- Angst-ridden teenager

- Robot
- Cat
- Trapeze artist
- Yoda
- Priest
- Biker

Keep going! Aim for at least thirty more perspectives.

Here are a few examples for my Mont Blanc Pen:

OPTIMIST: "It has never let me down."

DEVIL'S ADVOCATE: "What if you had a pencil instead? Would it work as well?"

MOM: "Make sure you have a pen and wear clean underwear."

GRANDFATHER: "When I was your age we had to make our own pen ink."

BOSS: "Take a note."

FAST FOOD WORKER: "Would you like blue or black ink with that?"

REALTOR: "Sign on the dotted line."

LAWYER: "My best friend."

PUNK ROCK GIRL: "Dude, it makes piercing your ears so easy."

ANGEL: "I'd sell my soul for this pen."

THOR: "It's like a hammer from the gods... that writes."

ROBOT: "I think I love you."

ALIEN: "Silly humans still write things down."

NOSY NEIGHBOR: "I saw her. She was up till the wee hours of the morning hunched over that notebook writing something in it with that pen."

DOG: "Is that food?"

CAT: "Oh look: a stabbing implement. Another way to kill you."

CREATIVE ANARCHY EXERCISE:

SCAMPER

RULE: Stay within your client's project objectives.
CREATE ANARCHY: Approach the project from left field.
RESULT: Shake out the old and bring in the new.

The SCAMPER concept is not new. It was originally created by Alec Osborn with the mnemonic developed by Bob Eberle. SCAMPER is typically used for business processes and marketing. Fortunately for us, it's adaptable to the design process and works particularly well for redesigns.

EXERCISES

What is SCAMPER?

SUBSTITUTE: What elements can be replaced?

COMBINE: How can an element be merged with another idea?

ADAPT: Can you take another idea and adapt it to fit this idea?

MODIFY: How can the idea be altered?

PUT TO OTHER USE: What is a completely different use for the product or service?

ELIMINATE: What element can be removed?

REVERSE: How can you rearrange or reverse in the idea?

 Let's do this

Take an advertisement you're working on or have done in the past. If you don't have one, create one for your favorite restaurant.

Use SCAMPER to sketch out new ideas. Aim for at least five new sketched ideas for each word in the mnemonic.

SUBSTITUTE: Take the type and imagery you have now, and consider what else will work. Stop being so literal. Use metaphor, simile and analogy. Play with puns. Think representative instead of literal. Audiences love associations.

COMBINE: Examine both the images and physical pieces of the design project. Consider how the elements can merge together. For example, merge the invite with the RSVP. Incorporate a promotional giveaway with the corporate brochure. Include an ad with the package. Think visually, too. For example, create an "Experience Fall in the City" campaign by manipulating an image of a leaf to form a skyline with its shape. Force all elements to do double-duty.

ADAPT: Look at successful ideas and adapt them for your own. Remember to modify and borrow, but *don't* steal or copy. Adapt from historical design, from nature, from an admired modern designer, from the pattern of sunlight on your kitchen floor, from an old lady's housecoat fabric, from anything. Shift to a new medium. If it's traditionally print, adapt it to digital or vice versa, or create a print interactive piece.

MODIFY: Take each element of your current design and change it. Modify all of it, one thing at a time. Change the typeface, image, size of the headline and image, placement of text, overall hierarchy, and color. Include the littlest details. If you don't like the way a letter looks, change it. Keep modifying until you have a distinctly new design; then change it all over again.

PUT TO OTHER USE: How else can the audience use your design? Create an innovative keepsake. Think beyond a pen or magnet adorned with the logo. Think more along the lines of an advertisement that can be origami folded into the product it advertises. How about a direct mailer that folds out into an awesome calendar poster?

ELIMINATE: Look at everything in your design. Is it all absolutely necessary? Go Bauhaus on it and declare "less is more." Add more negative space. Take out words. Simplify the image. Do you really need to give the street address when a URL is also listed? Are the sixteen pieces of paper contained in the direct mail campaign necessary, or can you get away with half that? "Eliminate" is a great opportunity to explore eco-friendly options.

REVERSE: Put on the brakes and go in the opposite direction with both the layout and concept. Switch up the sequence, pagination, hierarchy, layout, etc. Switch up the entire design. Change the concept by depicting a divergent point of view.

REVERSE ASSUMPTION

RULE: Understand your target audience.

CREATE ANARCHY: Shock and surprise the audience.

RESULT: Show the audience things from a different point of view via the unexpected.

Reverse assumption means taking what you think you know about a project and going with something completely different. The goal is to question everything, exploring what would happen to the visual and verbal elements of your design as if the opposite were true. Open your mind and challenge your assumptions. Remember too that it's common to have misconceptions about a subject with which you're not intimately familiar.

 Let's do this

Take an advertisement you're working on or have done in the past. If you don't have one, create one for a local bakery.

1. List five to ten things you believe about your subject. Put down the first things that come to mind.
2. Challenge each of these assumptions by writing down the opposite. Note: Don't be a Debbie Downer and assume that the opposite assumption has to be negative. Twist things to keep the vibe positive. Remember, you're selling something.
3. Use the second list to generate design concepts, shedding new light on your subject. This is applicable both to the headline and the image. It's a great opportunity to work on visual-verbal synergy.

Bakery Example

ASSUMPTION

1. Bakeries make pretty things.
2. Cake is meant to be eaten.
3. Wedding cakes are three or four tiers high.
4. Bakers are cute women who like to make sweet things.
5. Bakers' tools are piping bags and spatulas.

REVERSE ASSUMPTION

1. Bakeries make awesome zombie apocalypse cakes with filling that oozes.
2. Cake is meant to be more sculptural than edible.
3. Forget wedding cakes. Wedding cupcakes are all the craze.
4. Bakers are tattooed biker dudes.
5. Bakers use blow torches, jig saws and drills.

EXERCISES

DESIGN REFLEXES

Professional athletes have amazing focus and reflexes. They can see the ball, hit the ball, catch the ball, kick the ball... be the ball. Athletes train with the best technologies and methodologies. They practice constantly to get better at their craft. They live, breathe, eat and sleep their sport. Not unlike designers. (At least the successful ones.) The best designers challenge their problem-solving skills, practice design and develop their creative minds. The act of reading this book qualifies as creative mind development. This exercise will help you practice design and challenge your problem-solving skills via timed brainstorming.

 Let's do this

SUPPLIES:

- timer
- paper
- pen, pencil, marker, etc.
- twenty minutes of your time

1. Set your timer for one minute. In that minute, write down as many words as you can around the word *kids*; as in, "Kids are the next generation of great designers." Ready, set, go!

2. Set your timer for two minutes. List as many world problems as you can think of. Focus both on your own country and international issues. Ready, set, go!

3. Set your timer for one minute. Write down as many words as you can think of around the word *surfer*. Ready, set, go!

4. Set your timer for three minutes. Write as many ad concepts as you can about how kids and surfers can work together to solve the world's problems. Ready, set, go!

5. Set your timer for ten minutes. Sketch thumbnails of as many of those ad concepts as you can. Ready, set, go!

6. Set your timer for one minute. Go back to your lists and keep adding to them.

CHAPTER 2

BRANDING

What's the first thing that pops into your head when you see these words: Nike, McDonalds, IBM, FedEx, Coca-Cola, Pepsi, Gatorade, Disney, Harley-Davidson, World Wildlife Federation, New York Life, Apple?

If you are a design geek like me, I'll bet your answer was a visual of the logo. Powerful companies have powerful, memorable, logos—although logos are only part of the equation. Companies trigger that visual association by maintaining a consistent and unified look across all of their audience communications. This is called *branding*. Branding applies to every single thing the company produces—from product, packaging and advertising to the website, mobile app, internal communications and stationery. Nothing is left unbranded. Why? The more consistent and unified the brand application, the more recognizable the brand becomes.

Before you start slapping a logo on everything, stop. Branding is so much more than just logo. It is the company's essence. Branding includes the logo, the color palette, the design style, use of imagery, choice of type, advertising direction and the overall business concept of the company. But because the logo is the thing that people most commonly associate with a company, let's start with that.

THE LOGO

Modern logos originated with the ancient Greeks and Romans. Stylized monograms representing rulers or towns were found on coins. Monograms and other simple marks continued to be used by merchants, tradesmen and royalty through the Middle Ages. With the boom in advertising that followed the Industrial Revolution, logos became commonplace. By the nineteenth century, virtually every commercial business had a logo to identify the product or service being offered. Some of these logos are still in use today, albeit slightly modified to remain current, including:

Stunning vintage illustrative letterhead examples from the late 1800s and early 1900s.

- DuPont: oval-shaped logo designed in 1802
- Goodyear: famous winged foot developed in 1901
- GE: script *G* and *E* designed in 1900
- Coca-Cola: script type first used in 1886
- Volkswagen: *VW* letter combination designed in 1939
- Prudential: Rock of Gibraltar designed in 1896
- RCA: dog listening to a phonograph designed in 1910
- Johnson & Johnson: script type logo first used in 1886
- John Deere: leaping deer icon first seen in 1876

A logo makes its impact both literally and figuratively. Literally it identifies a company. Figuratively it is the company. Think of the logo as a calling card. Logos tell the audience what the product or service is, and from whom it comes. Logos also communicate the company's mission, values, goals and credibility. Companies want that logo to be recognized immediately and associated with their product or service.

07 ● **Folded Light Art + Design** is an
innovation light shade design brand
which investigates the tectonic relationship between form, material and
technique, digital fabrication, and
sustainable design.

That recognition and association can only happen, though, if the logo makes the right impression. That's your job! Creating brand recognition is a tall order, made all the more difficult by design and logo suggestions drawn on napkins by the client's well-meaning third cousin twice removed. As a designer, you understand the solid base of research and exploration behind good design. (If you don't, go back and read Rule 2: The Computer Is Only a Tool.) Now let's dive into what separates a good logo from an awesome one.

Type and marks,
that's what logos are made of

Logos generally consist of two main elements, the name and the mark. Either can exist without the other. Typography is what communicates the name (and its message) clearly. The mark creates a visual association that complements the typography, though it may be used independently. Both must be distinctive, memorable, versatile and appropriate for the target audience. Above all, they must stand the test of time. A poorly designed logo looks amateurish, leading the audience to assume the company is unprofessional or unreliable. When the logo looks professional, the audience will treat the company as such.

A company measures success by its customer base. Customers equal profits. Profits mean a company stays in business. To succeed, a company must prove to customers that its business is better than other similar businesses. The logo plays a role in getting those customers in the first place.

A logo that is more distinctive than logos for competing businesses will stand out and stick in the minds of potential customers.

K.I.S.S.

Keep It Simple, Sir. (Feel free to insert another *S*-based identifier here.) Simplicity is key in logo design. The quicker a viewer recognizes and understands a logo, the better. The logos of the great companies listed at the beginning of this chapter (and many others) are simple. Why? The more complicated the logo, the longer it takes to recognize. Complicated and complex are two different things. Complicated is fussy, confusing and contains many parts. Complex is well thought out, conceptual and intricately developed. In that vein, simple does not mean simplistic. Simple means functional, timeless, free of clutter and devoid of extraneous information. Simplistic means uninspired icons and generic type.

How do you create a simple logo that communicates a complex idea? Start with lots and lots of research. Ask the client questions, understand the business, understand their audience... all the due diligence required for any design. If you are doing your job right, the design solutions you come up with should range from literal to abstract, and from safe to really out there. They should also be inspired, fresh, ownable and simple.

A logo mark must capture the spirit of the business. The mark's representation doesn't always have to be literal, but it should mean something. A mark for the sake of a mark doesn't help the company, nor does a generic or wrong mark. I once had to develop a mark for a package series with a global audience. The client requested an icon that didn't mean anything, in order to avoid offending or misleading the culturally diverse clientele. My design team went through almost three hundred icons before settling on the winning mark. That exploration was one of the hardest I have ever done. I discovered it is difficult to disassociate meaning from a mark. Keep it appropriate and consider the associative meaning. Try to stay away from clichés as well. A photographer's logo could easily be a camera or an aperture icon—marks that are recognizable, but expected and boring. Dig deeper and explore more. Look at historical and cultural influence; bring in the Gestalt theory of closure. Investigate stylistic techniques to render a mark as well. A single-weight line is rarely interesting. How about varying line weight thickness, silhouettes, brush with ink, texture, linoleum cut, wood cut, eraser stamp, photography? Try rendering solutions by hand or generating them with a computer.

The logo's typography must work with the mark and vice versa. Successful logos often create this visual relationship through color or style. The process for creating the logo's typography is the same as the one for creating the mark. Choose a typeface with a connotative association. Then go one step farther. Don't use the font simply as it appears when typed. The most distinctive logos contain type that has been modified, manipulated or created by hand. These changes include letters that:

- have interesting or unusual ligatures
- interlock or overlap
- have parts added or removed
- are manually distressed
- are substituted with numbers or shapes
- are flipped or rotated
- are created from other objects or create an object.

The more the typography is altered, the more proprietary the logo. However, don't let all those extra flourishes and graphic elements detract from legibility.

09 ● "The imperfections found in hand-drawn illustration and type can make it feel more personal and contrast the sometimes cold and repetitive digital vector art commonly used in branding." —Mario Valdes

08 ● The objective was to create a contemporary brand identity system. It begins with a symbol and brand name, and builds exponentially into a matrix of tools and communications.

10 ● DroolInc.com

11 ● Emily J. Morris logo

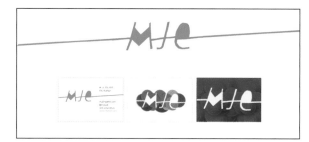

12 ● M.J. Eliot Logo & Business Cards

13 ● Three Fifty (350) Wine Lounge branding

Whatever you do, never forget practicality. A logo needs to work well at any size—shrunk for a business card and possibly blown up on a huge video screen—which is why it shouldn't be overly complicated. The mark needs to withstand the client's scrutiny and still be understood by the customer.

THE PAPER GOODS

Logos are rarely used on their own. They end up on everything. Stationery is the first thing usually addressed after client approval of the logo. Stationery has many components; that's why it's called a *set*. What do professionals do when they first meet each other? Exchange business cards, of course. How does a company get paid for services rendered? By sending invoices. How do their customers know they need to open an envelope they received in the mail? By looking at the return address. Stationery is the gateway of communication between company and customer.

The card

I find it ironic that the smallest piece of stationery contains the greatest amount of information. So much needs to be said in such a limited space. It's tempting to just cram the logo, name, title, company name, address, office number, cell number, URL and email address wherever it fits. But because there is no second chance to make a first impression, a well-designed card must accompany the meeting and greeting of a new potential contact. Excellent organization and design is needed to make an impression and communicate necessary information. The way information is arranged on the business card, how it feels to the touch, and the quality of its communication of the brand—all make a statement. The card serves as a memory jog to the receiver of the card, and you want that receiver to remember good things.

My research into business cards found that the company's logo is most commonly dead center, with the rest of the information evenly distributed in each of the four corners. This may seem to make the information more accessible;

14 ● MODhair Rome Rock 'n' Roll hair salon needed a groovy businesscard. This comb plays a classic rock theme when rubbed by fingernail, using the same principle as a music box comb.

in fact, it does the opposite, by leading your eye in four directions at once. I cringe just thinking about it. The best way to organize the information on a business card is to start by dividing the information into categories: contact information, name and title, and company-specific information. Then keep these categories together in your design. Use alignment, typeface, size and color to maintain consistency within the information, but do allow for some differentiation within text, perhaps setting the contact name in bold with the title in italic. This will assist with visual interest and hierarchy. Once you've done that, try playing with other arrangements of the text. Set the information in a different order. What about giving priority to the phone number or email, which are important bits of information usually presented with lower hierarchy. Try making the web address larger than everything else. Try holding the card vertically or horizontally. Go minimal; see how little information you can get away with. Or go extravagant. And don't forget the other side. Business cards give you two surfaces to work on—front and back—so take advantage of them.

The typical business card is 3.5" x 2" and may be held either horizontally or vertically. It's the perfect size for a wallet or the almost-extinct Rolodex. With more people relying on their phones and other mobile devices to hold contact information, business cards are increasingly considered more a keepsake than a traditional business tool. The artistic, cool and wow-factor cards are kept; the boring, uninspiring ones are thrown away after their data is digitized. Square, oversized rectangle, circular, interior die

cuts, rounded corners and other shapes are a surefire way to enhance a design and make a card stand out.

Using great paper is a simple way to make a card scream "Don't throw me away." Switching from standard card stock to something thicker or more distinctive can move your card into the "keep" pile. How about a textured stock or an unusual color? Use fluorescent, metallic or pearlescent inks. Printing techniques like embossing/debossing, letterpress, foil stamping, die-cutting, screen printing, and edge printing will give you a card that makes a distinct impression. Or you could move away from paper altogether. Wood, metal and plastic make great business cards that are virtually indestructible. Wood can be printed or engraved. Metal can be engraved, embossed, printed or die-cut. Plastic can be

15 ● Unique size, cool paper, letterpress printing—plus a great type layout with fun titles and icons for the employees—equals an awesome card.

LIGLIV Match Grip Music Workshop

16 ● Rebranding of Match Grip Music Workshop

engraved, embossed, foil stamped, printed, or die-cut. It can even be transparent.

The rest of it

The advent of email has greatly diminished the need for paper-based letterhead and envelopes, but not so much so that you can ignore these parts of the stationery set. Plenty of snail mail still exchanges hands. Professional correspondence, contracts, invoices and other business exchanges still make their way onto real paper. The typical letterhead has a clean design with plenty of white space (for the letter that has to go on it.) Don't let that inhibit your creativity, though. Create something that makes the receiver want to keep your fabulously designed letterhead instead of tossing it into the circular filing cabinet. All the paper, printing and finishing techniques discussed for business cards—aside from printing on wood, metal or plastic—also apply to the letterhead and envelope. As with the business card, the front and back of each are fair game.

Stationery works as a set. The logo and typography will automatically tie them together, but think about how they can become more than just mere copies of each other. If you have a multicolored palette, give each piece of stationery its own color. Use an illustration to tie the pieces together, or use a pattern or image that continues across the back of each piece. Work the business card into the letterhead

design by die-cutting slits to hold the card. Letterheads can be folded in many ways. Use the fold to your advantage: Create a reveal when the letterhead is unfolded or the envelope is opened.

CREATE THE BRAND

The logo and stationery are done. It's time to start forming. What's left to form the complete brand look? Oh, just a few things: brochures, websites, apps, advertising, publications, packaging, environment and any other design-based item a company could need. The public should see a unified design, from a tiny sticker to a giant billboard. There should never be doubt about which business they're seeing.

Style it

The *style guide* is the blueprint for a business's design program and is usually created by the design team. It helps guide the use of the business's design elements and serves to rationalize creative choices. A style guide helps any vendor, designer or agency working on the business's materials to consistently follow the same set of design guidelines. It's not a "you must follow every rule exactly or else feel my wrath" type of guideline, of course. No use stifling the creativity of those working on the project. Rather it should serve as a starting point, providing general usage rules and directional requests. At minimum it should contain:

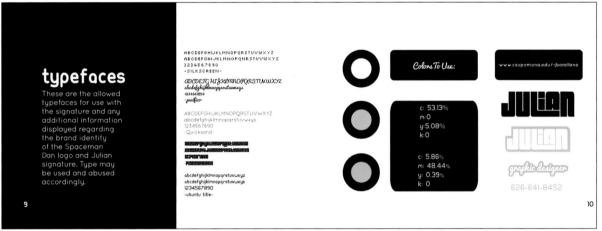

- The vision and overview of the company
- An overall design philosophy
- Imagery and information on usage of the logo, approved typefaces, color palette and overall tone
- Illustration and photography guidelines
- Collateral guidelines including suggested grid systems
- Description of usage restriction for any of the above

Think about the major brands out there today. The successful ones create a unified look. A woman walking 300 feet away with a hot pink rectangular shopping bag is immediately recognized as having visited a Victoria's Secret store. Say the word *angel* around most men in this day and age, and he will likely conjure up an image of a lingerie-clad model instead of an unearthly being. Consistency in message and style is what brands a company. An image of a person drenched in sweat guzzling a neon-colored liquid. An

advertisement in which all the products and background are either a single hue of red or white. A bright yellow billboard with bold black typography and nothing else. Cute animated polar bears sitting under a night sky drinking from a curvaceous bottle. A sleek electronic device on a bright white background. A light blue box with a white ribbon tied into a bow. Gatorade, Target, Livestrong, Coca-Cola, Apple and Tiffany & Co. (respectively) should have sprung to mind. If they did, the branding works. Please note that I only mentioned the most popular association to these brands. Each has a high degree of flexibility within the confines of the style guides. The overall tone is maintained even if the look changes from time to time.

While your client may not be on par with huge brands like Apple and Target, the takeaway message is the same: Consistency in branding will spark recognition. Flexibility in design will keep it interesting.

GALLERY

Magpie Artisan Pies

CREATIVE ANARCHY: Hand-rendered elements, Historical Influence

"Pie-making is an art. And no one knows this better than Magpie Artisan Pies. It was this handcrafted essence that became the driving force for the brand. We created an identity system that was as unique as the idea of starting a pie shop itself, speaking to the owner's heritage but with a chic and modern feel. Our goal was not just to create a celebration of pie but also to build a culture and community around it.

It is an ongoing, evolving brand identity that is updated week to week, with an in-the-moment feel. The imagery is not too contrived, but more visceral. The design links back to the owner's heritage and Pennsylvania-Dutch historical inspiration." **—20NINE**

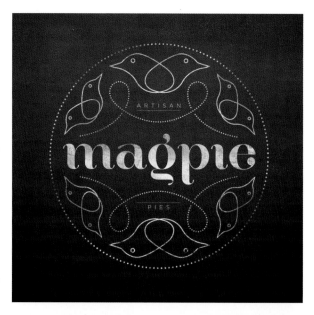

TITLE: Magpie Artisan Pies
DESIGN FIRM: 20nine
ART DIRECTORS: Kevin Hammond, Ashley Thurston-Curry
DESIGNERS: Jenna Navitsky, Justin Graham, Erin Doyle
WEB: 20nine.com
CLIENT: Magpie Artisan Pies

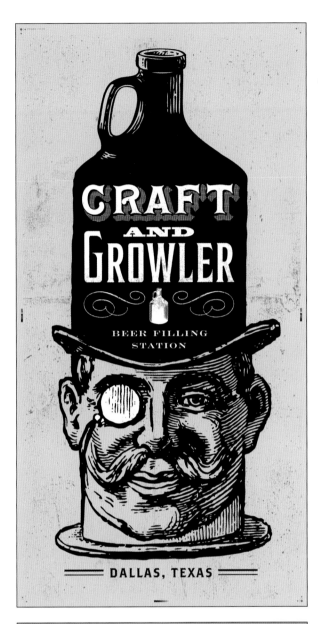

Craft and Growler Branding

CREATIVE ANARCHY: One-color printing, Style mash-up

"Craft and Growler is a start-up bar here in Dallas, Texas, that was going to be the first to offer growlers for the local craft beer folks. It needed to be creative, flexible and still somewhat supportive to the myriad of brands that would be featured at the bar. The final approach took a vintage 'dream of the 1890s' look with our own spin added, and mixed in some Steam Punk. We wanted a little tech, a little Monty Python and a healthy dose of hipster beer knowledge.

The fact that it is executed across print media, digital on-line, neon signage, glassware and in store—it shows the flexibility of the design. It communicates a serious passion for beer in a way that doesn't take itself too seriously." **—CALIBER CREATIVE**

TITLE: Craft and Growler Branding
DESIGN FIRM: Caliber Creative/Dallas Texas
ART DIRECTORS: Brandon Murphy, Bret Sano
DESIGNERS: Brandon Murphy, Catie Conlon, Kaitlyn Canfield
WEB: calibercreative.com
CLIENT: Craft and Growler

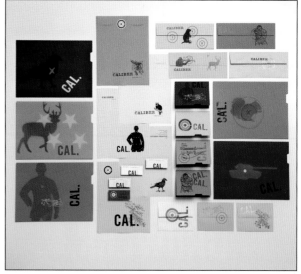

Caliber Stationery/Branding 1st Edition

CREATIVE ANARCHY: No boundaries

"Caliber Stationery/Branding 1st Edition is the initial branding for our new studio—a prime example of designers going nuts with (possibly) too much freedom. We created a kinetic system that changed and communicated our creativity through a variety of substrates, icons and looks.

I think it's successful in its sheer ambition and scope. It was like a growing thing that got away from us a bit. No boundaries is just that—no boundaries. It doesn't stop or end. Which can be problematic in terms of actual day-to-day application usage. Too much form, not enough function. Techniques employed included letterpress, foil stamping, spray paint stencils and photocopier toner." —**CALIBER CREATIVE**

TITLE: Caliber Stationery/Branding 1st Edition
DESIGN FIRM: Caliber Creative/Dallas Texas
ART DIRECTORS: Brandon Murphy, Bret Sano
DESIGNERS: Brandon Murphy, Bret Sano
WEB: calibercreative.com
CLIENT: Caliber Creative/Dallas, TX

Rock Lititz

CREATIVE ANARCHY: Altered letterforms, Flexible logo

"The objective was to develop an identity system for a corporate campus, Rock Lititz, that will become home to three unique, music-focused entertainment companies—Atomic Design, Clair Bros. and Tait Towers. The design concept visits the idea of triangular shapes—three sides to make one shape—and how triangles can be used in positive and negative space.

The typography system that was developed had functional considerations beyond what was considered aesthetically. All three companies frequently ship road cases of equipment to large venues (arenas, stadiums, etc.). Stenciling of names and logos on the outside of the cases is critical in order to quickly locate and track the cases once on site. The core triangular form used in the identity system was used to 'chop' the typography in ways that would expose the counter forms—providing a conversion to a stencil version of the font.

The identity's success is in its ability to flex and morph across companies, events and time, and it provides a tremendous range of expression. This is very important to entertainment companies that constantly adapt and reconfigure their skills to new clients and projects." **—CRAIG WELSH**

TITLE: Rock Lititz
DESIGN FIRM: Go Welsh
ART DIRECTOR: Craig Welsh
DESIGNER: Scott Marz
WEB: gowelsh.com
CLIENT: Rock Lititz

Bone Daddy's Branding and Collateral

CREATIVE ANARCHY: Illustration- and texture-heavy design

"Bone Daddy's House of Smoke is a popular Texas BBQ restaurant and bar. They approached us to rebrand all of their print and interactive collateral materials. The restaurants are filled with Southern folk art and a very funky junkyard vibe. To reflect this unique atmosphere, we incorporated hand-set wood type, rich colors, screen printed textures and the amazing illustrations of Nate Williams, whose quirky style brought the menu, website and collateral pieces to life." —THE MATCHBOX STUDIO

TITLE: Bone Daddy's Branding and Collateral
DESIGN FIRM: The Matchbox Studio
ART DIRECTORS: Liz Burnett, Jeff Breazeale
DESIGNERS: Liz Burnett, Zach Hale
WEB: matchboxstudio.com
CLIENT: Bone Daddy's

Europan Forum Oslo

CREATIVE ANARCHY: Experimental graphics, 3-D glasses

"The design work for this symposium on architecture and the jury meeting for the architecture competition EUROPAN included a program publication, website and banners for the location. All graphics were created as anaglyphs for viewing through red/blue glasses, bringing three-dimensionality into the graphics on this architecture event. The glasses were also used as name tags for the participants. It was a challenge to make it work in print, since the anaglyphs work a lot better on screen in RGB mode. A lot of trial and error was involved." **—ARIANE SPANIER**

TITLE: Europan Forum Oslo
DESIGN FIRM: Ariane Spanier Design
DESIGNER: Ariane Spanier
WEB: arianespanier.com
CLIENT: Europan Norway

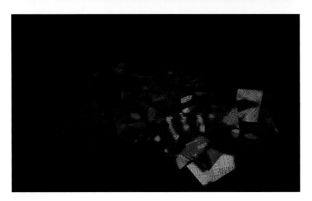

Contact 2.0

CREATIVE ANARCHY: Thermosensitive paper

"The Contact 2.0 project is a conceptual and contemporary approach to the business card. The usual function of the support is reversed, as it is totally black and devoid of any information. Only when in contact with the hand is the information revealed, before turning back to black. New technologies and sophisticated printing techniques resulted in a fun concept. The secret to the design's success is simple; everybody loves to touch things!" **—MURMURE**

TITLE: Contact 2.0
DESIGN FIRM: MURMURE
DESIGNERS: Julien Alirol, Paul Ressencourt
WEB: murmure.me

Deep Ellum Brewing Company Branding

CREATIVE ANARCHY: No boundaries,
Flexible design elements

"We approached the owners when they were just starting out in their garage.

They had a logo that was 'too clean' and we told them so. Not that it was bad—just bad for them. We wanted to capture the funk, the dirt and the smell of Deep Ellum. Nothing could be clean. Nothing could be 'out of the can' and nothing could be repeated. We decided to create the ultimate kinetic brand. There really isn't a graphic standard of any kind. Every employee gets up to five different designs for their business cards (that are just theirs). And each employee after that gets a different set and so on. Our design philosophy on this project? Draw it. Draw on it. Paint it. Scratch it. Tape it. Photocopy it." **—CALIBER CREATIVE**

TITLE: Deep Ellum Brewing Company Branding
DESIGN FIRM: Caliber Creative/Dallas Texas
ART DIRECTORS: Brandon Murphy, Bret Sano
DESIGNERS: Brandon Murphy, Maxim Barkhatov
WEB: calibercreative.com
CLIENT: Deep Ellum Brewing Company

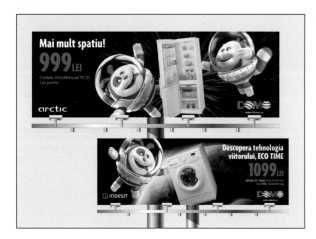

TITLE: DOMO
DESIGN FIRM: Brandient
ART DIRECTOR: Cristian 'Kit' Paul
DESIGNERS: Cristian 'Kit' Paul, Eugen Erhan, Alin Tamasan
WEB: brandient.com
CLIENT: DOMO Retail SA

Domo

CREATIVE ANARCHY: Selling cuteness

"Brandient designed the identity of the leading electronics retailer [in Romania], DOMO. Energized by the success of its new identity—remarkably the two striped balls in the logo, which infused the brand with a playful and friendly personality—the retailer came back after a few years and requested that the identity be taken to the next level.

Building upon a novel variation of the flexible identity paradigm, we came up with a pair of fully (and furry) constructed brand avatars: Do, the candid dog, and Mo, the mischievous cat—which would act as mascots, but also at times replace the striped elements of the logo. This identity design strategy enables accelerated consolidation of brand awareness while keeping the logo always new, always telling a story via strategically chosen themes.

The avatars contributed not only to increased brand equity but also to significant savings on advertising and communication, which become easier and cheaper to execute. In addition, the undisputed cuteness of the two avatars prompted the retail chain to eventually produce them as toys and trinkets and sell them in its own stores. People paying to take home your identity elements is a pretty cool measure of accomplishment." **—BRANDIENT**

Indygen

CREATIVE ANARCHY: Custom typography, Bold presence

"Indygen, a major telecom player [in Romania], was looking for an innovative way to build and secure the relationship with young consumers, amid major technological disruption facing the industry. The new brand was created to serve the specific interests, motives, aspirations, challenges and lifestyle of the Romanian youth. In addition, it had to serve as a digital platform capable of sustaining an ecosystem equipping the young generation with diverse self-development and entrepreneurial solutions.

The logo expresses the natural spontaneity of the kids as well as their desire to change. A custom typeface with three fonts was designed by Brandient to sustain the 'unrest' spirit of the brand, including the trademark 'Change' symbol as a glyph. All of it is captured in the 'positive rebellion' essence of the brand." **—BRANDIENT**

TITLE: Indygen
DESIGN FIRM: Brandient
ART DIRECTOR: Cristian 'Kit' Paul
DESIGNERS: Cristian 'Kit' Paul, Ciprian Badalan, Cristian Petre, Bogdan Dumitrache
WEB: brandient.com
CLIENT: Vodafone (Romania)

Seoul Fashion Week

CREATIVE ANARCHY: VARIABLE LOGO

The colors are closely related to the five cardinal elements of Yin and Yang—the basic principle of creation and symbolic ideas—and from colors observable in traditional Korean court dress. The variable logo options provide consistency within a flexible system, taking cues from the fashion world.

TITLE: Seoul Fashion Week
UNIVERSITY: James Madison University
DESIGNER: Jun Bum Shin
WEB: junbumshin.com

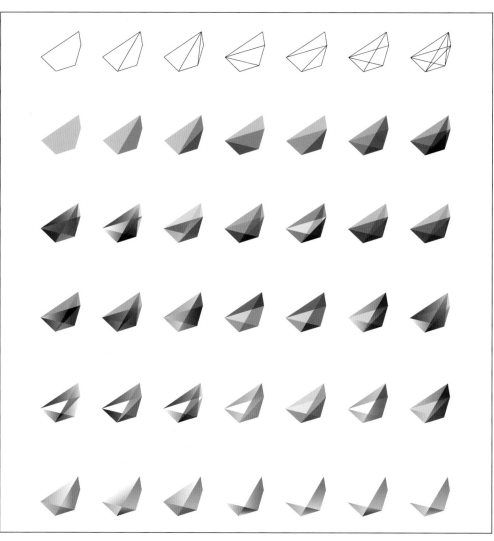

EXERCISES

ROLL THE DICE

RULE: Carefully consider all your design options.
CREATE ANARCHY: Let chance guide your design.
RESULT: Create logo design solutions you may not have otherwise thought of doing.

It's easy to get in the habit of doing the tried and true, always going with those fonts you know will work or a symbolic mark that's easy to create. But when was the last time you fully explored a logo for a client, where you didn't rely on the same old same old? Are you just getting plain ol' stuck for ideas? Here's a fun way to shake up your logo design.

 Let's do this

Grab two dice and a logo you're working on or have done recently. If you don't have one, create one using your last name plus some type of gadget (pick one to guide your sketches). Experiment with the placement of the mark relative to the type: left, right, center, bottom or middle. Roll once for the typography options, roll again for the mark/shape number. Do a sketch for each combination. Try at least twenty to start. If you roll the same number, either do a different sketch or roll again.

CHALLENGE ROUND: Incorporate a timer or compete against your colleagues to make it more exciting. Ready, set, go!

Typography

1. **SERIF**
2. **SIMPLIFY:** Break the letters down to basic shapes.
3. **CASE:** Try all uppercase, all lowercase or a combination of both.
4. **SANS SERIF**
5. **LIGATURE:** Combine two letterforms.
6. **TWO DIFFERENT FONTS** (even if it's just one word)
7. **LOCKUP:** Bring the words together in an interesting way.
8. **ALTERED LETTERFORMS:** Customize one or more of your letterforms.
9. **TAKE ON FORM:** Make the letters become a shape or object.
10. **DECONSTRUCTED:** Take the letters apart and put them back together again.
11. **HISTORIC:** Use vintage, retro or historic typography.
12. **HAND-LETTERED**

Mark/shape

1. **SYMBOLIC:** Try an implied representation of the product or service.
2. **GEOMETRIC:** Use basic shapes to form the mark.
3. **MONOGRAM/LETTER MARK:** Make a mark based upon a letterform.
4. **EMBLEM:** Make the type and mark one and the same. Use different shapes to house information.
5. **LITERAL:** Use clearly recognizable objects.
6. **SUBLIMINAL:** Hide a message in the mark (think FedEx and Amazon).
7. **ABSTRACT:** Develop a mark for the company without forming something specific.
8. **REBUS:** Replace a letter with an object.
9. **HIGH TECH:** Create a slick, web-esque look or pixel-based rendering.
10. **HAND-RENDERED:** Forego the computer to make any category of mark, but specifically one rendered with a traditional medium.
11. **SUM OF ITS PARTS:** Deconstruct the representative mark.
12. **ILLUSTRATIVE:** Make your characters simple or complex.

 4,7

 1,12

 11,3

 7,8

 8,1

RECIPE FOR DESIGN

RULE: Follow the brand standards.
CREATE ANARCHY: Take risks and manipulate the brand standards.
RESULT: Create new branding options with underutilized and unimagined materials.

We all have design recipes we use on a deadline. A certain fallback typeface, a stylistic approach, or a tried-and-true grid system. This is both good and bad. It's good because we know what works and it saves us valuable design time. It's bad because if we rely on our favorite recipes too often, our work starts to look all the same.

Brand standards have recipes too. Logo, color, typography, photography and layout usage are premeasured for us. The recipes tell us how to combine and format the designs. Primary elements become the main course; secondary and tertiary elements are the side dishes. Brand standards maintain consistency, which is a good thing. A brand needs to put forth a unified front. But it can also be a problem. Brand recipes get stale over time. While it's important to be in line with the brand's personality, it's also necessary to help it stay fresh. Whip up new brand creations by experimenting with the recipes.

 Let's do this

Take a brand standards guide you're currently working with or have worked with in the past. If you don't have one, use the brands standards from a major corporation. Most post their standards online or can easily be determined through their branded materials.

1. Carefully read the current brand standards. You may have been working with it for quite some time but it's prudent to read it again. Pretend you've never read it before.
2. Look for key words that will allow you to mix up the recipe. Words like *should* and *can* mean there's flexibility.

Take note of words like *must* and *cannot* as well. For example, the statement "the logo *must* be 100 percent cyan and *should* have the tagline whenever possible," can be interpreted to mean that the logo has to be the indicated blue hue but tagline inclusion is negotiable.

3. Closely examine all the secondary and tertiary elements. Can any of them become the main course? If the branding focuses on its primary blue color for all materials, try bringing in the secondary green or yellow as the dominant color instead. Don't abandon the blue, just minimize it in favor of a secondary or tertiary color. Same for typefaces.

4. Manipulate the image standards. The brand may call for happy smiling people. Who's to say the smiling happy people have to be shown all the same way? What if some are tightly cropped while others show the whole body? What if they are shot from interesting perspectives instead of the typical head-on view? Push the boundaries.

5. Be brave: Utter the words, "The standards don't say I can't _____ so I'm going to give it a try."

6. Expect some pushback from your creative director or client. Be prepared with well-thought-out reasoning for your design decisions. Use the brand standards as your argument for new brand recipes.

REBRAND YOURSELF DIY-STYLE

Unless you're looking for a new job, you probably haven't addressed your personal branding in quite some time. This is both good and bad: good because you are in a stable job environment, bad because you're a designer and you should have well-designed stationery. At minimum, you should have a great business card to hand out at networking events.

Digital presses have dramatically reduced the cost of printing. It's ridiculously easy to get anywhere from a few dozen to a few hundred cards on the cheap. Great for your wallet—not necessarily so great for first impressions with a punch. Think about memorable business cards you've seen. You know, the awesome ones—letterpress, thick-textured stock and magnificent die cuts. For large companies, cost isn't an issue. But for a smaller company or as an individual, the cost of die-cutting and other techniques are prohibitive. What's a designer to do? Do it yourself. Sure, it takes a little time, but given that you only need a few pieces at a time, it's totally worth it.

 Let's do this

1. Rebrand yourself: Make a new business card. Take all the branding skills you use for businesses and apply them to yourself. Let the logo, typography, color and layout project who you are and reflect your design sensibilities. **NOTE:** Don't rush this step. Rebranding yourself is tough. Make sure your decisions are just right.

2. Decide which special techniques you want to use. Cool for the sake of cool is never cool. Think carefully about what enhances your design while making sense with your concept. Consider some of the following:

- Create custom die-cuts with:
  - Corner rounders
  - Hole and shape punchers
  - Perforating and scoring tools
  - Fancy-edged scissors
- Emboss your stationery with embossing powder and a heat gun.
- Hand-sew or use a sewing machine to create a pattern.
- Spray paint a custom stencil.
- Have a rubber stamp made or cut your own linoleum block.

- Mount the card to another piece of paper to add texture and depth.
- The I'm-poor-and-have-zero-money options include:
  - Add color with markers, highlighters, paint or colored pencils.
  - Use a marker along the edge to fake edge printing (works best on uncoated stock).

3. Print your cards. Digital printers can be very inexpensive. Start with twenty-five to fifty cards. There's no sense in getting more unless you are actively looking for work. For an even cheaper option, print your cards from a desktop printer or photocopier.
4. Execute your special techniques.
5. Start handing out your cards. Watch as people *oooh* and *aaah* over them.

CREATIVITY EXERCISE:

WINDOW SHOPPING

Fashion and design have much in common. Both work to present striking images. Both use the Gestalt principles of carefully chosen color, balance and hierarchy. Both also go through cyclical trend patterns; what's old is new and what's new becomes old. It's probably not a stretch to say that fashion designers and graphic designers have similar work habits and are cut from the same cloth.

Therefore, what better way to look for inspiration than to go shopping? Seriously. Fashion provides a ton of innovation and ingenuity. More times than not, it is ahead of the design curve. Fashion is the perfect place to look for what's new and trendy.

 Let's do this

SUPPLIES:
- camera
- sketchbook/journal
- pen, pencil, marker
- money: just in case
- a friend: Shopping is always more fun with a friend.

1. Head to the largest fashion store or shopping mall in your area. The advantage of a mall is the ready availability of several different stores.
2. Start window shopping. Work your way through the entire store—men's, women's, children's, jewelry and accessories departments. Don't worry so much about the actual shirts, dresses or belts. Focus on the details. Record what you find.
3. Notice color and pattern trends. This is a great opportunity to see how colors or patterns work together. Pick up garments and hold them side by side. A reminder: Patterned and printed fabric are copyright protected. Use them for inspiration only.
4. Look closely at buttons, snaps, clasps, stitch detailing, fabric treatments, appliqué and other embellishments. Check out shoes, purses, scarves, belts, jewelry and cuff links too.
5. Visit specialty shops. Investigate high fashion and subculture trends. These are generally more interesting than typical department store offerings.
6. Before you leave the stores, sit down and make additional notes about your discoveries. Jot down why you noted the things you did. Was it color? Arrangement? Juxtaposition of patterns? The way the stitching swirled across the fabric? How an earring's shape inspired a typeface design idea? Write it down now before you forget.
7. Apply your findings to your current project or keep them handy for the next brainstorming session.

CHAPTER 3

POSTERS

Posters are great fun. It's a huge space that offers possibilities unlike any other type of design. What to do with all that great space? Use awesome images, create cool type, generate killer graphics and splash it across the page, right? Not so fast. A poster's job is to communicate a message. Period. All too often we look at a poster as a means to create a classic piece that will hang on someone's wall forever. It's an understandable goal because posters, unlike other forms of design, can have a second life as fine art. But it's not the primary goal of the design process. The message has to be the number one priority. It's not easy. A poster has to grab the viewer's attention in an environment where lots of other stimuli vie for attention. Think about where you see posters: hanging in busy school hallways, plastered to walls along crowded city streets, tacked to telephone poles, and fighting for space on message boards. Visual distractions on all sides threaten to pull the viewer's attention away from your intended message. Posters just yearn to be noticed.

Consider this: A poster is nothing more than an advertisement, invitation or promotion, just on a grander scale. It shouts to the public from the sidelines. Sometimes it calls out alone, a singular piece trying to grab your attention; at other times there's a whole chorus of them wallpapered side by side. Either way, success comes to the posters that command the most attention.

A BIT OF HISTORY

Posters date back to the early days of printing when *broadsides*, large sheets of paper printed only on one side, were produced as announcements, generally serving to promote and advertise local events and businesses. They were considered temporary and thrown away when no longer needed. In the beginning, they were composed of text, simple graphics and ornamental decorations, as these were the only available options for letterpress printing. As printing processes improved, illustrations were added. When color lithography became an affordable option, broadsides were replaced with posters.

Eventually, posters morphed into objects of desire, a phenomenon unique to this category of design. Not only did a poster advertise a theater event—now the same poster could hang on someone's wall as a piece of fine art. Some posters were—and are—so coveted that they are stolen from their public venue.

Among the many historically famous poster designers, few have seen as much sustained success as Henri de Toulouse-Lautrec. He became the preeminent designer for the Paris theater district in the early 1900s. His use of expressionistic portraits; flat, simple color; and dynamic layouts set his posters apart from the competition. To this day they continue to be highly sought after for private collections and museums.

Each art movement from the late nineteenth through the twentieth century produced famous poster designs. In the late 1800s, Art Nouveau's contribution to design history consisted of beautiful, elegant women surrounded by lavish organic typography and borders. A great example is Henri Privat-Livemont's poster advertising "Absinthe Robette" 1896. The woman exalts a glass of absinthe. This story-like setting was a common way to get the audience to engage with the poster. Art Deco (1920–1930) became well known for glamorous travel posters such as those featuring the Holland America Line, c.1932, by Hoff. Bold, airbrushed imagery and sans serif type combined to produce an idealistic view of travel. The International Typographic Style, also known as Swiss style, gave us Herbert Matter, who used bold photography and overlapping elements

18 ● (above) Reproduction of a poster advertising 'Robette Absinthe', 1896 (colour litho) Livemont, Privat (1861–1936); 19 ● (below) 'Dylan', poster advertising *Bob Dylan's Greatest Hits album*, 1966 (colour litho) Glaser, Milton (b. 1929)

20 ● Advertisement for the Holland America Line, c. 1932 (colour litho)

to sell products. A notable example is his 1934 Swiss Tourism poster that shows a large photograph of a smiling woman overlapping a montage of the Swiss Alps and skiers. The International Typographic Style is a favorite among modern designers. For instance, Paula Scher paid homage to Matter's work in the 1985 Swatch advertising campaign, and went on to a prolific career as, among other things, a poster designer. Her "Some People" poster, 1994, is illustrative of her long career producing posters for New York's Public Theater. Her work broke ground for the return to bold experimental typography during an era of relatively conservative designs. In addition to the aforementioned International Typographic Style, Scher was influenced by many other design movements, including Constructivism, Dadaism, Futurism and Bauhaus.

The Psychedelic Art movement (late 1960s) begat designs based on the sensory experiences associated with the use of drugs. Milton Glaser's famous 1966 poster portrait of Bob Dylan inspired many generations of designers to use bold, striking and organic imagery. These are just a few examples of historical influences on the beauty of modern poster design.

MAKE AN IMPACT

You can hold a brochure, direct mail piece or magazine in your hand. These are up-close-and-personal kinds of design. Subtle graphic elements and small type may be used when they're only a few inches away from your eyes. But because posters hang in a fixed location a significant distance away, you must devise a way to stop the potential viewer in his tracks and make him look at the masterpiece—*your* masterpiece—before him. Posters have about half a second to grab someone's attention. Once you do that you need to (1) divert him from his intended path, (2) bring him to the poster, (3) make him read it and understand the information it contains, and then (4) make him act on it. If you're really lucky, he will use his smartphone or other digital device to access further information from your poster right there on the spot. What's that you say? It's not easy? You are so right. In fact, it's actually quite a challenge. Here are a few things you can do to help the process along.

Another chance to K.I.S.S.

What is the focus of the poster? Develop your concept around that specific focus. Trying to communicate too many ideas will result in an overlooked poster. Think of a three-ring circus. With a lion tamer in one ring, the horseback riders in another ring, and the dancing dogs prancing around the third, can you watch them all at once? No. As your eyes flit back and forth trying to take it all in, you will inevitably miss something spectacular. Poster design is similar. Focus your poster on one ring only.

22 ● (left) Romeo & Juliet, Luba Lukova Studio; 23 ● (right) Poster advertising the ballet *Romeo and Juliet*, 1955 (colour litho) Russian School, (20th century)

Type and imagery on posters work best when kept simple. Focus is blunted by overly complicated type, hyperdetailed visuals and a rainbow of colors. The more visual information you present, the longer it takes for the viewer to see it all. Remember, you have less than a second to grab someone's attention. Strive for good visual-verbal synergy. Type and visuals that play off one another will minimize the information you need to add to a poster.

Keep the color palette simple. Remember that the poster hangs in a visually stimulating space. Full-color posters tend to blend into the environment. Contrast to the full-color world is best achieved with simple color choices. Consider using no more than two or three colors to present your concept.

Luba Lukova is a designer who knows how to make an impact. She is known for high-contrast, thought-provoking poster designs that shout a forceful message. One of her most famous posters is for a performance of Romeo and Juliet, designed for director Sir Peter Hall, the founder of the Royal Shakespeare Company in London. Clasped hands and a blood-covered sword beautifully and simply sum up the entire romantic tragedy in one large powerful image. Two colors and a small selection of hand-rendered text complete the poster. Nothing more is needed. When I interviewed Luba in October of 2009, she said this of her design:

> *I prefer the image to be the strongest in my work. And in design it's the correlation between the image and the text; that's what design is all about. When I use text, even if it's very limited, it should contribute to the whole picture, and it should be done so it really complements it. A bad typographical treatment can destroy even the greatest image.*

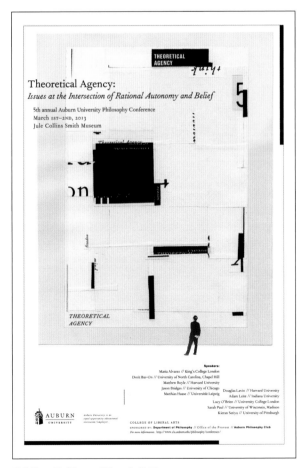

21 ● Theoretical Agency Philosophy Poster

Compare Luba's poster with the Russian School's poster for Romeo and Juliet from 1955. The illustration and typography are gorgeous and the color palette is limited. But the impact level is quite low to any viewers who might be standing more than a foot or two away. The image is generic and doesn't muster a passing glance.

Be relevant

Choose typography with appropriate connotative qualities. Nothing brings a poster down faster than a brilliant design with Comic Sans for its typography. This may be an extreme example, but you get the point. Think carefully about how the font speaks to the viewer. Does it communicate the right amount of romanticism, urgency, efficacy, comedy, tragedy or punk rockiness? Does it capture the essence of a performance or the seriousness of a lecture? Don't ignore all your typography lessons. Carefully consider your fonts, and choose ones that effectively speak both to the message and the viewer.

24 ● The Cripple of Inishmaan, Red Shoes Studio

The same goes for the imagery. Your poster's visuals need to at least hint at the subject matter. Obscure and meaningless visuals used merely for decoration or provocation may grab the viewer's attention but will not keep it for long, nor will they make the message any more memorable. Use powerful, high-quality, focused, relevant imagery. It doesn't always have to be large to be powerful. A bold image in a striking color can be small and still have a huge impact. Imagery can be photographs, illustrations or any manner of artistic expression as long as it communicates the message. The most powerful imagery tends to be the simplest.

COMMUNICATE CLEARLY

Every poster has an important message that you want your viewer to understand on his first try. For that, you need good hierarchy. If type and visuals compete for importance on the poster, you've lost your half-second window with your viewer, who needs to know why he stopped to look at your poster. Tell him right away whether it's a verbal or visual message, be it the title of a new play performance, the sheer beauty of a watch, or the visual difference between twenty-six breeds of goldfish. Once you've made your main point, remember to prioritize the rest of the information. For a play poster you'll need the date, time, location and contact information for tickets. An advertisement needs to tell the viewer where to find the desired object. Don't hide relevant information, and don't make your viewer work too hard for it.

Organize it

Yes, a grid is necessary, even for a single-page design. Whether you use a columnar, modular, irregular or some other creative rendition of a grid system, the underlying structure will give your design organization and consistency. Relationships between design elements create a sense of unity and allow the viewer's eyes to travel from one set of information to the next. After all, the viewer still has to get the message once you've gotten him to look at the poster. It doesn't have to be dull.

Tracy Kretz, PPO&S, describes her design approach to a poster for the Pennsylvania Apple Marketing Program, a program to showcase Pennsylvania apple varietals, "It was a challenge to incorporate so many bits of information, but

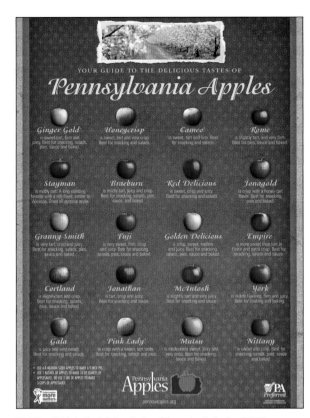

25 ● Your Guide to the Delicious Tastes of Pennsylvania Apples, PPO&S

once I nailed a great modular grid, the organization of all the elements fell into place."

The poster could easily have been a chaotic mess, with twenty apples haphazardly strewn hither and yon about the poster. The grid gives it clarity, which allows farmers' market patrons to easily see the types of apples available from Pennsylvania orchards.

Readability is key

You need to create a poster for the most amazing theater performance ever seen? Great. You want the poster to reflect the director's vision of an abstract expressionistic world? Wonderful. The type you've chosen is so abstract that the only people who know what it says are you and the client? Not so great. This is an extreme example, but if the poster can't be read, no one will act on the message. Cool design only goes so far. Make the message easily understood. This doesn't mean you have to set the headline type in 300 point Helvetica bold, but it does mean you need to take a step back and analyze your poster design. Can you read it from a distance? If you can't, neither can your reader. Don't forget the secondary type—the who, what, where, when, how and why of the message. Your viewers have to know what to do once they've absorbed your main message.

BRING IT ALL TOGETHER

It can be very tempting to use all the wonderful ideas generated in the initial brainstorming process of designing a poster, especially for a job consisting of a series of posters. Resist this urge. Poster series present the opportunity to create an awesome and cohesive set of posters, but only if done well.

Unify them

Unity is the most important principle in a poster series. It takes a lot of effort to create a singular piece that works well, but it takes dedication and patience to create an equally successful series. The easiest approach to a set of posters is to

26 ● Consistency in style, color and typography unifies the poster series even though they take on different looks.

POSTERS

49

27 ● 3 -color screen print

focus on elements that can remain the same. A strong grid, solid font choices and a well-developed color palette will greatly ease this process. Using the same or similar layouts can work. For instance, by placing the headline near the top, centering the visual and running the remaining information across the bottom each time, the layout will create visual unity across several posters. They shouldn't bore the viewer, though. This can be avoided with variation.

Finish it

Generally speaking, posters are not printed in huge quantities. Print runs tend to be in the hundreds instead of the thousands, allowing for alternative printing processes that can add lots of interest to a poster. Screen printing is a technique used for decades by poster printers because it has significant advantages over traditional or digital printing techniques. Screen printing can be done on just about anything, so a screen printed poster isn't limited to paper. It can be printed on chipboard, cardboard, sheet metal, wood or any number of other surfaces. Screen printing allows full opacity in a way not obtainable with the translucent inks used in traditional and digital processes. This is particularly useful when you want to use a layered or overlapping look

with no transparencies. Any color ink can be screen printed, which allows for specialty colors such as metallics and fluorescents. Because screen printing is done by hand, small nuances emerge between posters, adding a special one-of-a-kind feel to each piece. It also feels different to the touch because of the inks' slightly raised surface.

Letterpress is also an option, albeit more expensive. It's hard to find a large enough press, but worth it if the budget allows. The process pushes the tactile limits, with imprinted images and type. It also allows you to use one-of-a-kind wooden or lead type not available on a computer. At the other end of the spectrum, black and white photocopiers are a fantastic resource for a very low budget. Like other "hand" processes, the photocopier look also creates one-of-a-kind posters, as the "dirt" in the copier gets reflected in the prints. The 1970s punk scene started a trend with photocopied flyer-sized posters stapled to anything that could be stapled to. The Sex Pistols "God Save the Queen" poster is a perfect example of the collaged copied look emblematic of the era. The photocopy trend continues today; there are still plenty of start-up bands needing to cheaply get the word out about their music.

Paper is a great additive design element. Add another color to a limited-color print with colored paper. This is a useful resource when money is a concern and multiple colors aren't affordable. As an example, hot pink paper run through a photocopier gives a wonderful hit of color to an otherwise stark black and white design. Textured paper can also add a layer of visual interest to a simple design; many different types are available, including linen, recycled, felt and decorated. Be aware that the paper choice also influences the inks used for printing. Uncoated paper soaks up ink, producing a different appearance than a coated paper.

GALLERY

The Philadelphia Shakespeare Theatre: Othello Poster

CREATIVE ANARCHY: Experimental type and imagery

"The Philadelphia Shakespeare Theatre's Spring 2013 season's play, *Othello*, is a tragedy of love destroyed by jealousy. Themes of 'seeming,' jealousy, darkness, shadows and blood were throughout the play, so we wanted that to be interpreted through the poster. The letters of the title, *Othello*, were each assigned to a band in a diagonal line toward the bottom right corner, foreshadowing the imminent downward spiral of their lives. The play ends with death, so the last letter O was treated in a blood-red color to signify the ending. The juxtaposition of faces makes the viewer do a double-take, causing them to reexamine the poster." **—20NINE**

TITLE: The Philadelphia Shakespeare Theatre: Othello Poster
DESIGN FIRM: 20nine
ART DIRECTOR: Kevin Hammond
DESIGNER: Erin Doyle
WEBSITE: www.20nine.com
CLIENT: The Philadelphia Shakespeare Theatre

Caliber Holiday Poster

CREATIVE ANARCHY: Layering, Charitable concept

"The previous year, we had sent out an expensive mailer and in some cases food, wine and sweets to key accounts. But when approaching it again, we decided that it seemed a bit wasteful to send these types of items to people that really don't need them. We looked up what we had spent the year before and donated that to a charity where the funds would go to purchase livestock for tribes/villages in Africa. We were able to calculate the number of animals (chickens, cows, etc.) it purchased. From there, we wanted to communicate that 'purchase' to our clients." **—CALIBER CREATIVE**

TITLE: Caliber Holiday Poster
DESIGN FIRM: Caliber Creative/Dallas Texas
ART DIRECTORS: Brandon Murphy, Bret Sano
DESIGNER: Justin King
WEBSITE: www.calibercreative.com
CLIENT: Caliber Creative/Dallas, TX

AIGA Kickoff Party Poster

CREATIVE ANARCHY: Limited color, Experimental printing

"The AIGA Dallas-Fort Worth Chapter was having the kickoff party at a local craft brewery. We, happily, were tagged to create the poster/mailer that would go out to the club members. I'm a big fan of illustration and I think Jian brought a great flavor and style to it. The simple color approach has a wonderful classic feel too. For the main poster, we used standard two-color offset printing. For the additional smaller event poster, we photocopied black toner on black paper then silk-screened white over it." —**CALIBER CREATIVE**

TITLE: AIGA Kickoff Party Poster
DESIGN FIRM: Caliber Creative/Dallas Texas
ART DIRECTORS: Brandon Murphy, Bret Sano
DESIGNERS: Jing Jian, Brandon Murphy
WEBSITE: www.calibercreative.com
CLIENT: DFW/AIGA Chapter

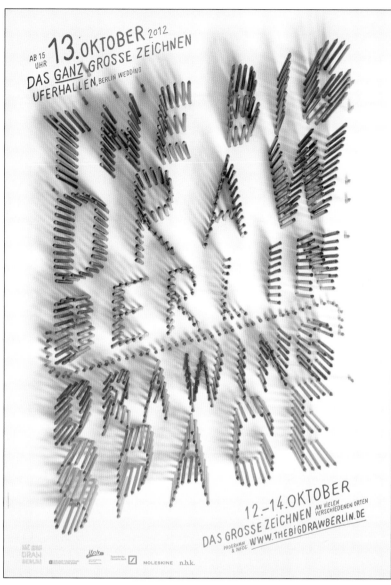

Big Draw Berlin
CREATIVE ANARCHY: Real-time creation

"The posters were created with colored pencils that were standing up and shot from above. They were slowly shaved down, dissolving into color dust. We created a little stop-motion animation out of these shots. It was a very dusty and slightly painful experience: We used more time than intended, and electric pencil shavers run on a very uncomfortable frequency." —ARIANE SPANIER

TITLE: Big Draw Berlin
DESIGN FIRM: Ariane Spanier Design
ART DIRECTOR: Ariane Spanier
DESIGNER: Ariane Spanier
WEBSITE: arianespanier.com
CLIENT: Kulturlabor e.V.

Gotye Concert Posters

CREATIVE ANARCHY: Typographic play

"Gotye needed a poster design that could be used for several different locations on a U.S. tour. When I was working on concepts for this poster, Wally from Gotye was much more hands-on than most musicians that I work with. While working with very opinionated, hands-on musicians can often be a hellish nightmare, Wally was extremely articulate with his feedback and vision. We decided to create an image that was clean, stark and vintage, just like his music. I constructed a landscape scene completely out of triangles, a reference to the triangles on his *Making Mirrors* album cover. The icing on the cake was making the sun double as the O in the band name, perfectly combining the typography with the illustration." —**DOE EYED**

TITLE: Gotye Concert Posters
DESIGN FIRM: Doe Eyed
ART DIRECTORS: Eric Nyffeler / Wally De Backer
DESIGNERS: Eric Nyffeler
PRINTING: The Half & Half
WEB: doe-eyed.com
CLIENT: Gotye / Second Hand Entertainment

Undead Ben Franklin Disco Biscuits Poster

CREATIVE ANARCHY: Twist on the familiar

"My main objective was to create a more modern representation of Ben Franklin, while appealing to the Disco Biscuits fan base. The concept behind the poster is the resurrection of the Disco Biscuits' performance at the Electric Factory. As Philadelphia natives, they played the Electric Factory more than any other band, but not in more than five years. This is represented by Ben Franklin coming back from the dead to attend the show. To accomplish this he must electrify his brain with lightning—a play on the iconic story of Ben Franklin and the electronic style of the Disco Biscuits music." **—JAKE BURKE**

The Felice Brothers

CREATIVE ANARCHY: Ink transparency, Unusual imagery

"This poster needed to fit into the band's aesthetic and reflect the personalities and sound of the band. I did research on brotherhood and what it means to be a brother. I wanted the idea of brotherhood, with all of its ups and downs, to be a large part of the image and illustrate what it's like having a sibling. The illustration of the two chicken men (read: cock fight) shows the kind of sibling rivalry we all experience at one point or another, even when well loved. Breaking the word *brothers* into a second line provided a much more even composition as well as a visual interest in the letterforms that might have been lost had the line not been broken." **—JEREMY FRIEND**

TITLE: The Felice Brothers
DESIGN FIRM: Jeremy Friend
CREATIVE DIRECTOR: Jeremy Friend
DESIGNER: Jeremy Friend
WEB: jeremyfriend.com
CLIENT: The Felice Brothers

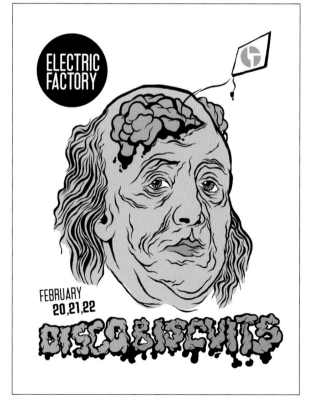

TITLE: Undead Ben Franklin Disco Biscuits Poster
DESIGN FIRM: Jake Burke Design & Illustration
DESIGNER: Jake Burke
WEB: Cargocollective.com/jakeburkecreativity

2 The Nines: Oblivion

CREATIVE ANARCHY: Challenging orientation

"The photograph chosen for the poster is intended to represent the idiom 'dressed to the nines.' The upside-down orientation of the image is meant to represent 'oblivion,' the title of the band's most recent album. The poster was exhibited in a show recently, and when I walked into the gallery, it had been hung with the photo right side up (text upside down). The installation crew was so embarrassed." —**JAMIE RUNNELLS**

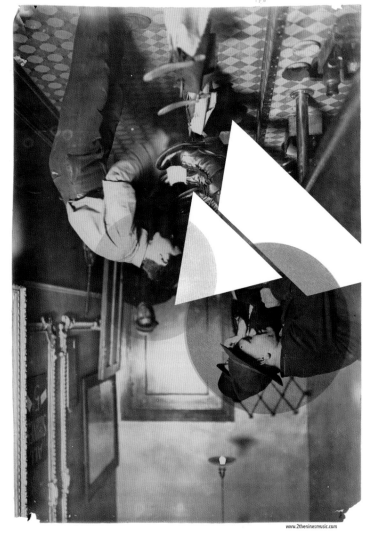

TITLE: 2 The Nines: Oblivion
DESIGN FIRM: Jamie Runnells Design
CREATIVE DIRECTOR: Jamie Runnells
DESIGNER: Jamie Runnells
WEBSITE: jamierunnells.com
CLIENT: 2 The Nines

Japandroids Poster

CREATIVE ANARCHY: Unusual imagery, Headline legibility

"The goal of the poster was to pack Schubas Tavern in Chicago, Illinois, shoulder to shoulder for an exciting New Year's Eve party. We wanted the poster to be, quite literally, a monster of a party. When we considered the name 'Japandroids,' we connected the dots to one of Japan's most iconic monsters—Godzilla. So, with a mix of city-squashing lizardry and, of course, the promiscuous flavor many NYE parties hold, the imagery of a sexy dino worked itself out.

We wanted the typography to make an obvious nod toward the 'monstrosity' direction put in place—large, round and in your face, yet still full of fun. In addition, the type doubles as the city the Japandroids will destroy when they rock the NYE shows." —**MIG REYES AND KYLE STEWART**

TITLE: Japandroids poster
DESIGN FIRM: Straightsilly
ART DIRECTOR: Mig Reyes
DESIGNERS: Mig Reyes, Kyle Stewart
CLIENT: Schubas

Dialogue, Censorship and Sudan; from the Social Justice Portfolio

CREATIVE ANARCHY: Visual metaphor

"I played with positive/negative imagery in *Dialogue.* The idea is that instead of having a dialogue, we create wars, represented by the nuclear mushroom dividing the two faces. There is a small line between the faces that reads: "War is not the answer." I wanted this to be really tiny so people make an effort to read it, and hopefully realize that peaceful communication can prevail over aggression.

The *Censorship* image initially appeared as a commissioned cover for the Art & Leisure section of the Sunday *New York Times* for a feature on how the Taliban regime in Afghanistan censored music. The article described how the Taliban beat the musicians with their instruments. So I thought that an image with the flutist's fingers nailed to the flute would be a strong metaphor for the issue. The art director was concerned the editor might not like it, 'since the paper normally doesn't want to disturb people while they're having coffee on Sunday morning.' But the editor loved it and it was printed without any changes.

For the *Sudan* poster, the message is about the contrast between the developed world, where we take food as a commodity and are concerned with low-calorie nutrients, and countries like Sudan, where food is a matter of life and death. The idea came after watching a television documentary about the impoverished country. At the end of the film there was a commercial promoting low-calorie food. The contrast was so striking that while watching the ad I had the idea for the image in my head and I completed it in an hour." **—LUBA LUKOVA**

dialogue

censorship

sudan

TITLE: Dialogue, Censorship and Sudan; from the Social Justice Portfolio
DESIGN FIRM: Luba Lukova Studio
DESIGNER: Luba Lukova
WEB: clayandgold.com

POSTERS

TITLE: The Gaslight Anthem Promotion Pack
UNIVERSITY: Mississippi State University
PROFESSOR: Jamie Mixon
DESIGNER: Alaina Anglin
WEBSITE: www.alainaanglin.com
CLIENT: The Gaslight Anthem

The Gaslight Anthem Promotion Pack

CREATIVE ANARCHY: Unexpected visual

"The objective was to create a work that spoke to the fans of the Gaslight Anthem and represented the music. The design was expected to function both as 'art' to be purchased by the fans and as an advertisement to promote the show.

The type is reminiscent of the raw, audacious, punk rock style. The poster denies the viewer a look into the woman's eyes; they only see her half-smile. The combination of aggressive brush-and-ink hand lettering combined with elegant negative space makes the design masculine and feminine, chaotic and ordered, beauty and beast." —ALAINA ANGLIN

EXERCISES

PICTURE PLAY

RULE: Use relevant imagery.

CREATE ANARCHY: Combine conceptual ideas to develop distinctive and unexpected visuals to communicate the message.

RESULT: Generate intriguing and thought-provoking dynamic imagery that will grab a viewer's attention and hold it through the entire message.

I'll bet your typical first reaction when presented with a visual design problem is to go with a literal representation of the message. For a poster advertising apples, show an apple. For a jazz concert, use musical notes, instruments or musicians. It's not a bad idea. Literal imagery will resonate quickly with a viewer. But what if you want something more exciting or dramatic or mysterious? Show something seemingly foreign and bizarre instead that turns out to make sense after all.

 Let's do this

Take a poster you're working on or have done in the past. If you don't have one, choose a local event and create a poster for it.

1. Pick out three key elements of your poster's subject and main message. Let's take a poster advertising an informational retirement talk by a leading financial firm. It has these key elements: company's public persona, retirement/future and money.

2. Create a word list for each element *individually*, without thinking about the end result. Ignore the other two lists. Just write. Jot down adjectives and representational visuals. Iconic visuals tend to work best. Build words off each other to generate your lists. Go wherever it takes you. There are no wrong words. Nothing is too random or obscure. Write whatever pops into your head. Try for at least twenty words per column.

3. Once you have your word lists, connect words across the columns. Again, don't get blocked by seemingly silly or crazy ideas. See if you can create some kind of story. Try for as many idea combinations as you can—the more, the better. Use these as jumping off points for new and intriguing visual concepts.

HERE'S THE EXERCISE FOR THE RETIREMENT POSTER.

FINANCIAL INSTITUTION	RETIREMENT/FUTURE	MONEY
Large	Home	Dollar bill
Trustworthy	Nest	Green
Friend	Birds	Bull
Foe	Golden egg	Bear
Strong	Finish line	Stock market
Ox	Picnic	Stacks
Paul Bunyan	Race	Coins
Dominant	The unknown	Bank
Savior	The abyss	Teller
Superhero	Compass	Paycheck

Ship	Living	Penn and Teller
Sailboat	Travel	Magic
Life preserver	Vacationing	Bling
Water	Rocking chair	Green back
Sea	Drowning	Dollar sign
Captain	Uncertainty	George Washington
Spy glass	Balancing scales	Benjamin Franklin
Pirate	High wire	Wallet
Sail	Zip line	Change purse
Rowboat	Skiing	Sock
Oar	Ski lift	Moths

IDEA ONE

WORDS: Superhero, Finish Line, Bull and Bear

VISUAL: Superhero shooting a starter's gun as a bull and bear race to the finish line.

ALTERED VARIATION ON THE IDEA: Include the word *picnic* and show the bull and bear in a sack race.

REASONING: Saving for retirement can be difficult, but a retiree can get there with the help of a financial partner.

IDEA TWO

WORDS: Rowboat, Abyss, Bull and Bear

VISUAL: A bull and bear in a tiny rowboat. Keep the image tiny, leaving vast negative space around the visual.

REASONING: Helps the viewer connect with the emotional state of the unknown future beyond retirement.

IDEA THREE

WORDS: Sailboat, Golden egg, Dollar bill

VISUAL: Two golden eggs wearing sunglasses lounging happily on the deck of a sailboat with a sail made of dollar bills.

REASONING: Entering retirement with smooth sailing and nest egg intact, presumably by working with your client.

IDEA FOUR

WORDS: Paul Bunyan, High wire, George Washington and Ben Franklin

VISUAL: An overhead view of Paul Bunyan tiptoeing along a high wire with a tiny George Washington, Ben Franklin and other "engraved" presidents in his back pocket.

REASONING: Retirement is a balancing act, but with big strong Paul (i.e., the financial institution) you can make it to the other side safely with all your investments intact.

THE "WHAT IF..." EXPERIMENT

RULE: Be on target with the client's goals.

CREATE ANARCHY: Question everything.

RESULT: Tap into the wonderment of the absurd to lead to fresh ideas.

Adult imaginations can be somewhat limited as life experiences train us to believe certain things are "true." Milk comes in cartons or jugs. Broadway musicals need to be heard to be experienced. Posters hang on a wall.

Children, by and large, haven't "discovered" these truths. They have amazing imaginations. Children see nothing wrong with an apron-clad carrot serving tea to a bevy of princesses. Or a cowboy squid rounding up a herd of wayward tricycles. Children also have a wonderful knack for asking why or, better yet, why not. Just spend some time around a three-year-old and you'll quickly see what I mean.

This exercise taps into your inner child and asks you to question everything you know about your project. Throw in a dash of imagination and you have the recipe for a fresh and innovative design solution.

 Let's do this

Take a poster you're working on or have done in the past. If you don't have one, create one for a local theater performance.

1. Create a succinct list of the project goals. Don't forget the target audience, proposed format and desired connotation.

SAMPLE QUESTIONS USING THE LOCAL THEATER PERFORMANCE EXAMPLE:

What if the lead character were a woman instead of a man, or vice versa?

What if the lead character was in drag?

What if kids ran the performance?

What if the people viewing the poster can't read?

What if the director cast animals instead of people?

What if the poster will be fed to a goat once the performance is over?

What if the theater is underwater?

What if the theater is in outer space?

What if the poster won't hang on a wall?

What if the audience is blind?

What if the audience is deaf?

2. Write a list of five "What if" questions for each project goal. Strive for ideas ranging from known "truths" to the absurd. Don't be afraid to write anything down. Let the ideas flow freely. A seemingly ridiculous idea often produces the best solution.

3. Go back through your list and answer each one of your "What If" questions with a visual or verbal solution. For example, what if everyone is blind? Answer: The world would be a lot more textural.

4. Take your answers and consider how each can be applied to your poster. Using my example above, texture can be added to the poster through paper, die-cutting or finish technique such as letterpress or screen printing.

5. Keep going. Before long you will have a plethora of ideas to explore and execute.

EXQUISITE CORPSE

A traditional Exquisite Corpse was an early twentieth-century parlor game. The game challenges each player to contribute words or images to a collective composition. The players are each given a rule to follow for their part in the game. The "exquisite" aspect of the game is formed by the purposeful secrecy of the other players' contributions, thus the result is a magnificent, or exquisite, surprise to the players when the final composition is revealed.

The phrase *exquisite corpse* originated with the Surrealists. The artists believed imagination was conveyed best through the unconscious mind, dreams and illogical thought. The original game formed creative sentences.

A modern version of this game is perfect for projects that would benefit from unconventional thinking. Or for when the team has hit a creative wall and needs a spark to get them going again. Or for a simple and fun brain break when the project has everyone fried.

 Let's do this

SUPPLIES:
- paper (the larger the better)
- scissors
- pens, pencils, markers and other quick-drying art supplies
- hat
- timer

1. Everyone on the team writes down as many statements, adjectives and nouns as they can think of to describe the project/client. For a brain break, anything goes. Write down whatever comes to mind. Cut the words apart, fold the individual pieces and put them into a hat.

2. Grab your paper and make a barrel-fold, creating one panel for each team member (i.e., if you have four people participating, fold the paper so you have four panels). The first person will write/draw on the first panel and so on. Fold a piece of paper for each team member so everyone is writing/drawing the whole time.

3. Pull the first word from the hat and set the timer. Start with two to three minutes and adjust as necessary.

When given the go signal, each team member should write/draw whatever comes to mind with the given word. The result does not have to be project related. This is your chance to use your imagination. Don't think too much, just write/draw. Note: Cover your paper or sit far enough away from other team members so they can't see what you're drawing.

4. When the time is up, take a few seconds to trail lines from the bottom of your panel to the next. This will give the next person a starting point. Fold your panel back and pass your paper to the next person.

5. Repeat steps 3 and 4 until all the panels are filled.

6. Repeat steps 2–5 to create several rounds of Exquisite Corpses.

7. Once completely done, unfold each paper and check out the team's handiwork. Be sure to have a good laugh before starting a conversation about the results, which may seem random, ridiculous and funny. But look more closely at the results. Consider both the individual panels and the complete compositions. Let these exquisite corpses spark conversation and further brainstorming for the final design concepts.

USE THE FAMILIAR

1. You are stranded on a desert island with only the clothes on your back, a knife, your glasses and a can of Spam. Your boss doesn't care that you're stranded and needs you to design the poster for the tropical-themed office holiday party by the end of the day. What do you do?

2. Zombies have taken over. You are fortunate enough to find a safe house with some supplies but are trapped in the bathroom because the zombies found the safe house too. You discover floss, toothpaste, mouthwash, a toothbrush, a hairbrush, some acetaminophen and toilet paper. In the trashcan are a few used tissues. Your zombie client needs their zombie hoedown poster before the bathroom door gets broken in and you become a zombie too. What do you do?

3. There's a power failure and you get stuck in your building's elevator all alone with nothing but your work bag, which contains a protein bar, gum, your date book, a shopping list, a thumb drive with neck cord attached, cell phone power cord (though you left your cell phone on your desk), a bottle of water and a jar of maraschino cherries you picked up on the way to work, and no writing instruments. Your boss yells down the elevator shaft that help is stuck in traffic. He also lets you know that the client is leaving for vacation tonight and he needs the charity gala event poster design he assigned you this morning. What do you do?

These may be extreme examples, but learning to use the resources at hand is good design experience, and opens you up to developing successful solutions without a computer. It's fun too!

 Let's do this

SUPPLIES:

- Create supply boxes for the aforementioned scenarios.
- (OR) Fill boxes with a few random office supplies, creating one box for each team.
- Include: cutlery; food; bathroom items; desk supplies, such as paper clips, paper, a stapler and pushpins; and other random objects. Also consider Popsicle sticks, pom-poms, glitter, pipe cleaners and other kid-friendly craft supplies. Avoid: traditional design tools such as ruler, pen, pencil, marker, scissors, X-ACTO knife, tape, glue.
- camera
- timer
- plenty of space

1. Set the timer for 20–30 minutes. (Zombies are strong, so work fast!) Give each team a closed box.

2. Give the assignment. If there's a current project in need of a creativity boost, use that job in your scenario. Any project works with this exercise. The stranded island or zombie infestation scenario is a fun way to break up a day and stimulate creative thinking.

3. When you give the signal, teams dump their boxes and get to work, using the contents to create typography, images and elements. Think like MacGyver. Encourage ripping, tearing, smooshing, stacking, stabbing... anything goes. Warn the teams every five minutes.

4. When time is up, sit back and discuss each idea. Take photos of the creations and keep them on display for the remainder of the day. Who knows, there may be a viable solution among the results.

CHAPTER 4

PUBLICATION DESIGN

There's something lovely about the printed word. It's the smell of fresh ink and the delightfully tangible texture and weight of paper in your hands. It's the accompaniment to peacefully lounging while sipping a cup of coffee as you page through the latest magazine or read a good book. It's the feeling of a printed publication that makes it so wonderful.

Publications—books, annual reports, brochures, magazines and newspapers—tend to take on a life of their own. Pages come alive between the front and back covers. Inside, they work collaboratively to spin a tale that moves from line to line, column to column, and page to page. The cover beckons seductively. In a world screaming, "Print is dead," publications remain a sensual pleasure. Besides, what else can you read while soaking in the bathtub?

Clay, animal hides, papyrus and paper hold records of man's history. Paper eventually became most widely used because of its portability and ease of production. The first known document dates back to Sumerian clay tablets, which not coincidentally correspond to the beginning of modern written language. It was called *cuneiform*, and it was made up of angular marks pressed into wet clay. Written language spread with merchants as they traveled from region to region. What we recognize as Western writing started with the Phoenicians, eventually evolving into Roman letterforms.

Johannes Gutenberg's moveable type printing press, invented around 1450, opened the floodgates for mass production of printed materials. The 42-line Gutenberg Bible, aptly named because it has forty-two lines on each page, is celebrated as the first mass-produced book. This technology may seem primitive in the age of computers, but moveable type was a huge innovation. It took another four hundred years for the Industrial Revolution and the steam-powered offset printing press to supplant it. Now that the masses have all kinds of books and documents, the publication design competition begins.

IT STARTS WITH A PLAN

Organization is a must when tackling publication design. Unlike other forms of design, you need all the text and imagery before developing a visual concept. Designing a multiple-page document without these key elements is a recipe for disaster. Many clients won't blink an eye if parts of a publication are missing in the design phase. But you have to know what information needs to be included to make appropriate decisions on grid and format. It is not unrealistic to ask a client to be prepared at the beginning of the project. Once you have the information, make a point of analyzing all the imagery and reading through all the text, where clues to the visual concept can be found. Pay close attention to the tone of the writing. Is it formal or casual? Cheerful or serious? Pedantic or clever? Allow the tone to influence the design.

Consistency and readability top the list of publication must-haves. The visual concept is what holds the publication together. Layout and font choice help the audience read it. Create that mood board and style guide. Choose fonts and stick to them. Be consistent with point size, leading, paragraph styles, grids, indents and space after, and for the love of Pete, kern the headlines. Do allow for some variation; a long publication that looks exactly the same from beginning to end is boring.

What do they need?

The type of publication influences the visual concept, so know what you're designing. A book is intended to be read all the way through and therefore should be designed for maximum readability; a visual concept will help the

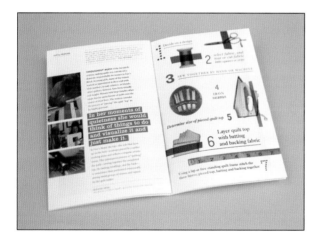

28 ● "This brochure is designed as three unbound nested french-fold signatures that can be unfolded to reveal posters on the reverse side. This form maximizes the delivery of content by utilizing a two-panel to four-panel layout that the viewer engages with. A highly nuanced and varied typographic system alludes to the improvised and intuitive approach to quilting. Expressive and normative typography integrate freely with scale and typeface selection, indicating a subtle division of content and creation of typographic hierarchy. Additionally, the pacing and sequencing of the written content is organized to be read in succession or non-sequentially." —Robert Finkel

pages flow well. Book covers need to grab the reader's attention, making him want to read the text inside. Corporate brochures communicate essential information about the company, presented in a favorable light. They tend to be information-heavy, so clarity is a must. Annual reports also disseminate information about a company—including progress the company has made, changes within the company, financial information, and the opportunity to highlight special aspects of the company—but their audience is investors, both current and potential. Information graphics—visual representations of numerical data—help the reader make sense of complicated numbers and add interest. A magazine's cover should be strong, simple and enticing. Faces sell best. The tone set by the cover should be a good indication to the reader of what she will find inside. Crazy, chaotic cover lines in screaming hues of lime and fluorescent pink give the impression that the magazine will be crazy and chaotic on the inside as well… which is appropriate for a punk audience but not the average housewife. Magazines consist of a table of contents, department pages, features and advertisements. A solid visual concept keeps everything organized while letting each element work on its own. The style guide should incorporate flexibility. Newspapers are similar, but produced on a daily, as opposed to monthly, timeline. The visual concept must be rock solid in order to meet the tight deadlines.

ON THE OUTSIDE

Covers are typically the only part of a publication that a consumer sees in a retail environment, which is why they need to be dramatic and dynamic. It needs to reach out and grab whoever's looking at it. Magazine and book covers are constantly competing with those of the publications surrounding them. You have to set yours apart, whether by image, typography, color or layout. I've picked up more than my fair share of books just because of the cover. I've even bought a few. One of my favorite book covers is *The Curious Incident of the Dog in the Night-Time*, by Mark Haddon. The fluorescent orange cover with an upside down die-cut poodle made the book irresistible. Covers are just as important for corporate brochures and annual reports even though they are generally handed out to people who need them.

30 ● "We wanted to bring this book home and truly translate the raw emotions that the patients, families and doctors were feeling prior to and after ViroPharma's help. Each photo is masked by a typographical overlay printed with white ink on vellum. The emotion of the subject is first portrayed as a negative emotion, with words like 'alone,' 'disconnected,' and 'defeated' covering the image. When the page is turned, however, the emotion of the subject is portrayed in a positive manner. Feelings of happiness and relief then shine through in the photos. This page-turning mirrors the before-and-after feelings that they go through with ViroPharma's help." —20nine

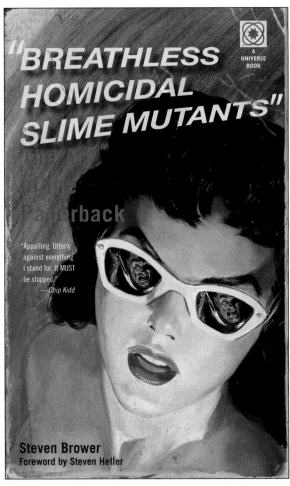

29 ● "I was extremely fortunate in that I was able to purchase the right to use the artwork by the great pulp artist Norman Saunders. I wanted the title to also be provocative. Together there's an "in your face" quality that is appropriate for the subject matter." – Steven Brower

A good cover is welcoming and encourages you to flip open the book or magazine to the first page. Lead the eye and use the Gestalt principle of closure and other visual clues to entice the reader to read farther. A little bit of mystery is good too, though. You don't want to give it all away on the cover. And don't forget to read the document. Design style and cover ideas come directly from the text.

ON THE INSIDE

The inside of a publication design starts with the grid, which carries the design through multiple pages. Imagery should enhance the tone set by the visual concept. Consider using silhouetted images in addition to boxed images. Continuance, unity and other Gestalt and relationship principles will help the reader's eye flow from one page to the next. The big danger in designing a publication is creating a boring layout.

31 ● The Kutztown University Communication Design recruiting brochure takes advantage of smaller half pages to both include and reveal additional information.

Keeping the idea fresh and exciting with each turn of the page is a challenge. A flexible or modular grid will give you more options. Varying the placement of images and body text—but not so much that the pages seem to separate from one another—creates interest. Break up the text with pull quotes, large headlines, subheads and exciting imagery. And above all, make sure you have adequate negative space. White space is your friend. Or you can take all this advice, throw it out the window, and emulate David Carson's *Ray Gun* magazine. His use of layered, grunge-inspired textural typography formed abstract and illegible layouts. Readability was hardly a priority. Wild or tame, classic or modern, let the content and subject matter set the mood.

FORMAT

Form follows function; but should it? Publication design falls into the bad habit of following the leader. A novel has to be 6" × 9"; the annual report has to be 8.5" × 11"; the corporate brochure has to fit into a standard envelope. Think about what would make the format interesting to you and reflect that in your publication design. Unusual sizes and shapes get more attention than the same-old same-old. Did you ever have a *Gray's Anatomy* book with the acetate pages? How exciting it was as a kid paging through that book. I was fascinated with the blood vessels and bones and organs and how they overlapped each other. That feeling is what's missing from publication design today. I know, I know, it all comes down to cost. But why not work with your printer

and see how you can add interesting paper, die-cut pages, vellum, acetate, fold-out panels, different size pages or a brochure within a brochure? I've even seen a recipe book that's completely edible: *The Real Cookbook* by the German design agency, KOREFE. Chris Ware's *Building Stories* is divided among thirteen separate books, each with a different format, all housed together in a box. It's an adventurous read with a graphic style that holds it all together. Format and design go hand in hand. If you have adventurous design, why not use an adventurous format too?

GO INTERACTIVE

Tablets and other devices are redefining what it means to read a book. Not only can you read the pages, but the pages can be enhanced with video and other interactive elements. Augmented reality means scanning a magazine page with an app and watching it explode with movement and color. Print is not dead, and books will continue to survive in this digital world, but the reality is that more and more people use a digital format. And that doesn't mean just saving it as a PDF. Exceed your audience's expectations. Push their boundaries. Help the publication grow. Why just explain how to make a soufflé when you can show it in a video? Why not enhance the latest fad workout with an animated series of illustrations? Share an awesome website by launching the actual website instead of showing a series of static screen shots. Technologies are advancing every single day. Take advantage of them.

GALLERY

TITLE: Viropharma 2011 Annual Report
DESIGN FIRM: 20nine
ART DIRECTORS: Kevin Hammond, Ashley Thurston-Curry
DESIGNER: Erin Doyle
WEBSITE: www.20nine.com
CLIENT: Viropharma, Inc.

ViroPharma 2011 Annual Report

CREATIVE ANARCHY: Hand-rendered elements, Experimental format

"2011 was a year of continued growth and further realization of ViroPharma's larger vision. New product introductions and expansion in Europe meant leaving an even greater impact on the world. 'Onward & Outward' was designed with powerful visual imagery and hand-drawn graphic treatments to create a unique experience for the reader. The book literally unfolds into vibrant, compelling, full-sized posters to stress how ViroPharma continues to expand and serve small patient populations. This annual report emphasizes the 'ripple effect' a disease can have on one person's life, and the unwavering commitment ViroPharma continues to give to its patients." **—20NINE**

TITLE: Caliber Armory Zine
DESIGN FIRM: Caliber Creative/Dallas Texas
ART DIRECTORS: Brandon Murphy, Bret Sano
DESIGNERS: Bret Sano, Brandon Murphy, Justin King, Maxim Barkhatov
WEBSITE: www.calibercreative.com
CLIENT: Caliber Creative/Dallas, TX

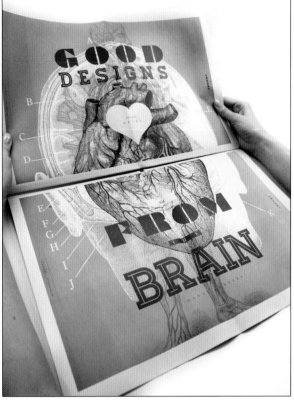

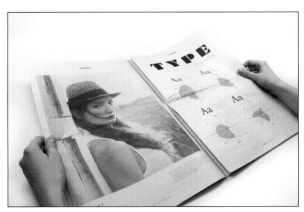

Caliber Armory Zine

CREATIVE ANARCHY: No boundaries

"We wanted to create a promotional piece for the studio that expressed our style or our interest in editorial layout. We didn't want it to really 'promote' much of anything else, [just be a] very 'soft sell' about us. We gave each designer in the shop some basic parameters: do an interview, create a piece of art, develop an infographic, but otherwise—anything goes.

I think the low-tech nature of printing one color on large format newsprint is a 'win' these days—at the least it's unique to see that kind of piece tackled that way. Otherwise, the pure randomness of it is very artistic and fun. And it was mostly born out of frustration in not getting clients to allow us to do a newsprint-format piece. So we decided to do one for ourselves." —**CALIBER CREATIVE**

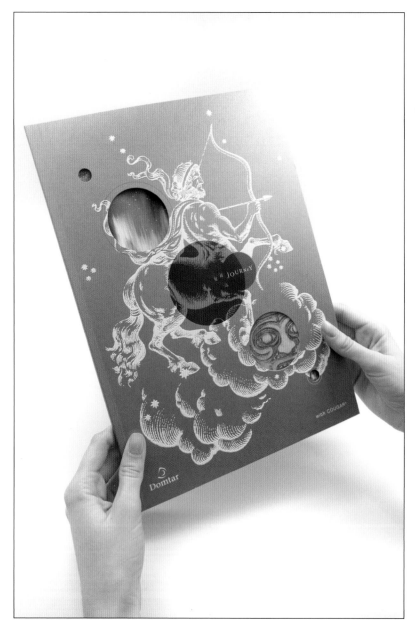

Domtar Paper/Cougar Journey Promotional Brochure

CREATIVE ANARCHY: Myriad of printing techniques

"Domtar asked us to create a paper promotional brochure that continued a story 'journey' regarding creative exploration—while showing great imagery and print technique. The core of the concept centered around travel and 'finding your way.' Throughout history, we've always wanted ways to keep us on course to our intended destination. The stars became a central element within this theme. The story is not confining, and the visual execution is unique. Wonderful imagery and some great tactile techniques help you understand that the paper substrate can be an excellent vehicle to communicate your message." —**CALIBER CREATIVE**

TITLE: Domtar Paper/Cougar Journey Promotional Brochure
DESIGN FIRM: Caliber Creative/Dallas Texas
ART DIRECTORS: Brandon Murphy, Bret Sano
DESIGNERS: Bret Sano, Justin King
WEBSITE: www.calibercreative.com
CLIENT: Domtar Paper

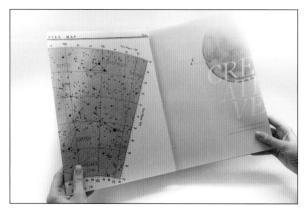

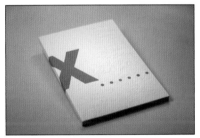

XTO Energy 25th Anniversary "Signature Book"

CREATIVE ANARCHY: Limited color, Varying grid

"The initial thinking was to create a book that said 'thanks'—that XTO would not be who they were without each person over the years putting their mark on the company. We wanted the book to be a 'yearbook on steroids' and needed a very loose framework to hold the tons of stories and images gained for the project. All totaled, we gained more than 2,400 employee signatures and hundreds of personal stories.

Its purpose was pure—to praise the employees—and it succeeded in that goal. Its production value was high, with a duplexed embossed cover and more than 120 pages of content. It was dense at times—open at others—sad and funny all mixed together." —CALIBER CREATIVE

TITLE: XTO Energy 25th Anniversary "Signature Book"
DESIGN FIRM: Caliber Creative/Dallas Texas
ART DIRECTOR: Brandon Murphy, Bret Sano
DESIGNER: Brandon Murphy, Maxim Barkhatov
WEBSITE: www.calibercreative.com
CLIENT: XTO Energy/Exxon

FUKT

CREATIVE ANARCHY: No boundaries

"Everything is more or less related to the current issue of the magazine, which always has a typographic cover. It seems people like cats with three eyes, naked dogs and letters inside of jelly. Quite a few of the typographic pieces are created as 3-D and photographed. The only thing that has been strict on the *FUKT* cover design is that we don't have a magazine logo that looks the same or appears in the same place." —**ARIANE SPANIER**

TITLE: FUKT
DESIGN FIRM: Ariane Spanier Design
ART DIRECTOR: Ariane Spanier
DESIGNER: Ariane Spanier
WEBSITE: arianespanier.com
CLIENT: FUKT Magazine

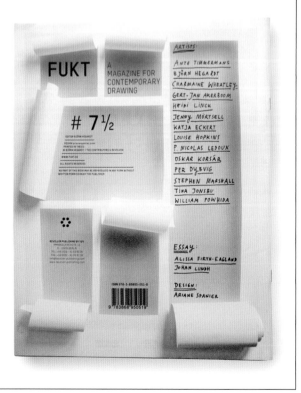

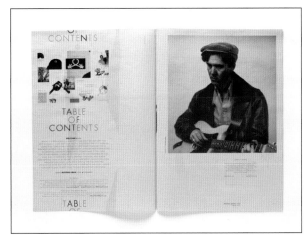

Matériel Magazine

CREATIVE ANARCHY: Unexpected content

"The goal was to pace the creative work so that the variety of visual styles intermingled in a compelling, thoughtful and, at times, surprising way. The folios are a complicated and increasingly untidy (and miniature) flip book; we suggest you give it a try." —**FRANKYLN**

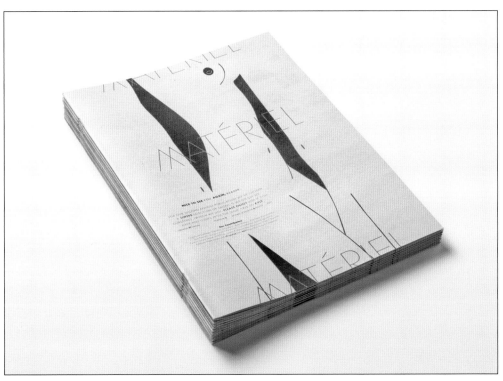

TITLE: Materiel Magazine Issue 002
DESIGN FIRM: Franklyn
ART DIRECTOR: Michael Freimuth, Kyle Poff
DESIGNERS: Michael Freimuth, Kyle Poff
WEBSITE: quitefranklyn.com
CLIENT: Materiel Magazine

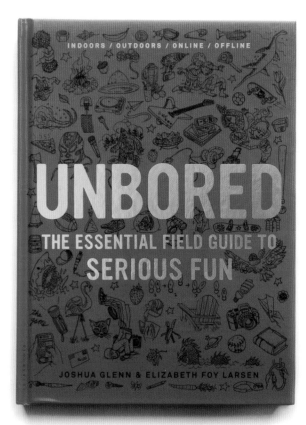

TITLE: *Unbored: The Essential Field Guide to Serious Fun*
DESIGN FIRM: Leone Design
ART DIRECTOR: Tony Leone
DESIGNERS: Tony Leone, Colleen Venable
WEBSITE: leone-design.com
CLIENT: Bloomsbury

Unbored: The Essential Field Guide to Serious Fun

CREATIVE ANARCHY: Varied layout, Playful Illustrations

"Contemporary books for kids tend to be very silly and/or gross, which communicates a 'For Kids Only!' message. Parenting books, meanwhile, aren't aimed at kids at all; and although strict, old-fashioned instructional books are trendy now, they primarily represent a nostalgia trip for adults. Our goal was to create a book that would, from an editorial and design standpoint, appeal to both parents and kids—thus encouraging them to engage in fun activities together.

Bloomsbury gave the *Unbored* project 350 full-color pages, which the design team packed with more than 850 illustrations by Mister Reusch and Heather Kasunick and hand lettering by Chris Piascik. The illustrators' complementary, loose, and sketchy styles lend to the witty DIY tone of the book. Designed to feel like a textbook that has been doodled in, torn up and pasted back together, *Unbored* walks the line between cool and constructive.

Unbored appeals to both kids and parents and has the presence of a high-end gift book. We successfully rode the line between playful and serious by orchestrating a balance between clean, somewhat traditional typographic principles juxtaposed against energetic, sketchy illustrations and torn-paper textured accents. As a fun aside, throughout the illustrations we subtly referenced pop culture that would resonate with adults of certain generations—1980s skateboarding, heavy metal and punk bands, song lyrics, Godzilla and even the Yeti!" **—LEONE DESIGN**

ADCN–Since 2012

CREATIVE ANARCHY: Destruction

"*Aufheben* is a word with several meanings: "abolish," "preserve" and "elevate." The German philosopher Georg Wilhelm Friedrich Hegel (1770–1831) used this term to describe reality. He saw the world around him not as a static reality, but as a continuous ongoing process, changeable and dynamic. In such a world there's no place for the individual and his quirky ideas. Ads are not convincing anymore and creativity doesn't disrupt. Everything is finished. In other words: the truth does not exist. But a deeper, more mature truth is within reach and at the tips of your fingers.

How? Simply by identifying as much as possible and counter-setting it at the same time. Assert and deny. Place it on the table and dismiss it. This is what we've done when we were asked to design the ADCN [Art Directors Club Nederland] yearbook. This yearbook is made from forty-five generations of yearbooks from the dusty archives of the ADCN. They are collected, dismantled and cut to raw materials to supply this unique book. The ADCN archive is no more." **—AUTOBAHN**

TITLE: ADCN-Since 2012
DESIGN FIRM: Autobahn
ART DIRECTORS: Maarten Dullemeijer, Rob Stolte
DESIGNERS: Maarten Dullemeijer, Rob Stolte
WEBSITE: www.autobahn.nl
CLIENT: Art Directors Club Nederland

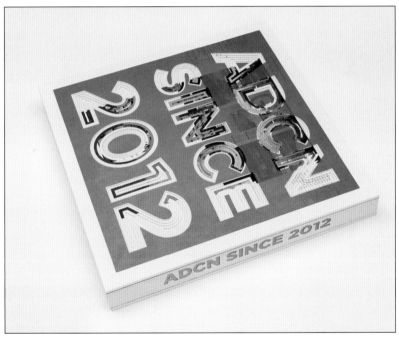

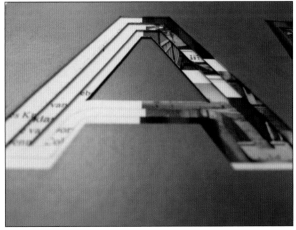

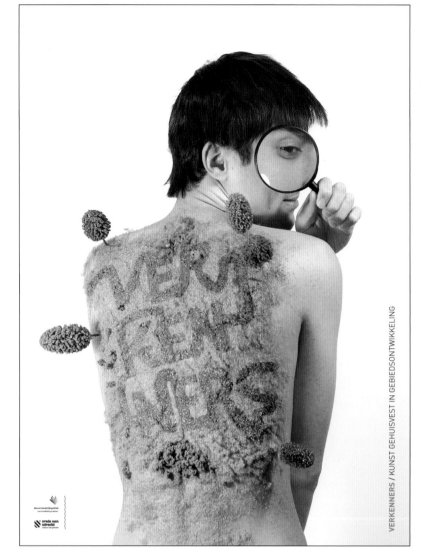

VERKENNERS / KUNST GEHUISVEST IN GEBIEDSONTWIKKELING

Verkenners

CREATIVE ANARCHY: 3-D typographic exploration

"Verkenners is a collaboration between artists and area developers [Netherlands]. Together they are looking for a way to use art in new development areas. Can the use of art and culture in area development projects contribute to improve the quality of area development? What opportunities are there for artists? And can we create involvement among the future residents of the area? We created an accessible publication with answers to these questions. The image concept for this book is inspired by the series 'Landscapes' by photographer Levi van Veluw." **—AUTOBAHN**

TITLE: Verkenners (Art in Area Development)
DESIGN FIRM: Autobahn
ART DIRECTORS: Maarten Dullemeijer, Rob Stolte
DESIGNERS: Maarten Dullemeijer, Rob Stolte
WEBSITE: www.autobahn.nl
CLIENT: Vrede van Utrecht / DLG

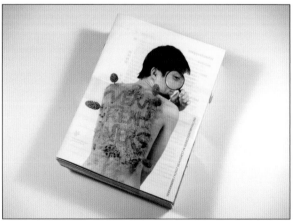

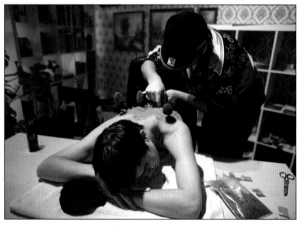

I Wonder What It's Like to Be Dyslexic

CREATIVE ANARCHY: Experimental typography, Experimental theme

"*I Wonder What It's Like to Be Dyslexic* is a coffee table book [created] to help people understand what it feels like to struggle with reading, and to challenge the common misconception that dyslexia is just people seeing letters jumbled up. Designing the book was a process of remembering what I struggled with when I was younger and finding different typographic and language methods that would slow the pace of the reader down. It was quite fun to see family/friends struggling with reading something and wondering whether I had done this on purpose." **—SAM BARCLAY**

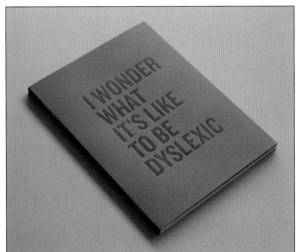

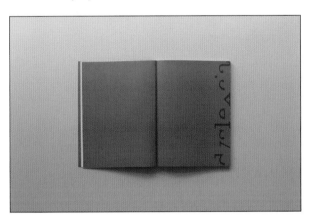

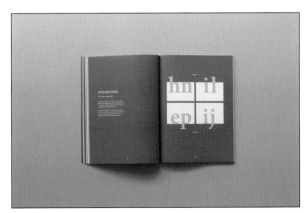

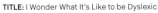

TITLE: I Wonder What It's Like to be Dyslexic
DESIGN FIRM: Sam Barclay
ART DIRECTOR: Sam Barclay
DESIGNER: Sam Barclay
WEBSITE: www.sambarclay.co.uk
CLIENT: Sam Barclay

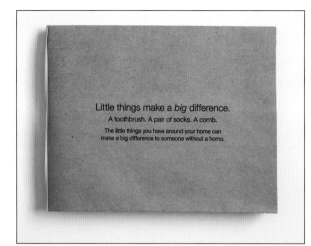

Central Iowa Shelter & Services Brochure

CREATIVE ANARCHY: Unexpected use

"Central Iowa Shelter & Services (CISS) needed a collateral piece to hand out after speaking engagements that would tell the story of the organization and inform readers about what they could do to help—and, understandably, the piece would have to do it all on a minimal budget.

We developed an ingenious piece that not only conveyed the mission of CISS, it literally gave readers the tools to help. A small brochure that told the story of CISS was covered by a simple paper bag. Printing on the bag listed the "most needed" items. Recipients were encouraged to fill the bag with donations.

A few weeks after distribution, paper bags began to appear at the front desk of CISS, loaded with donations for the shelter. Many bags include toiletry items and clothing while some simply held checks." **—SATURDAY MFG.**

TITLE: Central Iowa Shelter & Services Brochure
DESIGN FIRM: Saturday Mfg.
ART DIRECTOR: Brian Sauer
DESIGNERS: Brian Sauer, Annie Furhman
WEBSITE: www.saturdaymfg.com
CLIENT: Central Iowa Shelter & Services

The Times of Oman Layouts

CREATIVE ANARCHY: Unexpected grid, Unexpected imagery

"I have developed this visualization technique called *conceit*. By conceit, you start by questioning the possibilities and keep developing design ideas until the problem is resolved. As an example, I start with a question such as: 'Is it possible to use empty space as an illustration?' Or perhaps I may even ask: 'If the particular business story talks about fear, can I use and mimic the horror film poster to visualize the story?'

If you are working with editorial design, a successful design is a combination of a great headline and a great visual. So the headline must always connect with the visual."

—ADONIS DURADO

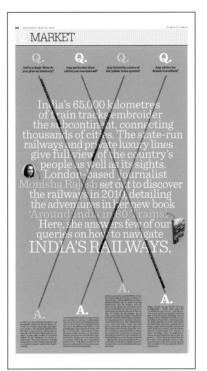

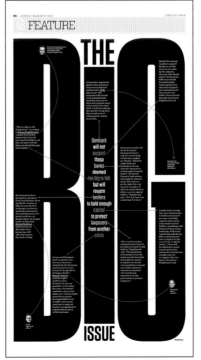

TITLE: The Times of Oman Layouts

DESIGN FIRM: Times of Oman

DESIGNER: Adonis Durado

WEB: timesofoman.com

EXERCISES

PATTERN IT

RULE: Avoid distracting elements.

CREATE ANARCHY: Use pattern as a primary design element in place of a photograph or illustration.

RESULT: Your design will be livelier and more interesting.

Patterns are a great way to bring additional visual interest to a design. Don't settle for typical stripes or dots though. Create new, vibrant and exciting patterns that hold their own against the design's type and imagery. Let the pattern take the lead.

 Let's do this

Take a publication design you're working on or have done in the past. If you don't have one, use a local nature center as your inspiration.

1. Generate a list of objects that relate to your project. Think of everything you possibly can. List it all!

2. For each object you listed, imagine holding it in your hands and inspecting it closely. For example, a nature center has lots of butterflies. What are a butterfly's basic shapes? What does it look like when it flies? What does it look like when it lands on a flower? What kinds of markings are on its wings? Include the tiniest details. Same for any other kind of object—medical instruments, office supplies, flowers, airplanes, computers. What do you see?

3. Sketch them out. Draw the object every way imaginable: silhouette through illustrative; the whole body to an extreme microscopic view.

4. Put together patterns. Try a "gift wrap" approach with the silhouettes and stagger the objects across the page. Throw in other objects with your illustrative versions and your results resemble toile (if B&W ink drawings) or an upscale wallpaper (if rendered as watercolor). Try them tiny or big or any size in between. Microscopic views tend to form pretty awesome patterns as is. See how many patterns you can create.

5. Incorporate the pattern into your design as a primary visual and prepare to wow your audience.

LET'S GO TO THE MOVIES

RULE: The type of publication influences the visual concept.

CREATE ANARCHY: Use your favorite movie to influence your publication, whatever the visual concept happens to be.

RESULT: A cinematic flow tells the design's story and entertains the audience.

We all have movies that resonate with our life. Either they closely resemble our situation, have influenced us to be better people, or act as pick-me-ups when we have a rough day. Think about your favorite. Why does that particular movie resonate with you? Why not another one? Is it the actors, art direction, theme, choreography, costuming, cinematography, color, emotion, historical context, graphics, suspense or music? Perhaps it's a combination of some or all of these things.

Approach your publication design like directing a movie. You are the director. Your goal is to win over your audience. There's a plot, a script, and a beginning, middle and end. You choose the tone, theme, art direction, image direction and flow. You make all decisions in the cutting room to put the final design together. You may even win a coveted award. Do enough of them and you can become a celebrity in your own right. Paparazzi may not stalk you, but you get the idea.

 Let's do this

Take a publication design you're working on or have done in the past. If you don't have one, redesign one from a large brand. Many companies post PDFs of their brochures and annual reports online.

1. Decide what movie to use. Describe it. Write out the plot and major theme(s). Detail the art direction, choreography, costuming, cinematography, color, emotion, historical context, graphics and music. This is the guide for your design.
2. Storyboard your design based upon the movie. Follow the plot curve. The introduction is where you establish the plot structure (grid), characters (type and image style) and tone (overall design style). As the movie progresses, situations happen (sidebars and pull quotes) until the climax is reached (large type, bold images or a visual surprise). Then it descends into the resolution, wrapping up the design with the closing credits. **NOTE:** Don't use a generic plot curve. Follow the movie's plot, which may have more ups and downs, before leading to the climax. The climax could also be at the very end of the movie with virtually no resolution, the like finale of *The Sopranos*.
3. Choose typefaces that connote the feel of the movie. Try to avoid cheesy and too literal. If your favorite movie is *Texas Chainsaw Massacre*, don't us a bloody-looking typeface. Instead, choose a typeface with an edge to it, like a Transitional style with pointy serifs. Do the same for color and image selections. If you have preselected images, manipulate the tone of them to reflect the feeling you need.
4. Execute your ideas. Consistency is important, but allow those plot twists into the design. Surprise your audience, or leave them weeping at the happy ending.

INTERVIEW CHALLENGE

Like many other people, designers can become complacent in their work. It is imperative to reevaluate your design skills from time to time. Also, given the vagaries of the economy, it seems prudent to be prepared for a sudden shift in your employment, ready and able to interview at a moment's notice. Would you know where to look? Would you know what to include in your portfolio? What are your strengths and weaknesses? Do you have a style? Preparing yourself for an interview not only has you prepared for the worst-case scenario but also helps you put your work into perspective.

 Let's do this

SUPPLIES:

- all of your work
- personal branding
- résumé information

1. Gather your best work and examine it. Create a list of the projects and make sure you have access to all of your files, images and type. Aim for ten to twelve projects.

2. Make note of the strengths in your work. What are you good at? What are you most proud of? Has any of the work won awards?

3. Make note of your weaknesses too. What needs work? How can you further develop your skills? What's missing in your design repertoire? Seek out opportunities to improve yourself with college classes, online tutorials and personal projects.

4. Prepare your work as if you were going on an interview. Or think about getting ready for a real interview if you are so inclined. Now's the time. Prep files. Mock up work to make it look "more real"—there are plenty of comp file formats available on the web. Take photos of work that has been produced or is 3-D.

5. Write a short blurb about each project that states the project's goals and how well they were achieved. Think of this as an elevator pitch for your project. Your interviewer and/or future art director will want to know this

information. This is your chance to shine; don't forget to highlight special features, such as custom typography or illustration.

6. Put together your physical portfolio. Decide whether you are going to use digital or print. Either way, show your work off at its best. Make sure to have large clear images and succinct blurbs.

7. Post your work online. Include several views of each project and your project blurb. If you already have an online presence, now is the time to update it. **NOTE:** Always include information about the entire project team. Also note that work done at your job may need to be cleared with your employer before you post it. There may be problems with your contract. Freelance work is fair game.

8. Develop your personal branding.

9. Refresh your resume.

10. Brush up on common interview questions and practice speaking about your work.

11. Go on a mock interview with a trusted designer friend. Ask her to review your portfolio and resume. Would she hire you? Ask for constructive feedback.

PLEASE NOTE: It is highly unethical to go on a job interview unless you are actually looking for a new job. Don't mislead a potential employer. The design community is tight knit, and word of your dishonesty will travel. It may even get back to your current employer. If you really want interview practice, video record yourself or see step 11 above.

CHAPTER 5

PROMOTIONS AND INVITATIONS

Promotions have been around just as long as advertising has, and it is often mistaken as such. This is not entirely invalid, as promotion is technically a form of advertising. Both promotion and advertising are marketing tools whose purpose is to drum up business. There are major differences, though. Advertising is used for long-term sales efforts, which generally involve a significant amount of money. It tends to be comprehensive and expansive in its reach. Advertising campaigns are designed to maintain audience interest over an extended period of time, taking time to build upon its message. It can be some time before any results are seen.

Promotion is the fast-acting version of advertising. Promotions are a quick hit to a specially chosen audience whose purpose is to generate immediate results. While long-term customer loyalty is certainly desirable, a promotion provides instant gratification. Promotions are the "Whoa!"— the in-your-face, holy-cow-I-have-to-go-check-that-out types of materials.

MORE RULES

The first rule for promotions is repetition. Let me say that again. The first rule for promotions is repetition. Companies who send out more than one promotion get the best results. Of course it's also a good idea for the promotion to knock their socks off. This leads to rule two: Make an impact. Not just a little bitty impact. A great big wallop-over-the-head impact. This is no time for subtlety. Rule three: Choose the best medium. Digital is usually the most cost-effective solution, especially if you are in the digital industry, interactive or video categories. Be careful though: Sometimes a print-based solution may work better even in those industries. Think about how many emails you get in a day?

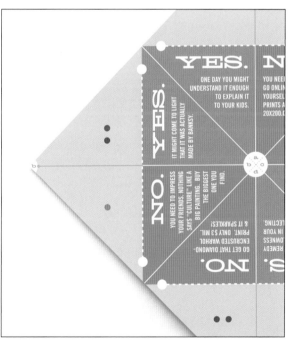

32 ● This fortune-telling promotion for 20x200 helps buyers decide if an art piece is right for them.

Ten? Forty? Three hundred sixty-seven? Unless an email is opened right away, the likelihood of it being read goes down dramatically with each hour that goes by. Why? People are busy, emails get buried under other emails or end up in the spam folder. A printed piece may sit on the desk a few days before it's opened, but the act of physically opening it shifts the odds in your favor. Not all promotions will get opened, of course. It is a form of direct mail, after all. But a promotion mailing list should be more specialized. It may have only a few names on it—current clients plus select others you think could use the company's services. Printed promotional materials can be hung on a wall, set out on a desk, interacted with, played with, touched, held and shared.

PROMOTION TYPES

Promotions shout successes, speak facts, sing praises, and say thanks. With so many different reasons to promote, and so many different options for design, look to your message to determine which promotion style work bests.

Brag promotions

Brag, or announcement, promotions are sent when something big happens. Wow, look how awesome we are. We won an award. We did great things for charity. We created an innovative solution. We developed something really cool and we want you to see it. Work with us and we'll make you cool too. It's the perfect time to remind your current clients how much they like you and maybe catch the eye of new clients. Show off a little. Have extra copies of award-winning projects printed, and send them along as part of the promotion. Include direct quotes to help support the genius of your accomplishment. Explain it, too. Saying you won an industry award doesn't necessarily mean anything to someone outside of your industry. Offer statistics and facts about the award itself to help explain why the award is such an honor. For example, if 2,785 people submitted work and only 150 received awards, then it proves your award is indeed a big deal.

Capabilities promotions

Capabilities promotions help grow the client base. This type of promotion doubles as a showcase for the company's work while educating potential clients about its services. Think of it as an awareness promotion. The kind of promotion that says, "Hey, look at me. I do/make stuff you need and I'm in

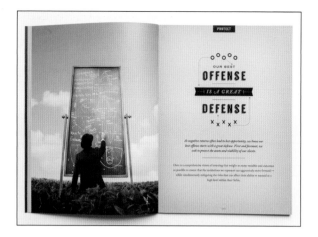

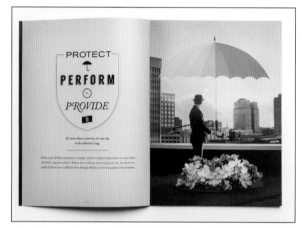

33 ● "The goal was to create a piece outside the bounds of normal marketing in the financial category. Most communication is dry, to say the least, in the investment sector. Our objective was to humanize the approach while showing category strength. The head of Verger had much success in investment management, having been ranked in the top 80 people under 40 in finance. He had the clout to depart from the norm in his marketing materials. The tone of the piece was meant to speak from a place of confidence, less about the "pitch" and more about philosophy and category relevance, knowledge, as well as category difference." —Hayes Henderson, Wake Forest Communications

your backyard." This kind of promotion should emphasize why your business is better than other similar businesses. Where to start? With whatever best shows what the company's got. A printer will want a design that touts all of his printing capabilities. It may include special techniques to entice clients. A self-promotional piece for a designer or design firm should show a sampling of the work they create. A company that makes widgets may want to include a miniature version of the widget.

Self-Promotion

Designer promotions are extra fun because, well, we're designers. This is our chance to show off what we do. You could assemble a portfolio of your work. Be sure to include a varied selection to show off your breadth to the potential client. Are you a stellar poster designer and want to do more posters? Send out a poster as your promotion. Is packaging your thing? Send out a promotion that either is a package or folds into one. Do you want more lettering jobs to come in the door? Create a series of hand-lettered quotes and mail them out every few weeks. Show your prospective clients what inspires you, and create what you want to do.

A WORD OF CAUTION: There's a very fine line between cool and cheesy. Think very carefully about what you use as a promotional tool. A custom-printed whoopee cushion will only work if you specialize in humorous design. If not, it's weird and might make the potential client say, "Huh?" I once had a design job applicant send me a boxed Ken doll dressed as him. He replaced the logo with his name and used the callout areas to highlight industry skills. He gave Ken a briefcase and other design-related tools. His résumé graced the back of the box. I thought the idea was clever because he was applying for a job in the packaging industry, but it was kind of creepy, too. The reason this applicant's idea ultimately failed was that the execution and craftsmanship were terrible. Type was placed haphazardly and the box itself was poorly crafted. I would have kept it on my desk—I love kitschy things—but instead it landed in the trash can as a waste of his money and my time. On top of that, the company I worked for didn't do kid-based packaging or work with Mattel.

Don't let this story stop you from taking a chance, though. Sometimes risk helps get the job. But do your homework. Be relevant and timely. Errors and bad assembly will ruin any great concept. Relate to the client and their

needs. Show off your strengths. Go after the work you want. Cater your promotions to appeal to your dream client without abandoning your current clients—who knows, your current clients may discover something new about you.

Just-because promotions

Holiday wishes, "Thank you because you're you," and "Just to say hi" promotions are perhaps the most fun to create. Just-because promotions are an opportunity to make a connection with the client without making it feel like you're trying to sell something. It can be friendly and casual. It's the equivalent to popping in with a box of donuts.

Holiday greetings are a no-brainer. Of course, you'll want your holiday greeting to look amazing, what with the hordes of other holiday greetings your client receives. This type of promotion is perfect for double duty. The design shows off your talent and reinforces your presence without resorting to the hard sell. Don't assume that holiday

34 ● "The greeting card was given as a gift to sponsors who supported the organization. We wanted to do a whimsical layout with non-traditional colors to create a unique holiday card and grab attention. The double sided die-cut also added an element of surprise." —Kong Wee Pang

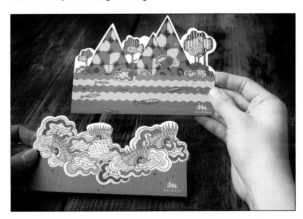

promotions have to be delivered in November and December. There are plenty of other holidays. In fact, there's a holiday almost every day of the year. February sports Kite Flying Day, May has No Socks Day, August features Bad Poetry Day, and November remembers World Kindness Day. How many clients do you think receive a promotion for Kite Flying Day? Not many. Think of all the creative ways you can commemorate a day like that.

Thank-you promotions serve a similar purpose. They express your gratitude to the clients who have helped sustain your business over the years and keep your name in front of them. Clients like to feel appreciated too. A "thank you" goes a long way to establish a collaborative working relationship. Just saying "hi" reinforces that idea as well. The promotion can be as simple as a greeting card or as complex as a 3-D cutout. Send something that the client will find useful or save as a keepsake. Your ultimate goal is to make an impression on the client. Useless items end up in the trash.

INVITATIONS

Nowadays, invitations are sent mainly for weddings, corporate events, baby showers and first birthday parties. Weddings are usually what we think of first when the word *invitation* is mentioned. They are a huge part of our society and are the most common cause for invitations. Second to that is event/party invitations. Styles range from traditional to modern to funky.

Invitations have a rich history. Town criers were the delivery method of choice for many years when the masses were mostly illiterate. Everything from weddings to hangings were announced. It was understood that anyone within hearing distance of the shouted invitation was invited to the event. The elite used monks to transcribe their invitations for private events using calligraphy, a beautiful form of writing. As the common people became more literate—thanks to the invention of moveable type and printing presses—invitations became more mainstream and were usually sent through the mail. Here's an interesting note about wedding invitations: The mail service was fairly unreliable for many, many years. During the 1700s, 1800s and even the early 1900s, invitations were hand delivered to ensure the recipients received them. This delivery method wasn't the cleanliest, given the dirt roads and other unsanitary conditions of the time. This was why invitations were

35 ● This save the date card and associated website were created to promote a wedding. Minimal design printed on wood makes it stand out from the crowd and reflects the couple's fun personality.

placed in double envelopes, a package that included the outer envelope with the address and a second inner envelope to hold the invitation itself. It guaranteed the inner invitation stayed in pristine condition for the intended deliveree.

36 ● (above) Bright bold colors and quirky illustrations set this invitation apart;
37 ● (below) Doll-Myers wedding invitation and program

This tradition continues today, though you would be hard-pressed to find a bride who knows why.

Wedding invitations

Summer Doll-Myers, a freelance wedding invitation designer, says, "Wedding invitations are an extension of the couple themselves. The look and feel is completely dependent on their personalities." Traditional invitations

with flourish script and expensive paper exist alongside nontraditional invitations with crazy type and experimental formats. There's no such thing as standard anymore when it comes to invitations. More and more couples want to highlight their personalities, the venue, the dress, the proposal or the best man who happens to be the groom's dog.

Jessica Hische took her wedding invitation to the world. The World Wide Web, that is. With the help of her fiancé and many talented friends, Jessica created an online wedding announcement/invitation. The invitation is a long scrolling story of Jessica and Russ's life. Their lives prior to meeting, their first date, first kiss, courtship, proposal and careers are told in a parallax website that features different artists' renditions of these moments. The innovative use of technology and traditional use of illustration makes for an incredibly memorable invitation. Those invited to the actual wedding received a code to enter at the bottom of the invitation to see the details. This invitation serves its traditional purpose while doubling as a showcase promotion for the artists involved.

Event invitations

Event invitations used to take the form of the traditional wedding invitation. Nice, but uninspired. People attended because it was the polite thing to do. Things changed, people got busy and out the door went obligatory event attendance. To boost turnout, designers started experimenting with the format, structure and design. After all, they figured, event invitations should instill in the recipient a desire to attend the event.

If you're designing an invitation, consider customizing the choice of format. A public event invitation often works best as a poster and/or advertisement, as these are best suited to reaching a broad audience. For a private event, anything goes. Reflect the event with your choice of materials and printing. Create a keepsake. Include a "key" for entry. Create a mini event highlight within the invitation to give the audience a taste of what's to come. Go tech and put the event invitation online. Give the recipient a special code to RSVP. This technique makes the guest feel elite—like they are part of something special.

GALLERY

Maddox Murphy One-Year Announcement

CREATIVE ANARCHY: Unexpected content, Indulgent

"This one-year announcement for Maddox Murphy [son of Brandon Murphy, one of the owners of Caliber] is a set of 'fact cards' featuring imagery and factoids about Maddox Murphy's first year. It's pure nonsense and self-indulgent for a designer to create something like this for his kid, but it's a heck of a lot of fun. Instead of having a big one-year birthday party (where Maddox shoves cake in his face), we decided to send out a mailer to friends and family documenting the first year of his life. An infographic with real (and fictitious) information was crafted to educate those that wanted to know more about him (like maybe Grampa and Gramma).

Production value is high (cardboard, letterpress, silk screening) and it's not what you normally see for a birthday announcement for a one-year-old. So, I guess the success is just going a bit over-the-top with it." —**CALIBER CREATIVE**

TITLE: Maddox Murphy One-Year Announcement
DESIGN FIRM: Caliber Creative/Dallas Texas
ART DIRECTORS: Brandon Murphy, Kris Murphy
DESIGNERS: Brandon Murphy, Kris Murphy
WEBSITE: www.calibercreative.com
CLIENT: Caliber Creative/Murphy Family

TITLE: Dear Stefan & Jessica
DESIGN FIRM: Go Welsh
ART DIRECTOR: Craig Welsh
DESIGNER: Craig Welsh
WEBSITE: gowelsh.com
CLIENT: Society of Design

Dear Stefan & Jessica

CREATIVE ANARCHY: Twist on the familiar, Unusual size

"We wanted to convince designers Stefan Sagmeister and Jessica Walsh to visit Society of Design as featured guest speakers. Sagmeister and Walsh are known as design risk takers, so the idea was to approach the invitation by designing something that was likely to be unlike anything they had seen before.

The studio has a very large collection of letterpress equipment and materials—hundreds of cases of wood type, varying in size from 1 inch to 13 inches. A constraint was placed on the project that it had to utilize the letterpress resources. Scale, quantity and materials are some of the primary design considerations when working to have the audience pay attention quickly. It was a combination of these that led to printing on paper towels. We placed the wood type directly on the concrete floor in the print shop. The greatest challenge was to keep the type in place (no way to lock up wood type on an open concrete floor). Total print length was 14 feet.

A happy accident occurred when the rubber-based ink wouldn't dry quickly. Instead of waiting to send the invitation after the ink had fully dried, the decision was made to send the paper towels with slightly wet ink. However, a note explaining the possibility of still-wet ink and a couple pairs of yellow rubber gloves were packed with the paper towels. The note and gloves made it apparent upon opening the box that something unusual awaited inspection.

The ultimate success of the project was Stefan Sagmeister agreeing to visit Society of Design. He presented to a sold-out crowd of more than 360 in February 2013." **—CRAIG WELSH**

Together At Last Kong Wee + Jay Crum

CREATIVE ANARCHY: Unexpected format,
Experimental materials

"Our goal was to invite our friends and family to our wedding
in New Orleans. We also wanted to make something fun and
whimsical. Jay is from New Orleans, and I am from Malaysia.
Since we met in art school in Memphis, we have always passed
hand-drawn notes to each other. We wanted to have our personal voices come through in this design. The limited color
palette was inspired by our background in silk-screen printing.
All of the type and drawings for this piece were drawn by hand.
The invitation came in a canvas bag stamped with our initials
from a handmade woodcut stamp. The invitation, printed on a
handkerchief, has the main image of two rabbits in a boat to
represent us. Since we met and live in Memphis, most of our
friends would be traveling from there to New Orleans. The main
concept was a romantic journey down the Mississippi River
that would be exciting and fun." —**KONG WEE PANG**

TITLE: Together At Last Kong Wee + Jay Crum
DESIGN FIRM: taropop studio
ART DIRECTOR: Kong Wee Pang
DESIGNER: Kong Wee Pang
WEBSITE: www.kongweepang.com
CLIENT: Kong Wee and Jay Crum

Matchbox Studio Matchboxes

CREATIVE ANARCHY: Unexpected format and scale

"Our goal with the matchboxes was to do a fun promotional piece that resonated with the vibe and brand of the studio. It was pretty easy to come upon doing matchboxes since our studio is called Matchbox. We wanted the matchboxes to be something that everyone in the studio had the opportunity to work on, so we did just that. Each designer was given parameters such as color palette, typefaces and other supporting elements to design with. It was a collaborative studio effort."

—THE MATCHBOX STUDIO

TITLE: Matchbox Studio Matchboxes
DESIGN FIRM: The Matchbox Studio
ART DIRECTORS: Liz Burnett, Jeff Breazeale
DESIGNERS: Zach Hale, Mark Travis, Katie Kitchens, Rachel Negahban, Josh Bishop, Liz Burnett, Jeff Breazeale, Bryan Lavery
WEBSITE: matchboxstudio.com
CLIENT: The Matchbox Studio

Nördik Impakt 13-Communication

CREATIVE ANARCHY: Phosphorescent inks, Experimental format

"Considered for the last thirteen years as the biggest electronic music festival in France, Nördik Impakt wanted to break off visually from its former iterations. Murmure was tasked with the mission of improving the festival's image with the creation of a more modern, elegant and conceptual graphic identity. The collateral was developed around electronic music and phosphorescence. We created posters and invitation cards that keep the graphic identity and reveal its electronic strength when the lights go out." —MURMURE

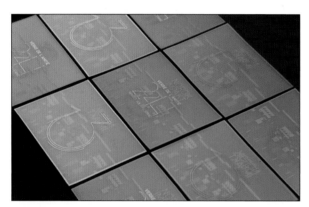

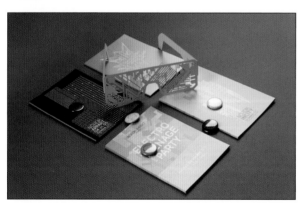

TITLE: Nordik Impakt 13-Communication
DESIGN FIRM: MURMURE
ART DIRECTORS: Julien Alirol, Paul Ressencourt
DESIGNERS: Julien Alirol, Paul Ressencourt
WEBSITE: www.murmure.me
CLIENT: ArtsAttack!

Shot Glass Card

CREATIVE ANARCHY: Unexpected format

"The concept for the design was to create a greeting card that would transform in some fashion into an origami shot glass for use in birthdays, celebrations, graduations and so on. The transformation of paper into something you aren't expecting sparks curiosity and wonder. It's made even better that the transformation is into something relevant and useful." —ROSS MOODY

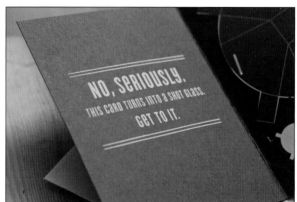

TITLE: Shot Glass Card
DESIGN FIRM: 55 Hi's
ART DIRECTOR: Ross Moody
DESIGNER: Ross Moody
WEBSITE: www.55his.com
CLIENT: 55 Hi's

In the Post Promo

CREATIVE ANARCHY: Experimental format

"For my personal branding I wanted to incorporate my passion for design and typography. I have always found manipulating how people read very interesting. I kept this in mind throughout my personal branding. The promo mailer is an A3 folded poster that is intended to lead the user through it. It's everything that would get me ready for the big wide world: logo/website/promo mailer/business card." **—SAM BARCLAY**

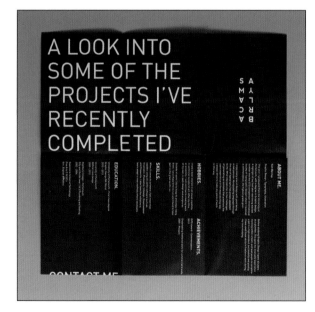

TITLE: In the Post Promo
DESIGN FIRM: Sam Barclay
ART DIRECTOR: Sam Barclay
DESIGNER: Sam Barclay
WEBSITE: www.sambarclay.co.uk
CLIENT: Sam Barclay

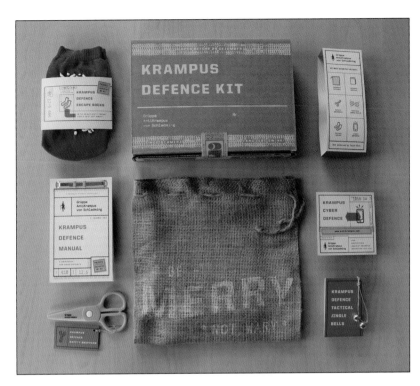

TITLE: Krampus Defense Kit
DESIGN FIRM: Swink
ART DIRECTOR: Shanan Galligan
DESIGNERS: Matt Riley, Yogie Jacala, Krista Farrell
WEBSITE: www.swinkinc.com
CLIENT: Swink

Krampus Defense Kit

CREATIVE ANARCHY: Unexpected theme

"Krampus represents the dark side of the holidays. Basically, Krampus is the 'bad cop' to Santa's 'good cop.' While Santa leaves gifts for the good boys and girls, Krampus is known to punish the naughty. He snatches them up at night from their beds, stuffs them into a burlap sack, and carries them away to his lair.

Under the guise of the *Gruppe AntiKrampus von Schladming* (the AntiKrampus Group of Schladming—a town known for one of the most raucous Krampus festivals), we sent out a defense kit to help arm our friends against this oncoming menace. Included in the package were a useful array of anti-Krampus paraphernalia: official Gruppe AntiKrampus scissors to escape from his burlap bag; a handy guidebook; special no-slip socks for quick, late-night escapes; and jingle bells. To be extra careful, we also made a Krampus detector for the iPhone and tracked his movements on his Twitter feed.

All the boxes and burlap bags were silk-screened. The interior items (manual, item tags, belly band) were printed with two spot colors on French Poptone. The yellow stickers and box seal were laser printed and trimmed in house. All kits were lovingly hand-assembled and held together with late nights and beer. The post office was nice enough to deliver them on our behalf." **—SWINK**

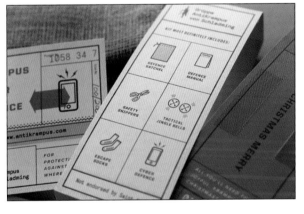

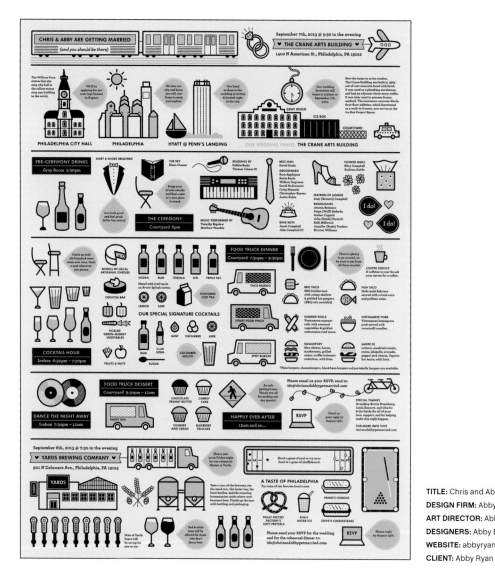

TITLE: Chris and Abby Get Married
DESIGN FIRM: Abby Ryan Design
ART DIRECTOR: Abby Bennett
DESIGNERS: Abby Bennett, Andrew Shearer
WEBSITE: abbyryandesign.com
CLIENT: Abby Ryan

Chris and Abby Get Married

CREATIVE ANARCHY: Experimental layout, Breaks tradition

"For our wedding invitation, I designed an 18" × 24" screen-printed infographic that works as an invitation, program and menu. The poster was designed with the rehearsal dinner invitation as the bottom section so it could be removed for guests only coming to the wedding." —**ABBY BENNETT**

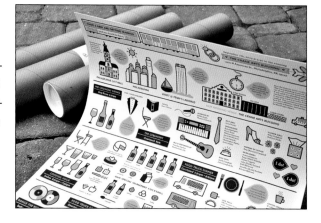

Build Your Own Wine

CREATIVE ANARCHY: DIY approach

"Part of our business is to create ideas for the drinks industry, so we wanted to come up with a self-initiated project to give our clients a laugh and a few bottles of great wine. We wanted to remind people who we were whilst having a bit of fun and a laugh at ourselves. All the star members were photographed, had their various features cut up and put on an adhesive label. The core idea was the play between 'bring your own' and 'build your own.' The typography was stenciled and then spray painted, further enhancing the handmade concept. The images were the central pieces of the idea, so most of the secondary typography was designed to be functional." **—THE CREATIVE METHOD**

TITLE: Build Your Own Wine
DESIGN FIRM: The Creative Method
ART DIRECTOR: Tony Ibbotson
DESIGNER: Tony Ibbotson
WEBSITE: www.thecreativemethod.com
CLIENT: The Creative Method

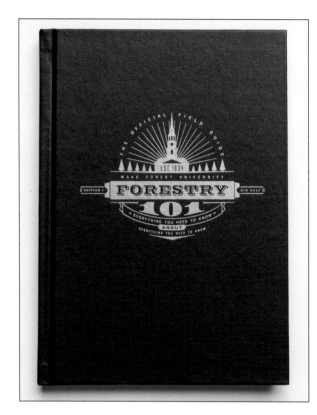

TITLE OF WORK: Wake Forest University Forestry 101
DESIGN FIRM: Wake Forest Communications
CREATIVE DIRECTOR: Hayes Henderson
ART DIRECTOR: Brent Piper
DESIGNER/S: Brent Piper, Stephanie Demarest Bailey
PHOTOGRAPHER: Ken Bennett
WRITER: Bart Rippin
CLIENT: Wake Forest University Student Life

Wake Forest University Forestry 101

CREATE ANARCHY: Unexpected layouts, Texture

"This is a piece given to incoming freshmen. Its intent initially was to be an information piece—relevant phone numbers, web addresses, locations and deadlines—to help new students learn their way around. First and foremost it needed to be a very functional quick-facts piece so students could use it to navigate the treacherous terrain of being a new student. But we also wanted the piece to have attitude, humor, coolness, and not take itself and the university too seriously.

The structure of the piece is a hardbound book, with a black cloth cover and gold foil stamping. It serves to both make the piece seem valuable and hard to get rid of, as well as lightly mock the pomp and circumstance of college books and the collegiate environment. While the book looks 'official,' lines foil-stamped on the cover like 'everything you need to know about everything you need to know' give a wink and some clue as to what follows." **—HAYES HENDERSON**

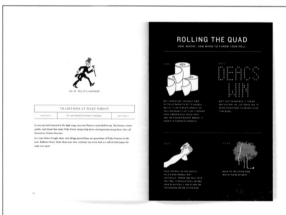

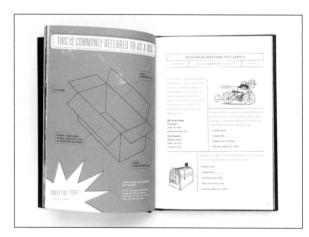

PERSONALITY TYPE

RULE: Only use two fonts in a design.

CREATE ANARCHY: Go crazy and use twelve.

RESULT: Create visually rich invitation or promotion that speaks to all of the personalities involved in the event.

It's not easy to choose typefaces that go well together. In fact, it's really hard. So why not give up trying to choose and just use all of them? I know this goes against every lesson you ever learned in design school. Here's the thing: Any rule can be broken if done with purpose, forethought and intelligence. That includes the use of more than two or three fonts. It can be done and done quite well—with proper planning.

 Let's do this

Take an invitation design you're working on or have done in the past. If you don't have one, do a quick search for an unusual holiday and create an event for it.

1. Research your event. Write down theme ideas, decoration ideas, colors, style of music and the kinds of people it involves.
2. Find or create a quote for your event. Five to ten words works best.
3. Start sketching out arrangements of words. Just use your own handwriting for now. Fancy lettering at this point will just bog you down, distracting you and taking too much time away from the layout process. These layouts can include but are not limited to:

   - stacked
   - center-aligned
   - left-aligned
   - right-aligned
   - sloped
   - circular
   - vertical (turn type on end like a book spine; having one letter sit on top of the other like Japanese writing is extremely difficult for Westerners to read)
   - interlocking/overlapping
   - shaped
   - spiral
   - a combination of the above mentioned

4. Now choose your fonts, thinking about all aspects of the event including the personalities of the people involved. Search for fonts that "feel" like the event and the people. Pick as many as you like—the more the better.
5. Choose a few of your layout sketches for the computer. Armed with your list of fonts, start executing your ideas. Carefully consider which font works with which word. Consider using one font for all the smaller words, like *it* and *the*, for consistency. Vary the fonts for larger words. Don't be afraid to alter letterforms to make them work. For instance, you could extend an ascender or descender, add a swash, or create a ligature. Switch fonts if you have to.
6. Pick the one you like best for the final invitation. Add in the event information and you've got it.

EXERCISES

OPPOSITE DAY

RULE: The design should be harmonious.

CREATE ANARCHY: Use opposites to create tension on the page.

RESULT: Visually exciting design reverberates with the audience and generates a sense of anticipation.

Contrasting elements are a good way to give your design that extra oomph. Opposites intentionally juxtaposed in the same design create tension. Tension creates suspense. The whole purpose of an invitation or promotion is to make the audience feel the suspense and anticipation of the event's big day.

 Let's do this

Take an invitation or event promotion you're working on or have done in the past. If you don't have one, create one for a celebrity wedding.

Using the list of opposites provided, create sketches using word pairs. Don't think too literally with this exercise. Go beyond the obvious and expected. It's easy to do this with imagery, but include type, color and layout as well. For instance, the first pair of opposites (abundant/scarce) can be rendered as:

- An intricately patterned area next to a stark background
- A type-heavy cover with little to no type on the inside panel
- Foil-stamped corrugated cardboard
- Multicolored dots interspersed with solid black ones

A abundant/scarce
advantage/disadvantage
alive/dead
ancient/modern
appear/vanish
artificial/natural
attractive/repulsive

B below/above
bitter/sweet
bless/curse
bold/timid
broad/narrow

C calm/frenetic
clockwise/counterclockwise
cold/hot
conceal/reveal
cool/warm
create/destroy
crooked/straight

D dangerous/safe
dark/light
decrease/increase
dry/moist
dull/shiny

E early/late
east/west
enter/exit
even/odd
expand/contract

F float/sink
fold/unfold
free/bound
frequent/seldom
full/empty

G gentle/rough
giant/dwarf
girl/boy
go/stop
good/evil

H hard/soft
harsh/mild
heaven/hell
heavy/light
hill/valley
horizontal/vertical

I important/trivial
include/exclude
inferior/superior
inner/outer
intentional/accidental

J join/separate
junior/senior

justice/injustice

K knowledge/ignorance
known/unknown

L laugh/cry
leader/follower
lengthen/shorten
lenient/strict
loose/tight
love/hate

M mad/sane
major/minor
melt/freeze
merry/sad
miser/spendthrift

N narrow/wide
near/far
neat/messy
never/always

O offer/refuse
old/new
opaque/translucent
optimist/pessimist

P poetry/prose
possible/impossible
pretty/ugly
pure/impure
push/pull

Q question/answer

quiet/noisy	sour/sweet	**U** under/over	weak/strong
R rapid/slow	sow/reap	upside down/right side up	white/black
rare/common	start/finish	us/them	win/lose
real/fake	sunny/cloudy	useful/useless	wisdom/folly
rich/poor	**T** tame/wild	**V** vast/tiny	**Y** yin/yang
rough/smooth	there/here	victory/defeat	young/old
S shrink/grow	tight/loose	virtue/vice	**Z** zip/unzip
singular/plural	together/apart	voluntary/compulsory	zenith/nadir
sober/drunk	tough/easy	**W** wax/wane	

CREATIVY EXERCISE:

PUNK IS NOT DEAD

The Punk Art movement is an amazing testament to the photocopier. Posters for gigs consisted of images culled from whatever materials were lying around, then photocopied together. These cheap, effective invitations were then stapled to anything that didn't move. Part of the appeal of the photocopier is the inevitable grit and degradation that occurs when images are shrunk or enlarged. The mechanical technology of the day also conferred its own imperfections, unlike the "clean" printers and scanners of today. The raw, edgy beauty of the genre hearkens back to the days when technology didn't mean as much as just rockin' out. Get in touch with your inner rebel by creating your own Creative Anarchist design show invitation.

 Let's do this

SUPPLIES:

- photos
- newspapers
- magazines
- anything else within reach
- markers, pens and pencils
- scissors/X-ACTO knife
- tape/glue
- paper
- photocopier: If you don't have one in your office, try the library or post office. Remember to bring coins.

1. Decide on the details of your Creative Anarchist design show. Pick a title, location, date and time.
2. Decide how you want to create your type. Will you write it by hand or use cutout images to create a ransom-note effect?
3. Photocopy all your photos and other materials to see how they translate into black and white. Pick your favorites.
4. Start making your image. Move the original around while copying to create blurs and smears. Enlarge and shrink over and over to get a gritty, degraded look. Superimpose letters. Layer, repeat, stack, reassemble and collage images together. Lighten or darken the exposure. Crumple, tear and scribble to create texture. Three-dimensional objects will copy with a ghostly edge due to the copier's shallow depth of field. Write or paste your text into place. Photocopy onto different colored paper to get different effects. Keep going until you have your desired look.
5. Photocopy a bunch and hang them all over your office. Go a step further and follow through with your Creative Anarchist design show.

EXERCISES

FAMOUS QUOTES

RULE: Don't copy.

CREATE ANARCHY: Steal your headline.

RESULT: Generate inspirational messages that resonate with the audience.

We all have our favorite quotes. We spout them in conversation. We hang them on the wall to motivate us. Sometimes we live by them. Why not use them to inspire our design? I'm not talking about using a quote in the design. I'm talking using the quote to generate ideas for the design.

 Let's do this

Take an invitation or event promotion you're working on or have done in the past. If you don't have one, create one for a charity event.

1. Find inspiring quotes relevant to the project. They can come from literature, film, cartoons, video games, comic books, children's stories, folktales, well-known speeches or something you once heard a college professor say.

2. Expand on the quotes with lists of words that they bring to mind. Write down visuals, emotions, adjectives, formats, colors, typefaces and anything else that pops into your brain. Don't edit yourself. Mind mapping works well for this. Use whatever method works best for you.

3. Look at your lists, and select words that resonate with the project.

4. Start sketching! Keep the essence of the quotes in mind as you work out your ideas. Think about using one of the quotes itself if you need inspiring text.

5. Narrow down your ideas. Choose ones that have a strong conceptual basis.

FOR EXAMPLE, FOLLOWING ARE QUOTES THAT COULD BE USED FOR THE SCHOLARSHIP PROGRAM CHARITY EVENT.

"I want to take the road that leads to awesome" —Kid

"Two roads diverged in a yellow wood, / And sorry I could not travel both." —Robert Frost

"Twinkle, twinkle, little star / How I wonder what you are! / Up above the world so high, / Like a diamond in the sky." —Jane Taylor, English poet

"The best presents don't come in boxes."
—Bill Watterson, creator of *Calvin & Hobbes*

"Without struggle, there is no progress"
—Frederick Douglass

CHAPTER 6

PACKAGING

We need to buy things from stores: food staples, home goods and personal items. Most of these items need some form of packaging. There's a lot of good packaging out there that serves its singular purpose—grabbing enough of your attention to make you purchase the item. But because the package is still competing against all the other packages on the shelf, "good" isn't always good enough. It needs to be desired. Have you ever walked into a store and bought a product just because of the packaging? I have. Innovative, creative, amazing wine labels are my weakness. What's yours?

Packaging is a form of advertising. A tiny little ad sitting there on the shelf trying to sell itself to you. It wants to make you want it. It wants you to desire it. It wants to come home with you. How do you design a package so that it triggers this response? By using your knowledge of design to create a package that not only communicates but also seduces.

ORIGINS

Ever since we began collecting food, we've had to store it. Early forms of packaging consisted of reeds, leaves, bark and skins. As materials developed, so did packaging. Pottery, wood crates and barrels, mass-produced ceramics, glass and paper followed. It wasn't until the 1600s that packages with labeling became standard practice. Labels distinguished reputable products from label-less, inferior goods. Fast forward four hundred years and the world would seem bare without the rainbow of colorful packages lining store shelves and filling our homes. Virtually every product sold or distributed now has packaging of some sort. The absence of identifying information not only is detrimental to sales but also can be illegal.

THE SEA OF CONSUMERISM

Unlike other forms of design, consumer packaging is entirely dependent upon its audience for success. Your package could be the coolest design ever created, but if the audience is unwilling to buy it, then the package has failed. The consumer is the ultimate judge of the design when they choose which products to examine and, ideally, to buy. Sure, advertising will drive some sales, but the packaging has to sit there and wait to be noticed by the consumer. It has to catch her eye, say the right thing, entice her enough to pick it up and then make it all the way to the checkout line. Not a simple task by any means. But if that package can make it into her hands, the battle is half won. The packaged product now has a good shot at going home with her.

There is stiff competition on those shelves. Think about the environment of a grocery store. Everything in that store is packaged and labeled, including the loose produce. It's a sea of design, and you have to be prepared to weather the storm. Wealthy Western cultures are all about choice. We believe that one of the symbols of democracy and freedom is having choices about what we do, say and are offered. Lots of choices. The more the better. Don't get me wrong: Choice is essential to our society. I don't want anyone telling me what I can or cannot have in my life. Still, this celebrated freedom of choice stumps us when presented with too many options. Diners are great examples of this. Have you ever gone to a diner where the menu is six pages long and offers three hundred different choices? Too many options make it harder to choose—you don't know what to eat, and then you second-guess yourself about your choice. Sometimes it's easier when there are fewer choices. This phenomenon affects the grocery shopper too. Which granola bar is the right one for the consumer when presented

38 ● "The vintage Cabernet Sauvignon had a limited run of 500 bottles. The label—with a folded lapel—is playing on the stereotyped lawyers' pinstripe suit, with a power, "Look at me" red handkerchief sticking out for real. Everything great on the computer screen, but without the dedicated production team, which assembled by hand the 500 red handkerchiefs, it would not have come to life so impressively." —Brandient

with thirty different options? Each granola bar package is vying to be the best.

This battle for attention is where the designer comes in. You are responsible for attracting the consumer through the use of imagery, type, structure and communication. What will make her pick your package instead of another one? Is it the delectable picture of the granola bar or the stylization of the product name? Perhaps it's the choice of color or the arrangement of information. Maybe it's the shape of the box, or the fact that the consumer can easily tell the product is organic. Knowing your audience will guide your design decisions to whatever will best appeal to them.

Sell by...

Packaging can stay on a shelf or in a warehouse for weeks, months or even years. It's a design medium that sticks around for a while. Even though individual products are sold on a daily basis, the design of the packaging tends to remain on shelf for quite some time. Once the grocery products, cleaning supplies, skincare regimen and hair care solutions are home, the packaging lasts only as long as it takes for a consumer to deplete the product or extract its contents. This varies with the product, of course. A bottle of olive oil can last for many months, whereas toy packaging is generally discarded about three seconds after a child realizes what's inside. Furniture boxes, on the other hand, sometimes have second lives as rocket ships or castles. Regardless of how long the package lasts in the home, the original design has the potential to be on the shelf in the store for years. Because the goal of any packaging is immediate brand recognition, the consumer can have a major freak out if a product's "look" is changed too often or too much. Just ask Tropicana about that. In 2009, Tropicana released a redesign of its famous juice packaging. Away went the iconic logo and orange with a straw. Away went the colored tab indicating the quantity of pulp. Away went clear differentiation between varieties of product. In their place was a clean, white, generic, uninspired design very much in keeping with the trend toward "generics" happening at the time. Sales dropped like a stone. It only took two months of plummeting profits and consumer outcry for the company to go back to the old packaging. This is an extreme example but a poignant one about how poor design decisions can obliterate sales of an otherwise good packaging structure and successful product. Updates and changes will be made from time to time of course. Formulas, features, brand ownership and marketing positions evolve. The trick is to update the design without alienating the consumer.

39 ● "The largest contribution to the brand's success came from the fact that the new logo had high visibility on a great variety of packaging—from large packages to very small bottles of natural essences." —Brandient

40 ● Creative typography and fun graphics make this specialty packaging stand out from its competition.

MASS MARKET VS. SPECIALTY

Mass market refers to large stores servicing a wide variety of consumers. Target, Walmart, Kmart, JC Penney, CVS, Rite-Aid and Walgreens, to name a few, are examples of mass-market retailers. These stores cater to everyone. Specialty stores are just that: niche retailers catering to a select audience. Not that they wouldn't appreciate the profits from a mass-market audience, but the nature of the specialty business is targeted to a specific crowd. The different audience changes the approach to packaging. On mass-market shelves, information needs to be bold and clear, because competition is stiff and shelf presence is a fight to the death. Because there are fewer competitors in the smaller specialty shops, designers can be a bit more subtle and experiment more. In a shop selling only one brand of product, anything goes.

3-D

The three-dimensional nature of packaging is what sets it apart from other forms of design. This is good news and bad news. The good news is that you have more space to work with; the bad news is that you have more space to work with. Packaging is picked up, held and fondled by consumers. You need to consider each surface, because packaging isn't always placed facing forward. Sometimes all that's visible is a side or top panel.

There are opportunities for communication on each panel, side and surface of packaging. Remember too that design doesn't have to be limited to just one package. *Billboarding*, the practice of allowing design elements to align from package to package, builds a strong presence on shelf because of Gestalt principles. The whole, all of the packages side by side, is greater than the sum of the parts, the individual package. Have fun making images and graphics flow from package to package. The Split Milk design concept for Earth Fare dairy products wraps the image of a cow around three sides of a carton. When placed on shelf, a full cow can be formed by both two and three side-by-side cartons. Even simple design decisions like placing the logo in the exact same spot and in the same color on a salad dressing label will create a unified front to that section of the store shelf.

Paper or plastic?

Another advantage to three-dimensional packaging is the opportunity to experiment with form. Paperboard and other paper-based structures can be folded, scored, manipulated, cut and glued to fit virtually any product. There are a few limits due to manufacturing and automation capabilities, but paper can hold almost any shape. Paper and paperboard are also considered sustainable technologies. Most manufacturing companies take great pains to replace and regrow the trees used in their process. Because of this,

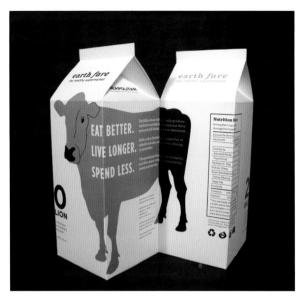

41 ● Split Milk

plus efforts to recycle used paper and paperboard products, paperboard packaging is an eco-friendly design solution.

When the laws of physics limit paper folding, plastics take over. There are seven categories of plastics: HDPE, LDPE, PP, PVC, PET, PS and Other (biodegradable, photosensitive, and plant-based plastics). Each category has its own unique profile of properties regarding the ease with which it can be shaped, and the kind of products it can contain. With few exceptions, plastic packaging is derived from a petroleum base, therefore even though most of it is recyclable, it is not considered as sustainable as paperboard.

If you get the chance to influence the packaging format, the number of options are incredible. I had the opportunity to work on a product rebranding that included a complete overhaul of both the graphic and packaging components. The graphic work was challenging, but my team came through swimmingly. The structural work was frighteningly new to me. We worked for months creating ideas for bottle and lid structure to contain the products. We went through every shape imaginable, and some that were beyond imagination. We made prototypes with a 3-D printer. We tested the structures with staff and in focus groups with consumers. We agonized over the exact hue for each piece of the package and worked tirelessly with the manufacturing plant to obtain the right color and clarity in the plastic. It was a grueling, fascinating experience. For instance,

I had no idea that plastic bottles started out as little plastic pellets that were superheated, melted and injection molded into whatever shape we wanted. I knew plastic bottles came from somewhere, but I always envisioned a huge vat of liquid plastic poured into a mold. Finding out about the pellets was a learning experience.

Other materials and special techniques

Paper and plastic aren't your only options for creative packaging. Campbell's soup shattered stereotypes when they introduced ready-to-eat "Soup on the Go" microwaveable cups in 2003. "Campbell's Go!" microwaveable soup pouches followed in 2012. Both the design on the pouch—black and white photography of happy people and hand lettered typography—and pouch itself were breakthroughs in design and garnered a lot of attention in the industry. The soup is quite tasty too. Then Ella's Kitchen adopted pouches as well, tucking baby food into adorably cute packages that doubled as serving containers from which toddlers could squeeze the food right into their mouths. Knob Creek took high-end whiskey packaging and turned it on its head with a bold typography-based label design, bucking a market dominated by Jack Daniels-esque vintage label designs. The typical clear vodka bottle got an upgrade when Chopin and Belvedere entered the stores in the mid-1990s. Frosted glass bottles featured clear "windows" on the front that revealed back side printing and etchings. The vodka bottles lit up the industry's perceptions of alcohol packaging. Au Bon Pain introduced triangular boxes for sandwiches, a logical solution for the lunch crowd that had, surprisingly, never been done before.

A great packaging designer considers how the graphics and the structure of the design work together. Explore paperboard, corrugated cardboard, glass, plastic, metal and natural materials. Don't forget that you can use different materials for different parts of a package, like a metal cap on a glass bottle. Consider how these materials complement your design. Create a reveal. Use flaps. Use visual-verbal synergy, Gestalt principles and plain ol' cleverness in the design solution. Make the experience of opening a package like opening a birthday present. Zig where the rest of the industry zags. Do anything you can to stand out in the crowded marketplace.

GALLERY

TITLE: Alfaro Barroco
DESIGN FIRM: Dorian
DESIGNER: Gabriel Morales
WEB: estudiodorian.com
CLIENT: Palacios Remondo

Alfaro Barroco

CREATIVE ANARCHY: Minimal design, Typographic surprise

"The design created is a tribute to Alfaro, the town where the winery is located, and its Baroque history. The six wine labels are an homage to this land. The illustrated letters' baroque ornamentation is inspired by the altar of the Virgen del Rosario from the Colegiata de San Miguel, which is the symbol of the Riojan Baroque and the center of the event activities." **—DORIAN**

Alternative

CREATIVE ANARCHY: Unexpected materials, Sustainable

"Alternative was created to reflect a new way of looking at organic packaging. The concept simply shows a vine, from the leaves to the bark to the wine. Every aspect of the packaging was organic; this includes the laser-cut balsa wood, the string and wax that is used to affix the label to the bottle, the outer paper wrapping and even the inks used to print the image.

When creating this label, we came across numerous production and technical hurdles. At each one it would have been very easy to ditch the ideas and look at something easier. Through hours of hard work we were able to get around these issues and produce what is ultimately a very original pack. We believe that through perseverance and an unwavering desire to create something original we were able to achieve something ahead of its time." **—THE CREATIVE METHOD**

TITLE: Alternative
DESIGN FIRM: The Creative Method
ART DIRECTOR: Tony Ibbotson
DESIGNER: Tony Ibbotson
WEB: thecreativemethod.com
CLIENT: Marlborough Valley Wines

Fire Road Wine

CREATIVE ANARCHY: Unexpected visuals,
Creative printing techniques

"Storytelling is the oldest form of branding and is the easiest way for a brand to be remembered. If you can bring a story to life on a label in a simple and bold way, chances are people will remember it. We used print techniques to enhance the story. The split label with the rough burnt gap helped create disruption on the shelf and reinforce the story.

After the redesign, sales increased by more than 100 percent. This opened up more opportunity for The Creative Method, gave our client confidence in what we did, and ultimately gave us more scope to be creative in future projects."
—THE CREATIVE METHOD

TITLE: Fire Road Wine
DESIGN FIRM: The Creative Method
ART DIRECTOR: Tony Ibbotson
DESIGNER: Tony Ibbotson
WEB: thecreativemethod.com
CLIENT: Marlborough Valley Wines

Maria's Beer Packaging

CREATIVE ANARCHY: Primitive design

"Most beer packaging is atrocious, or overdesigned. These look like they were made by a talented eight-year-old, which you don't see too often on an alcoholic beverage." **—MICHAEL FREIMUTH**

TITLE: Maria's Beer Packaging
DESIGN FIRM: Franklyn
DESIGNER: Michael Freimuth
WEB: quitefranklyn.com
CLIENT: Maria's Community Bar & Packaged Goods

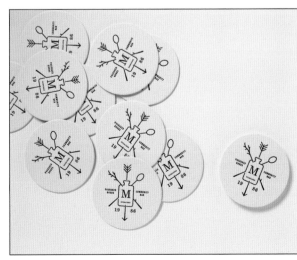

Thelma's Oven Box

CREATIVE ANARCHY: Unusual format

"At one of our first meetings, our art director, Brian, said, "The box could be anything. Any shape. Any design." "Anything?" said Derek. "Yeah, like, even an oven shape," said Brian. "That would be awesome," said Derek. And the sketches began.

"We set out to give a nod to grandma's kitchen without making the product seem dowdy or old-fashioned. We landed on words like *homemade*, *wholesome*, *sweet* and *full of goodness* with a brand promise of joy. This positioning gave Thelma a voice and spirit. The packaging was truly born from the brand. Our goal in creating Thelma's packaging was to re-create the feeling of enjoying warm cookies straight from your favorite grandma's oven. The oven box concept was the most logical, perfect piece to accomplish that." **—SATURDAY MFG.**

TITLE: Thema's Oven Box
DESIGN FIRM: Saturday Mfg.
ART DIRECTOR: Brian Sauer
DESIGNERS: Brian Sauer, Annie Furhman, Karen Weiss
WEBSITE: www.saturdaymfg.com
CLIENT: Thelma's

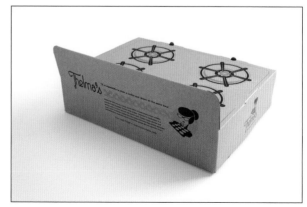

Real McCoy Whiskey

CREATIVE ANARCHY: Historic influence

"The design solution was based on the Real McCoy story. This was of Bill McCoy, who was a smuggler during the Prohibition era of the 1920s. We spent a lot of time investigating this era and how it looked in the day. It was here that we got the graphical cues that drove the design. During the 1920s, letterpress was prevalent and this formed the core of the label.

As we could not change the bottle shape, we needed to create some cut-through and standout in the label. It was placed on an angle to reflect the rushed and slightly shonky nature of the smugglers. This gives the overall pack some visual disruption on shelf. Also the mandatory information was incorporated in the design as 'customs and excise' style stamps and official marks—all further elements to visually bring the story to life and drive authenticity." —**THE CREATIVE METHOD**

TITLE: Real McCoy Whiskey
DESIGN FIRM: The Creative Method
ART DIRECTOR: Tony Ibbotson
DESIGNER: Tony Ibbotson
WEB: thecreativemethod.com
CLIENT: Diageo Australia

Choiselle Packaging

CREATIVE ANARCHY: Creative printing techniques

"The client wanted these products—which are very high quality—to be sold in high-end spas, so the packaging needed to reflect that. Since the typography was simple and sophisticated, we felt it was important to infuse a bit of the products' all-natural quality into the overall package design. We did this by designing the C in the logo to feel very plantlike.

We used a mixed printing technique for the bottles and labels. All of the generic information was silk-screened directly on the bottles before a scent-specific label was applied. The paper used for the printed labels also had a very luxurious feel, which enhanced the high-quality nature of the products. Last, the tiny hit of color in the illustration of each product's scent was a small element that made a big difference to us." **—SEAN COSTIK**

TITLE: Choiselle Packaging
DESIGN FIRM: Projekt, Inc.
DESIGNER: Sean M. Costik
WEB: projektinc.com
CLIENT: Choiselle

Holiday Beer Packaging

CREATIVE ANARCHY: Unexpected format

"Carlson Capital approached us with the need for an invite for their annual holiday party. The theme for the party was "Game Night!"—shuffleboard, card games, Monopoly, dominoes, and so on. The client wanted the invite to be really kitschy and fun. The quantity was only a hundred, so they could be hand delivered. This really gave us the opportunity to try something different without having to deal with mailing restrictions.

The beer package acted as both a gift and an invite. We wrapped it in a nice patterned paper to make it feel like a gift you might get around the holidays. It definitely breaks the rules for a traditional invitation." —**THE MATCHBOX STUDIO**

TITLE: Holiday Beer Packaging
DESIGN FIRM: The Matchbox Studio
ART DIRECTORS: Liz Burnett, Jeff Breazeale
DESIGNER: Zach Hale
WEB: matchboxstudio.com
CLIENT: Carlson Capital

PACKAGING

Minima Moralia

CREATIVE ANARCHY: Unexpected visuals

"The name *Minima Moralia*, borrowed from the philosophers' realm, brings the values of honor, respect, devotion, hope, gratitude and honesty together. There is truth in wine, the saying goes, and also in the people's eyes. The packaging identity depicts real people with an archetypal visual character, explored through the unique detail, texture and bokeh of wet plate photography (collodion and tintype)—an old technique kept alive by aficionados." **—BRANDIENT**

TITLE: Minima Moralia
DESIGN FIRM: Brandient
CREATIVE DIRECTOR: Cristian 'Kit' Paul
DESIGNERS: Cristian 'Kit' Paul, Ciprian Badalan, Cristian Petre
WEB: brandient.com
CLIENT: Domeniul Coroanei Segarcea

TITLE: Übernuts
DESIGN FIRM: Brandient
CREATIVE DIRECTOR: Cristian 'Kit' Paul
DESIGNERS: Cristian Petre, Adrian Stanculet
WEB: brandient.com
CLIENT: Pangram SA

Übernuts

CREATIVE ANARCHY: Unexpected visuals

"The name Übernuts is using the German *über*—which permeated both English and Romanian vernacular as a cool word for 'over, super'—to position the brand as a self-proclaimed quality standout, but in a light-hearted way. The multiple meanings of *nuts* add to the mojo of the brand, aimed primarily at the young demographic.

The package design is poking pop-culture fun at a celebrity-obsessed world, where even the smallest grain in the crowd would dream to become a celebrity, be that a rock musician, a football player or an illusionist. The vivid neon color is a strong brand property, clearly standing out on the shelf, triggering curiosity and building brand awareness. As an aside, it was great fun to take photos of raging popcorn kernels and rock star nuts!" —**BRANDIENT**

EXERCISES

WW_ _ _ _ _D? (AKA WHAT WOULD _ _ _ _ _ _ _ DO?)

RULE: Design in the now.
CREATE ANARCHY: Look to historical movements to develop design concepts and visuals.
RESULT: Vintage/Retro/Historical inspiration is reinterpreted into relevant and modern design.

You've already heard that there are no new ideas, so why not go back to historical materials to see how the design issues were resolved in the past? Look at typography, graphic elements, imagery and layout from bygone days. Examine the conceptual ideas behind the designs. Look for themes.

 Let's do this

Take a design you're working on or have done in the past. If you don't have one, go to the dollar store and pick out a product. Choose something with a particularly bad design so that you're not tempted to salvage any part of it.

1. Grab your art history book or design history book, or do a search of historical design archives, and start making a list of designers who made (or make) an impact on you. If you aren't familiar with designers in history, now's the time to start. Make your list. No one is off limits. Paul Rand, Stefan Sagmeister, Herbert Bayer, Paula Scher, Saul Bass, Neville Brody, Louise Fili, David Carson, Chip Kidd, Michael Bierut, Herbert Matter, Jessica Walsh, Cipe Pineles, Milton Glaser, Seymour Chwast, George Lois and Herb Lubalin are a few names to get you started. Don't discount a designer whose style you like but you think may not be relevant to the project or client. You're still in the idea stage, and remember, there are no bad ideas. Look at the designers' work. Understand their philosophies. It's never too late to learn.

2. Now figure out what makes each designer iconic. Is it a particular approach to design or the philosophy behind the concepts? Perhaps it's a signature style. Whatever it is, write it down.

3. Put yourself in the designer's shoes. How would he handle your design project? What would he do with your type, your images and your concept? Bold or subtle? Obscure or mainstream? Try to let go of everything you know, or think you know, and put yourself wholly into the mind of the designer.

4. Start sketching. A lot. Use all the references at your disposal and sketch out your design concepts in the designer's voice.

NOTE: Do not copy the designer's work directly. That's just plain lazy. Your job is to interpret his way of working as your own. Copying is never OK, and the last thing you need is a copyright infringement lawsuit. You're looking at influence and style rather than exact concepts, typography, shapes, elements and layouts.

DREAM A LITTLE DREAM

RULE: Work within the client's budget.

CREATE ANARCHY: Forget the budget and design for the dream job.

RESULT: Explore what you can do instead of what you can't.

Every job has budgetary restrictions. There's no way around it unless you're working for a gazillionaire. Your job is to produce the best results within the budget. But what if there were no budget? What if you could do anything at all? What would you create?

 Let's do this

Take a package design you're working on or have done in the past. If you don't have one, create a package design for a new wine.

1. Write down everything you know about your project. Include all the information that needs to be listed on the packaging, the predetermined packaging structure (or restrictions if a structure has not been decided upon), the proposed printing method and all other relevant information. Also write down your current ideas and design direction, if any.

2. Crumple up the list and throw it away.

3. Start a new list. This time write/sketch everything you'd love to do with the project, including stuff that's cool just for the sake of being cool. Include everything from the type and package structure to printing method and point-of-sale display. Dream big. Use language like *custom bottle*, *foil stamping*, *letterpress printing*, *minimal type*, *musical labels* and *flashing lights*.

4. Now take those big dreams and turn them into attainable project goals. For each dream item, list an alternative solution that fits within the budgetary constraints. For instance, an alternative to a custom bottle with a wavy profile is a shaped label, and letterpress printing can be faked on the computer.

5. Don't be too quick to give up all your dream ideas though. Consider reallocating funds to make some ideas work. A less expensive printing method allows for extra money to purchase a more expensive or custom bottle, or a less expensive stock bottle can free up enough to add a musical microchip. Some of your ideas may not cost as much as you think they will, and who knows? Your client may be impressed enough with your design to increase the budget.

6. Go forth and think positive thoughts about what you *can* do instead of what you can't. Keep dreaming big!

PARKING LOT NOTEBOOK

When you work in a field that relies on creativity, it's important to have a way to keep track of your ideas. It's equally important for that recording method to be available to you at any time, because we all know that creativity strikes anytime, anywhere, often from unexpected things (ribbon cuttings, a discarded piece of paper, a feather). You need someplace to record your ideas. You need a parking lot notebook.

"Don't I just need a nice, pretty journal to record my thoughts?" you may ask. No, you need a place to park your ideas, *all* your ideas. You need something that can get messy and withstand abuse. We are creatives, after all. Our brains aren't nice and pretty. Our brains are a frenzied mess of ideas, thoughts and artistic craziness. Your journal should reflect that.

 Let's do this

SUPPLIES:

- heavy duty journal with a good binding
- pencil, pen, marker, watercolor, paint, crayon, etc.
- tape
- glue
- sheet protectors
- scissors
- found objects
- random creative thoughts
- permission to hold nothing back

1. It's quite simple. Write it all down. Everything. Any and every creative idea that pops into your head. Write it; draw it; record it. No filter. No second-guessing. Your ideas will range from logos and grid concepts to cool color combinations and how to decorate your mom's next birthday cake. Record all of it.

2. If you forget your journal, write down a creative idea on another piece of paper, napkin or other surface. Then tape or glue the idea into your journal. Keep it all together so you never have to say, "Now where did I put that scrap of paper?"

3. If you find a small object that inspires you, tape or glue it into your journal. Secure a modified sheet protector or envelope to a page if you don't want to ruin the object. Again, anything goes. A piece of chewing gum, a butterfly wing, a fabric scrap, a logo with a typeface you love, an ad for a new desk, or a wine label. Put it in the journal.

4. If you have no choice but to take a picture of your inspiration, print it out and tape it into your journal the first chance you get. It's amazing how fast images get forgotten on your phone/camera. Same goes for images you find on the internet. Pasting everything into your journal means you never have to go searching for it.

5. Carry the journal with you whenever possible. Make sure you have a writing utensil as well. There is absolutely nothing worse than having an idea with no way to record it.

6. Be consistent and use the journal every day. Soon it will become a satisfying and creative habit.

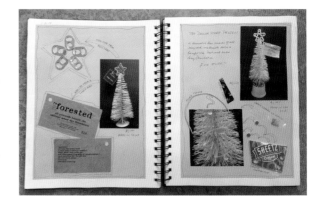

VACATION PACKAGE

When was the last time you were on vacation? What was it like? Relaxing on a beach sipping a tropical treat, or did you head for an exciting city and party the whole time? How wonderful it would be to access that trip anytime you wanted, just by picking it up at your local grocery or department store—a vacation in a box. What would the package look like? What would it be called? How would you design the graphics and sell copy to reflect your experience?

 Let's do this

SUPPLIES:

- vacation memories
- journal for sketches
- pen, pencil, marker, etc.
- packaging materials

1. Gather your vacation memories, including memorabilia and other physical items. Write down everything that made your vacation special. It could be just the fact that you lay on the beach for a week. Maybe it was the food, the people you were with, the fabulous nightlife, or zip-lining through the forest. List the feelings, smells, sights and anything else you can remember.

2. Determine the structure of your package. Is it a bottle, box or bag? Is it large and complex or simple and small? The structure sets the stage for your design.

3. Begin designing. Develop a product logo. Name your vacation something enticing. Make the consumer desire it. Consider all sides of your package. Don't forget the sell copy and ingredients.

4. Keep the finished package on your desk and look at it when things get crazy. Thinking about a magical vacation will get your brain feeling better in no time.

CHAPTER **7**

INTERACTIVE

In this day and age, the word *interactive* means technology-based media such as apps, websites and other digitally created design. Interactive design focuses on the use of software to create user experiences for both business and pleasure. But if you think about the word aside from digital media, it suddenly means a whole lot more. Every design, digital and print, seeks a response—a touch, an action or a reaction. All design speaks to the audience and waits for a response. Interactive design doesn't wait: It invites. It welcomes. It demands a response on the spot.

Some would argue that books are the first true interactive design—via the act of turning pages. Pretty boring, if you ask me. Pop-ups, pull-outs and other paper-based motion elements are more entertaining. The Braille alphabet contributed to a completely interactive book in "print"; fingers had to touch the paper to read it. It wasn't until the 1960s that computers developed the capability for interactive design, though it wasn't until the mid-1980s that the average designer could even use the technology. Early room-size computing monstrosities gave way to small desktop computers. It really is amazing how far computer technology has come in such a short time.

Sometimes it seems technology changes too quickly. Just when you learn one thing, it's updated or replaced by something else more advanced and so much cooler. What's cutting edge now won't be tomorrow, next week or next month. Access to this technology changes quickly as well. We used to be able to access the internet just through a computer. Now we can get it through so many more devices. And the types of devices keep multiplying too. What's a designer to do?

The first thing to recognize is that while innovations will alter technology, the fundamentals of design do not change. Technology is just another tool to help us explore

42 ● Wordless - Universal Wrap

43 ● The site's big numbers, bright colors, geometric elements and bold messages really set it apart from any other similar companies.

44 ● Based on an art and food theme, this lighthearted and expressive site uses collage to represent the content and spirit of the monthly e-journal.

and execute great concepts. The approach to interactive design is no different than designing publications, posters or branding: You need solid concepts, good grid structures, awesome typography and intelligent design decisions.

DIGITAL INTERACTIVITY

Designing for the screen offers so many opportunities for interactivity. This is why digital design is so special and, let's face it, cool. Interactivity creates a multidimensional atmosphere that invites the viewer to become involved with the page on a deeper level. On a website about cats, for example, a viewer can read about a cat, click through a gallery of photos, follow links to articles, listen to cat songs, watch video of cats, live stream zoo footage of big cats, use an app to determine your cat's personality type, play a virtual reality cat game, fill in a survey, leave a comment, post photos and converse with other cat owners worldwide. It's this interactivity that encourages a viewer to stay and play. You just can't do that in print. There is a downside though. With so many bells and whistles available in digital design, it can be hard to know when to stop. Do not sacrifice good design for the sake of all the cool add-ons. It's not worth it.

Technology will always offer a way to do something bigger, faster, stronger or better. Take advantage of it, by all means, but don't let it ruin your design.

Interactive design

Websites are made with the same common elements: navigation, text and images. It's easy to create a website. Put the navigation across the top, set up a couple columns of text, pop in a few images here and there, maybe throw in a video, and you're done. Right?

You should know better than this by now. Interactive design is about the user experience. It should be friendly and simple, magnificent and magical. Think beyond the necessary requirements for communication. Of course, you want your audience to understand the information you're giving them, but don't bore them. Leo Burnett had a fantastic website in the early 2000s. Not only did it show off the portfolio of his worldwide advertising agency, but it also allowed the viewer to use a virtual pencil to draw on the home page. Warby Parker's 2012 digital annual report scrolls in a circular motion, completely sidestepping the vertical and horizontal standards of web design. In addition to the innovative programming, the annual report is also filled with great infographics and excellent text. Tablets, smartphones and other digital devices have opened up new and exciting possibilities for digital design. The devices themselves are now part of the design. You can physically move the device and have it react with your design—the ultimate in user interactivity.

Make it worth his while

The goal of interactive design is to enhance a user's life. Productivity, mood, relaxation or distraction—whatever they're looking for. Design always comes first. Be wary of technology for the sake of thrills. Consider what's most necessary for the viewer. Tease him with enough to get him interested but not so much that he's overwhelmed. Entice and seduce him into delving deeper into the design. Make it useful. Make it fun. Make it entertaining and easy to use. Make him lose track of time. Make it beautifully designed. Make it easy to share. Make the programming solid. Make it fast-loading and responsive as well. Yes, interactive design has to do a lot. Ultimately it comes down to the needs of the client and the user's response. All the technology in the world won't help if your design misses the mark.

INTERACTIVE IN PRINT

Designers found ways to interact with their audience long before the appearance of smartphones or computers or apps or any kind of digital environment. We're not talking QR codes either. We're talking print materials that actually interacted with their audience, increasing the chance that the viewer would hang onto it.

Print has its limitations. Or does it? Print can bend, fold, twist, turn, dial, tear off, punch out and play music. An audience can see through it, assemble it, write on it, draw on it, color it in, open it, pull it out, spin it, make something with it, scratch it off, crumple it, paint it, reuse it, display it, lift it up, lick it, stick it, see it in the dark, throw it, catch it, laugh over it, be surprised by it, piece it together, and even burn it. Not all that limited after all, wouldn't you say? As a bonus, print is also tactile. Unlike with digital, an audience can feel the paper. Treatments like foil stamping, embossing, die-cutting, letterpress and screen printing layer on textural elements that appeal to the senses.

Pop up and tear off

I love it when print expands into interactive territory. It's especially exciting when it comes as a surprise to the viewer. Pop-ups are a particular favorite of mine. I've been fascinated with them ever since I was a kid. It's as if my imagination physically climbs out of the book. It's probably the source of my obsession with paper. It's a link to childhood. The viewer has permission to play with the paper, even if it's something as simple as tearing off the RSVP card. Or perhaps it's more than that. Maybe it's because we're so immersed in the cold digital environment that interacting with paper is a kind of release. Think about your design piece. Is it enough to just look at it? Can you interact with it? How? Think about that huge list of things paper can do; will any of those work? Will it benefit the design? Something cool for cool's sake won't cut it. Can the design have more than one use, or a second life?

45 ● Mad Cahyo's Tokyo architecture exhibition display featured his semi-finished house idea as a minimalist miniature model juxtaposed with an illustrated infographic teaser.

46 ● The interactive poster lets the viewer confront both death and eternal bliss by physically ripping the poster.

Katy Perry used seed-infused paper for her *PRISM* album. She encouraged her fans to "Plant the PRISM and spread the light." Granted, the quote is a little bit cheesy, but her heart is in the right place. [As an aside, Australia didn't agree. The original U.S. version was deemed a biohazard there because it would introduce invasive plant species into their environment. Perry created a second album with Australian seeds. Remember to do your research.] There's no sense in creating a card with pop-out pieces if the paper is too thin. Or having a client's album banned because it uses the wrong kind of paper.

BLURRED LINES

Where do print and digital meet? Print isn't dead and technology is increasingly taking over our lives. Is there room for both to live in harmony? I don't think that question will be answered anytime soon, but there are opportunities now that incorporate both. Recordable and musical greeting cards have been on the market for quite some time. Teeny tiny minicomputers have brought digital innovation to the stationery industry. Other advances are based on the same technology. Motorola recently introduced a new print ad that displays a Moto X phone that changes colors when a viewer presses tabs at the bottom of the page, using polycarbonate paper lined with LED digital circuitry. Is this print or digital? Magazines and advertisers are introducing augmented reality (A.R.), digital technology that interacts with print to add layered levels to their material. Viewers focus their digital device on an A.R.-marked image on a page and it automatically springs to life within their device. A food magazine can now have a video pop up, enhancing the recipe shown on the printed page. An ad for a music festival could have links to an interactive map to help you get around the city while enjoying the music scene. It can even trigger social media to respond to a new product. The page is still printed, and A.R. is digital, but together they become something more. (The whole is greater than the sum of its parts... Now where have you heard that before?) Whether it's paper-thin microchips or whatever technology will be invented next, this is the future of print and digital design—side by side and hand in hand.

GALLERY

50 x 50

CREATIVE ANARCHY: Unexpected materials, Thermosensitive ink

"50x50 is an experimental tour guide that collects fifty different views about Hong Kong culture in our surroundings. The project involved fifty writers expressing their views associated with fifty different visual images, presented in a playing cards format. The logo was simply inspired from a local game called 15.20 from our childhood.

We used thermosensitive ink because this tour guide is a Hong Kong discovery journey. When people touch the package, color fades out and selected words from the cards appear." —**C PLUS C WORKSHOP**

TITLE: 50x50
DESIGN FIRM: c plus c workshop
ART DIRECTORS: Kim Hung Choi, Ka Hang Cheung
DESIGNERS: Kim Hung Choi, Ka Hang Cheung
WEBSITE: www.cplusc-workshop.com
CLIENT: Hong Kong Ambassadors

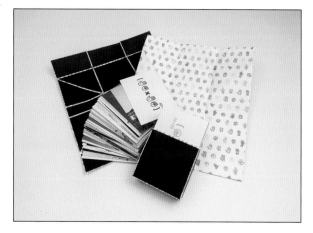

The Distillery Media Website

CREATIVE ANARCHY: Long and lean

"In a nutshell, it's a single drop-down parallax approach. Progressive in some of the tech, but very basic and fast in terms of working through the site to find the info you need. The clients of Distillery Media are often art directors and designers from large agencies. Therefore, the visual language of the site needed to be progressive and 'artsy.' It had to be cool enough for a snobby designer (like me) to look at it and say 'Cool, let's call that guy.'" —CALIBER CREATIVE

TITLE: The Distillery Media Website
DESIGN FIRM: Caliber Creative/Dallas Texas
ART DIRECTORS: Brandon Murphy, Bret Sano
DESIGNERS: Brandon Murphy, Bret Sano
WEBSITE: www.calibercreative.com
CLIENT: Distillery Media

Finca de la Rica

CREATIVE ANARCHY: Interactive

"The packaging focuses on the moment of relaxation and pleasure that accompanies a good glass of wine. The fun and original label invites consumers to participate directly on the bottle
itself by completing the puzzles." **—DORIAN**

TITLE: Finca de la Rica
DESIGN FIRM: Dorian
ART DIRECTOR: Gabriel Morales
DESIGNER: Gabriel Morales
WEBSITE: www.estudiodorian.com
CLIENT: Finca de la Rica

Adult Swim Comic Con Brochure

CREATIVE ANARCHY: Interactive, Unexpected form

"The Adult Swim booth and brochure were designed in a way that would react when viewed through polarized 3-D glasses. Inserting the glasses into the front of the brochure to make them part of the illustrated body/head was just a fun way to incorporate them. The type was all hand drawn, to work well with the illustration but also to stand out. Comic Con is a very corporate, shiny, slick event where big Hollywood studios spend millions of dollars on promotional displays and handouts. By using rough hand-drawn type and imagery, we felt the brochure would feel more real." **—JOSEPH VEAZEY**

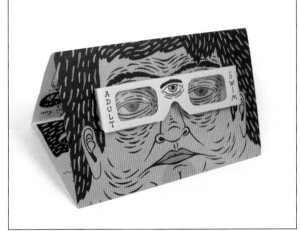

TITLE: Adult Swim Comic Con Brochure
DESIGN FIRM: Adult Swim
ART DIRECTORS: Jacob Escobedo, Brandon Lively
DESIGNER: Joseph Veazey
WEBSITE: josephveazey.com
CLIENT: Adult Swim

INTERACTIVE

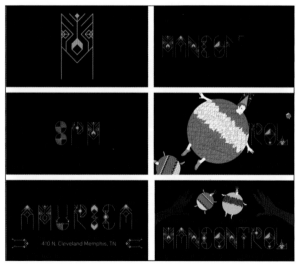

>mancontrol< Poster and Animation

CREATIVE ANARCHY: Music as inspiration

">mancontrol< is a unique band that incorporates elements of improvisation, crowd participation and light-manipulated instrumentation. Their show is a spectacle that has to be seen to be believed. The poster tried to represent the uniqueness of their show and sound. The abstract sounds that the band produces served as inspiration for the concept for their show during the holiday season. The main elements are the two figures that resemble Christmas ornaments. When they collide, strange sound waves are produced. Even the type gives off this abstract electronic energy." —KONG WEE PANG

TITLE: >mancontrol< Poster and Animation
DESIGN FIRM: archer>malmo
DESIGNER: King Wee Pang
WEB: kongweepang.com
CLIENT: >mancontrol< band

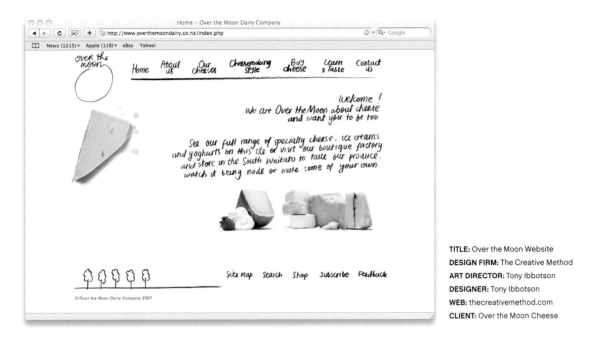

TITLE: Over the Moon Website
DESIGN FIRM: The Creative Method
ART DIRECTOR: Tony Ibbotson
DESIGNER: Tony Ibbotson
WEB: thecreativemethod.com
CLIENT: Over the Moon Cheese

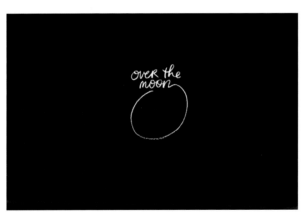

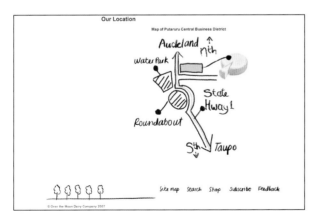

Over the Moon Website

CREATIVE ANARCHY: Hand-rendered elements

"The boutique New Zealand cheese company's personality, craft and contemporary edge is reflected in the final hand-penciled solution. It breaks from the traditional historical approaches of the competition. Their letterhead was designed with a handwritten 'Hey Diddle Diddle' nursery rhyme on the back. This gives an immediate warmth and reinforces a motherly nature to the cheese-making process. As much as we could, we looked to use images to reinforce and drive the hand-crafted feeling into the website." —**THE CREATIVE METHOD**

TITLE: Martin Treu Website
DESIGN FIRM: Projekt, Inc.
ART DIRECTOR: Sean M. Costik
DESIGNER/S: Sean M. Costik
ILLUSTRATOR: Scotty Reifsnyder
WEB DEVELOPER: Dustin Caruso,
WEB: projektinc.com
CLIENT: Martin Treu

Martin Treu Website

CREATIVE ANARCHY: Experimental navigation

"The concept for this website was simple: Design and illustrate a bustling streetscape scene where each building's sign would also act as a navigation button to one of Martin's pages. Each building and sign would then become the header graphic for a corresponding back page. The architectural details and typographic styles were pulled directly from reference material within Martin's recently published book *Signs, Streets, and Storefronts.*

The challenge in creating this streetscape image was to make it look interesting and energetic, while not being overly busy. We discovered that we needed to mute many of the elements within the illustration so that the signs and main buildings popped. This was important because they also doubled as the main navigation buttons. In addition, we also created animated GIFs for the signs that really helped draw the user's attention to them and gave the entire illustration some added visual interest." **—SEAN COSTIK**

Giving Gala Invitation

CREATIVE ANARCHY: Movement

"This invitation was for an annual fundraising event put on by the Real Estate Council in Dallas, Texas. The Gala was an over-the-top, cowboy-fair-themed party. The execution was focused with a moving wheel, like a spinning Ferris wheel, that revealed certain information about the event. It also incorporated another window that revealed funny cowboy slang or things that a cowboy would say. This was combined with Western and fair-inspired type and illustration that brought this invitation to life." —**THE MATCHBOX STUDIO**

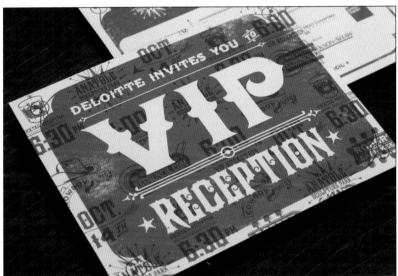

TITLE: Giving Gala Invitation
DESIGN FIRM: The Matchbox Studio
ART DIRECTORS: Liz Burnett, Jeff Breazeale
DESIGNER: Zach Hale
WEB: matchboxstudio.com
CLIENT: The Real Estate Council

Sandra Lovisco, Hair and Makeup Artist

CREATIVE ANARCHY: Unusual grid

"The whole design concept is inspired by the values of fashion, class and excellence. The usage of serif font, black, white and gold colors and the diagonal line express the femininity and the technical precision offered in hair and makeup services by Sandra Lovisco. The diagonal layout, used on every communication tool of the visual identity, is perceived as innovative yet simple, subtle yet striking, and makes the project consistent and recognizable." **—MATTEO MODICA**

TITLE: Sandra Lovisco, Hair and Makeup Artist
DESIGN FIRM: Sublimio - Unique Design Formula
DESIGNER: Matteo Modica
WEB: sublimio.com
CLIENT: Sandra Lovisco

Visual Phonetics

CREATIVE ANARCHY: Organized chaos

"Visual Phonetics is all about discovery and references the visual and tangible aspect of music. You can freely scroll through the site to create visual interaction, discover intimate details, and reveal tidbits behind a tight-knit community of musicians. The use of a collage-inspired interface of handwritten type, imagery, and artifacts was driven by people's interaction with the artist. The untraditional approach to web design catches the user off guard, yet rewards them with a sense of wonder, sincerity and understanding." **—WENDY VONG**

TITLE: Visual Phonetics
UNIVERSITY: Kansas City Art Institute
PROFESSOR: Marty Maxwell Lane
DESIGNER: Wendy Vong
WEB: wendyvong.com
CLIENT: Marty Maxwell Lane

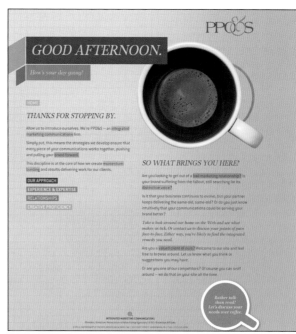

PPO&S Website

CREATIVE ANARCHY: Time reactive

"The concept centers around an invitation to the prospective client to learn more about PPO&S and ultimately have a cup of coffee with the firm's president to discuss his or her organization's specific needs. The salutation at the top changes messages that acknowledge the time of day the visitor has arrived, reinforced by the amount of coffee or coffee stains in the primary image. An energetic palette allows highlight devices to be called out and, when clicked, self-guides the visitor through to various layers of information about the integrated marketing communications firm." —**JOE KNEZIC**

TITLE: PPO&S Website
DESIGN FIRM: PPO&S
CREATIVE DIRECTOR/COPYWRITER: Joe Knezic
DESIGNER: Tracy Kretz
WEB: pposinc.com

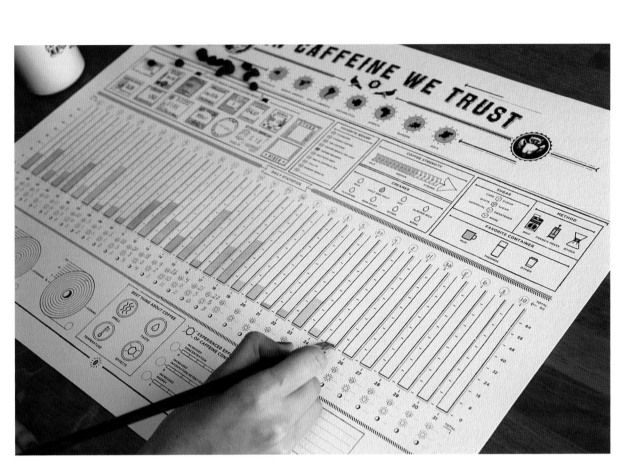

In Caffeine We Trust

CREATIVE ANARCHY: Caffeine-based interaction

The real-time interactive poster helps the viewer visualize his caffeine consumption. Collected data is recorded through painting with the viewer's choice caffeinated beverage. The personal experience makes the poster a collectable.

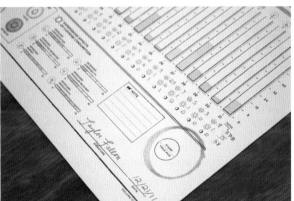

TITLE: In Caffeine We Trust
DESIGN FIRM: Column Five Media
ART DIRECTOR: Ross Crooks
DESIGNER: Andrew Effendy
WEB: columnfivemedia.com

EXERCISES

STOP IT!

RULE: Infographics should communicate at a glance.

CREATE ANARCHY: Entertain the audience.

RESULT: A motion-based, hand-done infographic incorporated into a digital environment is sure to turn heads... and maybe even go viral.

Infographics are all the rage these days. You find them everywhere from the web to annual reports to newspaper articles to backs of organic food packaging. People love them. It makes sense. People "get" pictures faster than words. Given the choice between reading a paragraph that describes the inner workings of a government office and looking at a picture that shows the same thing, most people will take the picture. It's been shown that people remember verbal information when coupled with imagery better than verbal information alone. This is a solid argument for presenting data in a sexy, inviting, graphically-designed pictorial environment. It doesn't hurt that they're also great fun to create. The downfall is that, too often, an infographic overwhelms the viewer with the sheer volume of data crammed into it. People will forget half of it even if presented in a stunning layout.

Help your viewer out by splitting the information into manageable chunks. Animate it for the client's website. It's just the same old information, except that it moves, right? Why not have some fun with it? Communicate your information with a stop-motion infographic, breaking the traditional ideas about both infographics and the digital environment. It's the perfect marriage of old-school animation and new-world technology. Creative anarchy at its finest.

 Let's do this

SUPPLIES:

- infographic information
- infographic crafting materials
- good lighting or access to large windows
- table to set up your creation
- a consistent backdrop
- camera
- empty camera card
- tripod
- stop-motion software (many free options are available)

Take an infographic you're working on or have done in the past. If you don't have one, create one about an unusual animal.

1. Gather all of your supplies and information. Sketch out your infographic idea in storyboard form. Designate which information will be shown when and how. Do not skimp on this step. This is your guide for making your stop-motion creation. Map out the characters, words, figures and scenes needed to make your idea work. Carefully consider how to transition from one set of data to another.

2. Craft your infographic "character" props. Use whatever makes you feel comfortable and fits the client's personality: Legos, dolls, clay, cut paper, felt, Popsicle sticks or dinosaur figurines you picked up at the dollar store. Make everything you need ahead of time. If a prop will talk or walk, you'll need various mouth and body positions. Create every iteration of your objects. Create your data as well. You can write it by hand, print out computer-generated text, or form it with your crafting materials.

3. Set up your backdrop and camera. Maintain consistent lighting. This is going to take a while.

4. Set up your props and start taking pictures. Take your first picture, move your props slightly and take another picture. Try not to move your objects more than an inch at a time. Continue until your infographic is complete. Be patient. Depending on the length of your infographic, you may need hundreds of images.

5. Import your pictures into any stop-motion software. Follow the software's directions to turn your individual images into a stop-motion masterpiece.

6. Export your video to a web-friendly format and post!

Blobfish are unusual animals that are also facing extinction. I created an infographic stop-motion video about these fascinating creatures and the fishing trawlers threatening their demise. Construction paper "characters," markers and the toy net served as our props.

START WITH THE BEAT

RULE: Web design should be friendly and simple.
CREATE ANARCHY: Let music dictate the design.
RESULT: Generate a digital design with a spring in its step and rhythm in its flow.

Music is a huge part of our lives. Most designers I know have killer playlists and headphones practically growing out of their ears. But unless a designer is specifically working on a gig poster or other musical event, those tunes rarely play a role in the design. It's time to change that.

Music is nonvisual design. In fact, music without design is nothing but noise, just as a web page without design is nothing but a glorified text document. Whether it's classical, rap, rock, techno or country, music is a layered mixture of elements working in harmony with each other, just like type, images and layout work together to form a design. Occasionally there's an auditory surprise, not unlike a pull quote or pop-up window. Why not bring the qualities of your favorite music into your design? It's the best of both worlds.

Let's do this

Take an interactive design (web or app) you're working on or have done in the past. If you don't have one, redesign the worst website you can find.

1. Get out your favorite playlist and tune in. Let your mind wander around the songs. Mentally translate the musical sound into visual elements; think *Fantasia*. What do the beat of the drum, the guitar riff or the vocalizations look like? Home in on the songs that reflect the things you want in your client's design.

2. Choose one song to start. Wireframe the musical flow. Consider how your audience will access information. For example, "Sabotage" from the Beastie Boys demands powerful pages with a visual heaviness, while Tchaikovsky's "1812 Overture" works better as a single page with parallax scrolling, beautiful flow and sophisticated organization.

3. Base your grid on the beat. For instance, irregular beats project an irregular grid, with columns of different widths and dimensions.

4. Select your type and images. Think about connotation. Choose complementary type pairs for the harmony and melody. Gritty black and white images connote a heavier sound; watercolor for a softer sound.

5. Incorporate type and graphic elements to divide the text. Use a pull quote to reflect an auditory surprise in the song. Utilize graphic elements to visualize the intricate smaller qualities of the song.

6. Continue working with the design until the visual and musical work together in harmony. Challenge: Do a different design option for every song in your playlist.

CREATIVITY EXERCISE:

SWITCHEROO

Creative blocks happen. Of course they almost always happen at the most inopportune times, like when you're on a crushing deadline or have to be especially innovative with a design. Your brain goes blank. Nothing. Nada.

It's times like this that you grab the closest design magazine, desperate for anything to spark an idea. Maybe you surf the web looking for inspiration, only to get sucked into the black hole of mindless Internet browsing. Get your head out of design for a minute. Take a break. Switching tasks, and in this case views, gives your brain a virtual restart. Changing your environment works wonders. Get up, get out and take a breather. Ultimately, though, you end up back at your same old desk in the same old environment. Why not change up that view too? A fresh new environment is sure to invigorate and inspire creative thinking.

 Let's do this

SUPPLIES:

- dusting cloth
- elbow grease
- petty cash

IF YOU ARE IN A SEVERE TIME CRUNCH:

- Ask someone to switch desks with you.
- Pull your chair around to the other side of your desk.
- Go sit in another room.
- Grab a box and clear everything off the top of your desk.

- Print out an image that makes you happy and tape it to your computer screen.

IF YOU HAVE A MORE TIME:

- Turn your desk so that it faces a different direction.
- Take down everything hanging up around your desk and replace them with all new things. If you have a child, ask him or her to make you new art.
- Get all new office supplies. Get a funky lime green stapler, patterned file folders and a slick new pen. Donate your old office supplies.
- Paint your office a new color if you can.
- Get a bunch of cool stickers and decorate your printer.

- Totally geek out. Break out your collection of wind-up toys, ponies or action figures (and give yourself permission to play with them).
- Get a new lamp, set out a candy dish (without too much candy; you don't want to trade Internet browsing for munching), add a plant, bring in a favorite mug and make your desk feel more home-y.
- Bring in an area rug to cover the typical industrial office flooring.
- Hang a modern art mobile over your desk.
- Switch up your playlist. Pipe new tunes into your space, preferably without headphones.
- Ask an office mate to switch desks with you. Bonus: You both get new creative environments.

PERSONAL SCAVENGER HUNT

This exercise is meant to push your boundaries, challenge you and expand your design horizons, pushing your comfort zone to the breaking point. This exercise is the hunt for the better designer within you.

 Let's do this

You earn points for every challenge you complete. The point value of each task is listed next to the challenge. I strongly suggest that you do these challenges with a design friend or with your team, though it's perfectly OK to do them solo. Either way, post your challenges publicly. Putting it out there for all to see is scary, but also liberating. Show the world who you are.

Set a time limit for your personal scavenger hunt—one week, one month, three months. Be realistic but challenge yourself too.

Are you ready?

PERSONAL CHALLENGES

+1 Read a book about an influential person, design or otherwise.

+1 Give a business card to ten new people.

+1 Get a headshot of you looking cool to use in the social media challenges below.

+5 Attend an event hosted by a local design organization.

+5 Take a class (online or in person) for a skill you always wanted to learn but never did.

+5 Expand your design library by 10 percent.

+5 Send a thank-you note to a mentor, professor or other influential person in your life.

+10 Volunteer your time to a good cause.

+10 Mentor someone.

+10 Spend an afternoon with someone you love and teach them a little about what you do. In return, ask them to talk to you about their life.

SOCIAL CHALLENGES

+1 Start a social media site for posting the results of this exercise.

+1 Write a blog post about your favorite designer.

+1 Write a blog post about a design you admire.

+5 Intelligently comment on three other people's posts about a design-related topic.

+5 Write a review for a favorite design book on Amazon or other book retailer site.

+5 Write a glowing review for a colleague or client and post to social media.

+5 Interview yourself about why you love design and post it.

+5 Create a video post.

+10 Teach something through a written or video post.

+10 Post about a mistake you made and how it was resolved.

DESIGN CHALLENGES

+1 Create a meme and attempt to make it go viral.

+1 Design a book cover for a best-selling novel about your life.

+5 Make a personal portfolio website (or update it if you already have one).

+5 Perfectly kern a headline.

+5 Create an infographic about a topic in your life.

+5 Design a clever T-shirt about a design-related topic.

+5 Submit a design to a competition.

+5 Create a concept for an awesome app (+20 bonus points if you make it happen).

+10 Learn to screen print or letterpress.

+30 Create a daily design project for yourself and do it for the duration of this exercise. Examples include designing a letter a day, monster a day, robot a day, album cover a day, poster a day, etc.

ULTIMATE CHALLENGE

+50 Do every exercise in this book and post it online (#creativeanarchy).

SCORING:

- **223 POINTS:** You are the ultimate designer. You live, breathe, eat and sleep design. It is your life. You rock!

- **109–173 POINTS:** You are making great strides in your life and are on track for a great design career. Keep it up!

- **49–108 POINTS:** You're a good person and designer. You may not be as hard-core as others, but you try hard and do your job well.

- **11–48 POINTS:** Strive to better your skills. You have great potential.

- **0–10 POINTS:** Consider another career.

IMAGES

CHAPTER 1:
ADVERTISING

01 ● **TITLE:** Times of India: Gully Gully
Mein Ganesha
DESIGN FIRM: Taproot India
ART DIRECTOR: Abhishek Sawant
DESIGNERS: Santosh Padhi and
Agnello Dias
WEB: taprootindia.co.in
CLIENT: The Times of India

02 ● **TITLE:** Malmö Festival Papertheme
CLIENT: City of Malmö
DESIGN FIRM: Snask
ART DIRECTOR: Fredrik Öst
DESIGNERS: Jens Nilsson, Richard Gray
WEB: snask.com

03 ● **TITLE:** Author Headphones: Mark Twain,
Oscar Wilde, William Shakespeare
DESIGN FIRM: McCann Worldgroup India
CREATIVE DIRECTOR: Talha Nazim,
Rohit Devgun
DESIGNERS: Talha Nazim, Rohit Devgun,
Nobin Dutta, Lamanoestudio.cl
WEB: mccann.com
CLIENT: Penguin Group (India)

04 ● **TITLE:** The New Dolls of Albion
DESIGN FIRM: Danny Warner Design
DESIGNER: Danny Warner
WEB: danny-warner.com

05 ● **TITLE:** Tom's Shoe Ad
UNIVERSITY: Kutztown University
PROFESSOR: Josh Miller
DESIGNER: Megan Ewer
© 2013 Megan Ewer

06 ● **TITLE:** Font Paralysis,
Fear of No Ideas, Nitpickers
DESIGNERS: Ann Lemon, Monique
Maloney
PHOTOGRAPHER: Michael O'Donohue
CLIENT: Art Director's Club of New Jersey
51st Annual Awards
© Michael O'Donohue 2014; © Ann Lemon
2014; AD © ADCNJ.ORG 2014

CHAPTER 2:
BRANDING

07 ● **TITLE:** Folded Light Art+ Design
DESIGNER: You Zhang
WEB: behance.net/youzhang
CLIENT: Tacit Design LLC

08 ● **TITLE:** Seoul Fashion Week
UNIVERSITY: James Madison University
DESIGNER: Jun Bum Shin
WEB: junbumshin.com

09 ● **TITLE:** Zoo Valdes sticker
DESIGN FIRM: Zoo Valdes
DESIGNER: Mario Valdes
WEB: zoovaldes.com

10 ● **TITLE:** DroolInc.com
DESIGN FIRM: Department 99
DESIGNER: Kevin Amter
WEB: kevinamter.com
CLIENT: Drool Incorporated

11 ● **TITLE:** Emily J. Morris logo
UNIVERSITY: Auburn University
PROFESSOR: Samantha Lawrie
DESIGNER: Emily J. Morris

12 ● **TITLE:** M.J. Eliot Logo & Business Cards
DESIGN FIRM: Jeffrey D. Creative
DESIGNER: Jeff Deibel
WEB: www.jeffreydcreative.com
CLIENT: M.J. Eliot

13 ● **TITLE:** Three Fifty (350) Wine Lounge
Branding
UNIVERSITY: York University /
Sheridan College
PROFESSOR: Paul Sych
DESIGNER: Yosub Jack Choi
WEB: yosubjc.com

14 ● **TITLE:** Musical Comb business card
DESIGN FIRM: FMD
DESIGNER: Fabio Milito
WEB: fabiomilito.com
CLIENT: MODhair
© 2013 Fabio Milito

15 ● **TITLE:** Caliber Business Cards 2nd Edition
DESIGN FIRM: Caliber Creative/
Dallas Texas
ART DIRECTORS: Brandon Murphy,
Bret Sano
DESIGNER: Maxim Barkhatov
WEB: calibercreative.com
CLIENT: Caliber Creative/Dallas, TX
Caliber Creative—Dallas TX © 2014

16 ● **TITLE:** Rebranding of Match Grip
Music Workshop
DESIGN FIRM: OMFG
CREATIVE DIRECTOR: Billy Cheung
DESIGNER: Billy Cheung
WEBSITE: www.billy-cheung.com
CLIENT: Match Grip Music Workshop

17 ● **TITLE:** Self Branding Identity Manual
UNIVERSITY: Cal Poly Pomona
PROFESSOR: Raymond Kampf
DESIGNER: Julian Arellano
WEB: jbarellano.com

CHAPTER 3:
POSTER

18 ● Reproduction of a poster advertising
'Robette Absinthe', 1896 (colour litho)
Livemont, Privat (1861-1936) / Private
Collection / The Stapleton Collection /
Bridgeman Images

19 ● 'Dylan', poster advertising Bob Dylan's
Greatest Hits album, 1966 (colour litho)
Glaser, Milton (b.1929) / The Israel
Museum, Jerusalem, Israel / Gift of Mel
Byars, Paris / Bridgeman Images

20 ● Advertisement for the Holland America
Line, c.1932 (colour litho)
Hoff (fl.1930s) / Private Collection / DaTo
Images / Bridgeman Images

21 ● **TITLE:** Theoretical Agency
Philosophy Poster
DESIGN FIRM: Kelly Bryant Design
CREATIVE DIRECTOR: Kelly Bryant

DESIGNER: Kelly Bryant / Designer and Illustrator
WEBSITE: cargocollective.com/kellybryant
CLIENT: Auburn University Department of Philosophy

22 **TITLE:** Romeo & Juliet
DESIGN FIRM: Luba Lukova Studio
DESIGNER: Luba Lukova
WEB: clayandgold.com
CLIENT: Ahmanson Theatre
© *Luba Lukova*

23 Poster advertising the ballet 'Romeo and Juliet', 1955 (colour litho)
Russian School, (20th century) / Private Collection / DaTo Images / Bridgeman Images

24 **TITLE:** The Cripple of Inishmaan
DESIGN FIRM: Red Shoes Studio
CREATIVE DIRECTOR: Wade Lough
DESIGNER: Wade Lough
CLIENT: James Madison University Department of Theatre and Dance

25 **TITLE:** Your Guide to the Delicious Tastes of Pennsylvania Apples
CLIENT: PPO&S
DESIGNER: Tracy Kretz
© *2014 PPO&S; © 2014 Pennsylvania Apple Marketing Program*

26 **TITLE:** Appel Farm Rebrand
UNIVERSITY: Moore College of Art & Design
PROFESSOR: Rosemary Murphy
DESIGNER: Samantha Emonds
WEB: samanthaemonds.com

27 **TITLE:** Mates of State
CLIENT: The Casbah - Durham, NC
DESIGNER: Jeremy Friend
WEB: jeremyfriend.com

CHAPTER 4:
PUBLICATION

28 **TITLE:** Alabama Workshop[s]
DESIGNER: Robert Finkel (Auburn University)
WEB: robertfinkel.com
CLIENT: Alabama Workshop[s] / Sheri Schumacher

29 **TITLE:** Breathless Homicidal Slime Mutants
DESIGN FIRM: Steven Brower Design
DESIGNER: Steven Brower
WEB: stevenbrowerdesign.com
CLIENT: Universe/Rizzoli

30 **TITLE:** Viropharma 2012 Annual Report
DESIGN FIRM: 20nine
ART DIRECTOR: Kevin Hammond
DESIGNER: Erin Doyle
WEBSITE: www.20nine.com

CLIENT: Viropharma, Inc.
© *2014 20nine Design Studios, LLC*

31 **TITLE:** Kutztown University Communication Design Recruiting Brochure
ART DIRECTOR: Karen Kresge
DESIGNERS: Alexa Flinn, Peter Hershey, Griffin Macaulay
CLIENT: Kutztown University Communication Design Department

CHAPTER 5:
PROMOTIONS AND INVITATIONS

32 **TITLE:** Clairvoyant
DESIGNER: Kelli Anderson
WEB: kellianderson.com
CLIENT: 20x200
Kelli Anderson © 2014

33 **TITLE OF WORK:** Wake Forest University Verger Capital Management
DESIGN FIRM: Wake Forest Communications
CREATIVE DIRECTOR: Hayes Henderson
DESIGNER: Kris Hendershott
PHOTOGRAPHER: Heather Evans Smith
WRITER: Bart Rippin
CLIENT: Wake Forest University/ Verger
Wake Forest University © 2014

34 **TITLE:** Bridges Holiday Card
DESIGN FIRM: Taropop Studio
DESIGNER: Kong Wee Pang
WEB: kongweepang.com
CLIENT: Bridges, USA
Bridges Holiday Card © 2014

35 **TITLE:** Save The Date
DESIGNER: Josh Miller
WEB: joshloveskelly.com
Joshua Miller © 2014

36 **TITLE:** Wedding Invitation – Jeleni and Mariu
DESIGN FIRM: Endak & Liubi
ART DIRECTORS: Katarina Endak, Dolores Liubi
DESIGNERS: Katarina Endak, Dolores Liubi
CLIENT: Jelena Lazi

37 **TITLE:** Doll Myers Wedding Invitation and Program
DESIGN FIRM: Doll Myers Creative LLC
ART DIRECTOR: Summer Doll-Myers
DESIGNERS: Summer Doll-Myers & Cory Myers
Doll-Myers © 2014

CHAPTER 6:
PACKAGING

38 **TITLE:** Lawyers House Wine
DESIGN FIRM: Brandient
CREATIVE DIRECTOR: Cristian 'Kit' Paul

DESIGNERS: Cristian Petre, Ciprian Badalan
PRODUCTION: Peggy Production
WEB: brandient.com
CLIENT: Tuca, Zbarcea & Associates

39 **TITLE:** Solaris
DESIGN FIRM: Brandient
CREATIVE DIRECTOR: Cristian 'Kit' Paul
DESIGNERS: Cristian 'Kit' Paul, Ciprian Badalan, Cristian Petre
WEB: brandient.com
CLIENT: Radix Plant

40 **TITLE:** Mrs Tinks Dinners - food packaging
DESIGN FIRM: Kary Fisher Ltd
DESIGNER: Kary Fisher
WEB: karyfisher.com
CLIENT: Tinks Food

41 **TITLE:** Split Milk
UNIVERSITY: University of Alabama at Birmingham
PROFESSOR: Doug Barrett
DESIGNER: Alyssa Mitchell
WEB: amforshort.com
CLIENT: "Earth Fare"

CHAPTER 7:
INTERACTIVE

42 **TITLE:** Wordless - Universal Wrap
DESIGN FIRM: FMD
ART DIRECTOR: Fabio Milito
DESIGNERS: Fabio Milito, Francesca Guidotti
WEB: fabiomilito.com
Fabio Milito / Francesca Guidotti © 2010

43 **TITLE:** Hard Eight Trading Website
DESIGN FIRM: UpShift Creative Group
ART DIRECTOR: Richard Shanks, Nicholas Staal
DESIGNER: Richard Shanks
WEB: upshiftcreative.com
CLIENT: Hard Eight Trading

44 **TITLE:** AEQAI Web Site Splash Page
DESIGN FIRM:
SCHELLHAS DESIGN
DESIGNER: Hans Schellhas
WEB: schellhasdesign.com
CLIENT: AEQAI

45 **TITLE:** Semi Finished House
DESIGN FIRM: butawarna
DESIGNER: Andrew Budiman
PHOTOGRAPHER : Erlin Goentoro (chimp chomp)
WEB: butawarna.in
CLIENT: Mad Cahyo Architect

46 **TITLE:** Eternal Bliss
UNIVERSITY: Kutztown Unversity
PROFESSOR: Vicki Meloney
DESIGNER: Nicholas Stover
WEB: nicholasstover.com
Nicholas Stover © 2014

INDEX